Presented to the T.

by

Dr. C.F. Amerasinghe

(matriculated 1951)

This book was awarded a ~~prize~~ Certificate of Merit by the American Society of International Law

THE DYNAMICS OF INTERNATIONAL LAW IN CONFLICT RESOLUTION

THE DYNAMICS OF INTERNATIONAL LAW IN CONFLICT RESOLUTION

by

JOAQUIN TACSAN

MARTINUS NIJHOFF PUBLISHERS
DORDRECHT / BOSTON / LONDON

Library of Congress Cataloging-in-Publication Data

Tacsan, Joaquín, 1955-
The dynamics of international law in conflict resolution / Joaquín Tacsan.
p. cm.
ISBN 0-7923-1450-6 (acid free paper)
1. International law. 2. Pacific settlement of international disputes. 3. Negotiation. 4. Conflict management. 5. Central America--Foreign relations--1979- I. Title.
JX3096.T33 1992
341.5'2--dc20 91-39251

ISBN 0-7923-1450-6

Published by Martinus Nijhoff Publishers,
P.O. Box 163, 3300 AD Dordrecht, The Netherlands.

Sold and distributed in the U.S.A. and Canada
by Kluwer Academic Publishers,
101 Philip Drive, Norwell, MA 02061, U.S.A.

In all other countries, sold and distributed
by Kluwer Academic Publishers Group,
P.O. Box 322, 3300 AH Dordrecht, The Netherlands.

Printed on acid-free paper

Printed in the Netherlands

To my father

ACKNOWLEDGMENTS

The framework I advance in this work was conceived during my doctoral studies at Berkeley and developed with the assistance of a Fulbright grant funded by the United States Information Agency.

A weaker framework would have resulted from my academic efforts if I had not encountered Professor Ernst B. Haas at Berkeley. His teaching and comments helped me widen and shape my perspective of the complex setting of international relations.

At the Law School I had the opportunity to work with Professor David D. Caron. A friend with a deep vision and knowledge of international law, David Caron was always there to give me his invaluable advice and support during the conception, development, and completion of the study. Having said so, however, I am solely responsible for the faults and gaps of my argument.

Linda Durston Dubrovsky edited earlier versions of my study. Eloise Schmidtt, Graduate Assitant at Boalt Hall School Of Law, U.C. Berkeley, deserves my appreciation for her friendly support on all kinds of administrative matters throughout my years at that school.

Finally, this work is dedicated with love and gratitude to my wife, Irene, and to my daughters, Natalia and Valeria, for their ability to temper my frustrations and sustain and reward my efforts throughout the full extent of this enterprise.

Joaquín Tacsan
Berkeley, California

TABLE OF CONTENTS

TABLE OF FIGURES AND DIAGRAMS

PREFACE

This study proposes a framework that I call "International Legal Dynamics" (ILD). The framework is intended to evaluate the effectiveness of international law in conflict-resolution processes and to study the ways international actors affirm, change, or disregard that law in their efforts to solve disputes. Thus, the ILD approach should help us trace both the ways international law affects changes in international actors' decision-making styles and the implications such changes have for international law itself.

The ILD approach views international law as legal knowledge. In so doing, it considers far more than just the information contained in international legal norms. It also takes into account the expectations participants derive through legal reasoning from the language of conventional legal rules, customary norms, international adjudication, and international legal theory. On the basis of this definition, ILD locates the dynamics of international legal knowledge in the exchange and interpenetration of actors' actual or assumed beliefs of what the law is as illustrated by the legal arguments they make and the various actions they take. Thus, ILD is suited to monitor actors' similar or dissimilar normative expectations and the ways some of these expectations manage to prevail over others and shape the larger bargaining process.

In using ILD to monitor normative expectations, we must certainly acknowledge that non-legal, that is, various economic, political, sociological, or psychological, factors, also substantially affect the outcomes of disputes. We also observe that international law is more effective in some disputes than others. We see too that certain norms frequently are utilized with many different meanings, while the meaning of others are more agreed upon.

Nevertheless, viewing international law as a body of knowledge that bargaining parties may consider, ILD advan-

Nevertheless, viewing international law as a body of knowledge that bargaining parties may consider, ILD advances a concept of international law that is no longer limited by the fact that no central supra-national entity exists to apply and enforce the law and that international actors are the major operators of international legal norms. It recognizes that international law is both a set of rules--not necessarily objective and always determinate--and a decision-making process that undoubtedly incorporates the individual will, interest, and ideology of the actors. International legal knowledge, as such, is never free from interest, habit, and/or ideology, but neither is it devoid of normative restraint.

While international law, in other words, is not self-defined, that is, while it leaves margin for different and divergent normative expectations, international legal knowledge helps parties to narrow uncertainties and may even shape the actors' decision-making and bargaining styles. It also exerts normative restraint on actors because actors tend to adopt the legal expectations that most participants share and advance. Indeed, international operators may debate their normative expectations--through negotiation and/or adjudication--either to solidify their conflicting positions or to yield to more consensual expectations. Such consensual expectations are the product of debate; they are truly consensual when most participants accept them as the authorized meaning of the legal norm in question. Consensual normative expectations are, thus, the basis for authoritative legal knowledge. They become the knowledge about or understanding of the law that the parties are willing and able to use as common criteria for settling their conflicts.

The foregoing concept of international law as legal knowledge does not reject the idea of the law as a body of norms. It represents an eclectic approach to the study of international law that draws on the work of both the New Haven and the Neopositivist schools of international law. This approach is also the direct result of the application of a "bridging" technique--the author's particular version of linkage theory as recently introduced by some theorists of international relations.

In introducing and advocating the eclectic ILD framework for evaluating the effectiveness of international law in the process of conflict-resolution, I use the past decade of peace negotiations in Central America as case material. As such, I do not intend to develop a new theory of international law or rigorously to exhaust one or various legal technical issues of the Central American conflict. My intention here is to introduce some variables and indicators--but certainly not a fixed taxonomy--that international actors might use to bring some order into the intricacies of international crises and that international analysts may use to appraise the effectiveness of international law in framing and shaping policy. Notwithstanding the above, I will be gratified if my framework would at least help explain the role of the complex legal expectations that developed in Central America during the 1980's.

Part I introduces the central problem of the study and the difficulties arising from any attempt to explain it according to either one of the pre-existing approaches to the study of international law. This part also explains the origin and nature of the bridging technique I apply to build the ILD framework from two leading theories of international law, namely, the New Haven and the Neopositivist schools.

Part II explains the various diplomatic efforts and normative expectations for putting to an end a decade (1979-1989) of border tensions, guerilla warfare, hegemonic intervention, human rights violations, general violence, and suffering in Central America, in terms of the guiding variables I introduce in Part I and detail in Part III. I focus on the key events in the region in four procedural phases: the Contadora process, the proceedings instituted by Nicaragua against the United States, Costa Rica, and Honduras before the International Court of Justice, the Esquipulas process, and the role of international organizations throughout the conflict. In so doing, I first highlight the uncertainty that prevailed among the parties before and during the Contadora process regarding the most appropriate conflict resolution approach and common normative criteria. Second, I explain why legal means for settling disputes achieved more relevance than forcible methods of self-help and the important role of the International Court of Justice as the adjudicatory determination process by which Nicaragua's normative expectations prevailed and became the common normative criteria for settling the controversy in the Esquipulas phase. Third, I indicate the distinctive features that differentiated the negotiations held in Esquipulas after the Arias Peace Plan in 1987, from those conducted under the auspices of the Contadora Group between 1983 and 1986. The most salient feature of the Esquipulas negotiations in this latter respect, is that the five Central American Presidents were able then to share the normative expectations that prevailed at the International Court of Justice and to use them as common normative criteria for settling the original conflict.

Part III spells out the framework and its sequential application to the peace negotiations in Central America during the 1980's. It concludes with some remarks about the potential of the framework to analyze other conflicts and to prescribe and predict some implications of international law for decision making and *vice versa*.

Overall, I argue that international law played a significant role in the Central American conflict of the 1980's, but only after the International Court of Justice re-defined and explained the notions of self-determination, nonintervention, collective self-defense, and use of force in the regional context. The Court's ruling in effect determined the normative expectations that finally prevailed regarding the U.S.-sponsored Contras' military activities in Honduras and Nicaragua. Right or wrong, the Court's analysis and interpretations established the expectations that oriented the peace negotiations in the region during the following years. The substantial international support received by the Court's decision on the *Nicaragua case*, the constraints that Nicaragua's applications against Costa Rica and Honduras exerted on the leaders of these Central American nations, and the renewed leadership and alliances in the region led the five Central American Presidents to accept the advice of the Court in the *Nicaragua case* and to re-conduct their negotiations on more similar, and therefore meaningful, normative grounds. The United States refused to follow the decision of the court, but, in the final analysis, it adapted to the development of events in Central America and allowed for the consolidation of a process that led to democratic elections, peaceful transfer of power, and the end of the contra-war in Nicaragua.

PART I

CHAPTER I

METHODOLOGICAL QUESTIONS

A. The Problem

On June 27, 1986, the International Court of Justice (the Court) rejected by twelve votes to three the argument of collective self-defense that the United States of America (U.S.) had used to justify its military and paramilitary activities in and against Nicaragua.[1] In doing so, the Court further decided "that the United States of America, by training, arming, equipping, financing and supplying the contra forces or otherwise encouraging, supporting and aiding military and paramilitary activities in and against Nicaragua, has acted, against the Republic of Nicaragua, in breach of its obligation under customary international law not to intervene in the affairs of another State."[2] Among several other findings, the Court also determined that the United States, by attacking Nicaraguan territory and by declaring a general embargo on trade with Nicaragua on May 1, 1985, "has committed acts calculated to deprive of its object and purpose the Treaty of Friendship, Commerce and Navigation between the parties signed at Managua on 21 January 1956."[3] Notwithstanding the decision of the Court, the Reagan administration not only sustained its general embargo on trade against Nicaragua, but openly and covertly continued to train, arm, equip, finance, and supply the contra forces "in order to pressure the Sandinistas toward fulfilling their commitment to democratize."[4] United States support of the contras was thus targeted to control internal events in Nicaragua in such a way as would exclude the left from power. The publicized assumption behind this policy was that such de *facto* veto control over the character of regimes in the region was necessary to protect

American national interests.[5] At the same time, however, U.S. foreign policy towards Nicaragua throughout the Reagan administration ignored international legal precepts, judicial decisions, and legal procedures. Indeed, the United States seemed immune to legal enforcement and punishment, as if no decision had ever been rendered. The United States failed to participate in the proceedings to adjudicate the merits of the case. [6] Just months before the 1984 Court ruling on jurisdiction and admissibility, the United States terminated its general acceptance of the Court's compulsory jurisdiction.[7] The judgment of the International Court of Justice was repudiated by the United States, and there is no real possibility of its being enforced in any domestic legal sense. International enforcement of the judgment is equally unlikely in light of the United States' persistent veto against such action within the United Nations Security Council.

Facts such as these regarding the *Nicaragua case* certainly can promote pessimism about the efficacy of international law and institutions.[8] An outline like this, as just described, incomplete though it is, may indicate to laymen and scholars alike that international law is unable to cope with breaches of law in which hegemonic national interests are at stake. In the present case, it would seem that international law is little more than opinion, but one weak voice in a crowded corridor.

However, this example has not been raised here to emulate previous criticism against the United States or suggest more efficacious enforcement methods for international judicial decisions. The important question of the legality or illegality of U.S. actions has already been discussed by the ICJ and commented upon by international legal scholars representing both the position of the United States and Nicaragua. The limitations to enforce the ICJ decisions on the *Nicaragua case* and others have been pointed out in many occasions. I need neither duplicate nor recreate what has been extensively debated elsewhere.[9] While, moreover, instances of conflict in Central America provide the historical material for the present study, the issue here is broader than whether or not the United States, by pursuing hegemonic policies in Central America, did or did not act legally. My objective is rather to trace the normative aspects of a difficult case, such as the one just mentioned, in order to challenge the conventional understanding of international law as a mechanism of questionable efficacy and to propose an alternate view of international law both as legal knowledge and as a mechanism with potential and actual impact on decision-making in times of conflict.

B. In Search of a Methodology

The task of appraising the role of international law in decision making requires a theoretical framework. But selecting a framework from extant international legal theory raises several problems. International law has such a long and pervasive history of dividing currents of thought that the whole discipline has evoked skepticism from laymen as well as lawyers.[10] Indeed, important conceptual gaps seem to exist between modern theories and approaches for the study of international law.[11] This chasm is especially evident when we contrast the two leading approaches to the study of international law. These are the methods defended on the one hand by neopositivists and on the other by the policy-science instrumentalists of the "New Haven School."[12]

These two schools of thought advance certain theoretical devices that I find useful as the basis for a framework to study the effectiveness of international law in the actual world. I deliberately overlook the natural law position, both in its theological and its secular versions, as well as the classical positivist approach, because the former two theories are commonly believed to have superseded these latter currents of thought.[13]

A brief exploration of the two theories I have selected suggests at the outset their limitations for use in this study; their focuses and modes of analysis lead to explanations which, though illustrative for their immediate purposes, are dissimilar.[14] The one analysis has, moreover, been criticized as being utopic and the other as apologetic. Neopositivists are considered utopic in the sense that they defend the existence of a systemic set of binding and objective rules and yet cannot explain how these international legal norms actually affect the motivations of decision makers. Instrumentalists are categorized as apologetic for their inability to shed light on situations in which a legal subject manifestly refuses to conform to well established rules of international law.[15]

However valid these criticisms, these two theories certainly present a divided outlook of the law. The one views the law as a body of norms, while the other views it as part of a larger social process. While neopositivists perceive the concept of a systemic international association as being endowed with a structure of rules that determines the behavior of the individual states, policy-scientists see the law as a process that is reflected through the decisions of the international participants themselves. Thus, instrumentalists view the law as policy guidelines for decision-makers; neopositivists defend its authoritative character as a body of restraining commands.

On the fringes of each of these two theoretical perceptions are outstanding pieces of legal scholarship that mainly describe state behavior without necessarily trying to provide a theoretical model or framework to prescribe or predict it.[16] Intermediate positions have also been introduced, most of which maintain the distinctiveness of the legal order while managing to respond to the extralegal setting of politics, history, and morality.[17]

I am not interested in elaborating on any of these intermediate positions, since it may be impossible to achieve full neutrality between the two major opposite positions. My intention here is to apply some epistemological devices to link the most compatible elements of neopositivists and policy-scientists. For that purpose, I have adopted an eclectic/selective approach in the sense that I take from leading theories what I find useful to explain the impact of international law on situations where the political seems to overshadow the legal. My attempt is not to construct a general theory on the basis of a single case study, but to test whether various theoretical linkages can help to improve future research.[18] By identifying the key elements of the authors' "levels of analysis" and the biases they hold toward specific "independent variables,"[19] I expect to observe how these theoretical positions actually do but in fact need not necessarily limit arguments to logical frameworks that produce irreconcilable outcomes.[20] The object, again, however, is not to reconcile outcomes--though this may result from our linkage--but rather to take from the theories what I believe are their most useful explanatory constructions. In doing so, I will also do what I think is necessary to overcome these two theories' mutual "external conceptual problems," that is, the source of what critics regard as their major gaps and deficiencies.[21] Before undertaking this exercise, it will be useful to describe the basic arguments of the New Haven and the Neopositivist schools.

B.1. International Law As Process: The New Haven School

Among the scholars who have attempted to work beyond traditional views of legal inquiry and present a comprehensive framework of study are the founders and disciples of the New Haven school of International Law.[22] Professors Myres McDougal and W. Michael Reisman, prominent representatives of the New Haven school, have sought to demonstrate that the positivist vision of international legality does not explain many different types of decisions that are embraced in the determination of "lawfulness." They also endeavor to show that the positivist approach is inappropriate to identify the factors that affect different types of decisions.[23] In their view, none of the following intellectual tasks--"clarifying goals, testing past trends in decision for conformity to those goals, understanding past decisions by reference to the context of conditions in which the decisions were made, trying to predict alternative trends in future decision and devising alternative courses of action"[24]--would be possible to accomplish if, as positivists suggest, international law were simply a body of rules. According to the New Haven school, this concept is inadequate for describing, prescribing,and predicting policies as well as for projecting alternatives to action. In McDougal and Reisman's words:

> It [the positivist approach] is inadequate for descriptive purposes: first, because technical rules are not simply given but are continuously being created and recreated; and, second, because technical rules, with all their complementarity, incompleteness, and ambiguity, do not afford precise comparison of trends in decision through time or across state boundaries. It is incomplete for scientific purposes because technical rules do not make precise and comprehensive reference to the factors which in fact influence decision. It is confusing for purposes of policy clarification because technical rules do not clearly express contemporary community policies or provide appropriate procedures for relating general policies to concrete cases. It is unreliable for predictive purposes because future decision-makers may be affected by many factors other than summaries of past experience. It is inadequate as a projection of alternatives in action because new institutions and principles may be more economic than past technicalities in promoting and achieving desired outcomes.[25]

Furthermore, McDougal and Reisman argue that since the devotees of positivism can observe no global "sovereign," with central legislative, executive, and judicial institutions, the positivist formulae by definition preclude a conception of international law as law.

The New Haven school of international law also criticizes the "natural law" position because "the intellectual task most emphasized by this frame (naturalist), that of syntactic derivation, could scarcely be expected, even when supplemented by an occasional revelation of divine will, consultation of the oracles, or transcendental cognition of absolutes, to provide the theory and procedures adequate for inquiry about empirical decision affecting trans-community interests."[26]

Thus, for the New Haven school, a better understanding of international law should be sought outside these traditional methods. International law, as viewed by policy scientists, is an accumulation of past trends in decision making, trends that conform to the shared and preferred expectations of the international community on how policy makers' behavior can achieve a "minimum world order." In McDougal and Reisman's terminology, those expectations about policy-making criteria constitute "authority" or "a set of conditioned subjectivities shared by relevant members of a group" that indicate appropriate behavior.[27] International law, according to McDougal and Reisman, is therefore a comprehensive process of authoritative decision and control, that builds up as standards of conduct from human interaction and that transcends the different territorial communities. It is formed by "constitutive" decisions or receptacles of accumulated experience, and "public order" decisions that protect and regulate the participation of different actors in global community process. It therefore comprises much of the information regarding past policy-making decisions and more or less accurately represents the expectations of international audiences.

In this context, international law can only be conceived within the dynamic process of decision-making, the so-called "World Community Process." Within this process, international actors--individual human beings who represent different groups--engage in many different "interpenetrating" patterns of interaction, by which the communities they represent affect each other and influence the more comprehensive process. The process unfolds through the actors' exchange of expectations about "values." These are the values that individuals demand through all their identifications, and which they accumulate and employ as bases of power to influence outcomes in particular interactions. In the final analysis, values are shared and shaped allowing for mutual control, authoritative decision, and the development of a global world order. Every phase in the process of authoritative decision is affected both by past and present distributions of values and by the perspectives (demands, identifications, and expectations) of community members about future distributions.

To McDougal and disciples, this all encompassing explanation of international law as process should allow the "observer" or analyst to realistically describe the events in the community process and the claims to authoritative decision that precipitate from these events. To describe events this way, the analyst may adopt and employ value-institutional categories. The New Haven school proposes the following list of such value categorizations: *Enlightment:* gathering, processing and disseminating information and knowledge; *Respect:* freedom of choice, equality and recognition; *Power:* making and influencing community decisions; *Well-Being:* safety, health and comfort; *Wealth:* production, distribution and consumption of goods and services, control of resources; *Skill:* acquisition and exercise of capabilities in vocations, professions and the arts; *Affection:* intimacy, friendship, loyalty, positive sentiments; *Rectitude:* participation in forming and applying norms of responsible conduct.[28]

According to the New Haven school, people equate authority with law, at least in part because people subconsciously expect that authoritative decision is necessary to maintain "minimum world order." A problem arises when some policy makers more or less freely violate the value expectations of the larger international community, and may even change the larger community's perceptions about what authority is. In this connection, McDougal and Reisman must concede that "the greatest defect in global public order ... is, unhappily, ... the failure of constitutive process to establish enough effective control over the different territorial communities, aspiring to aggrandize their own power, to preclude resort to unauthorized coercion and violence".[29] In the constitutive process of decision making, legal norms are items of evidence which might influence further decision; but being nakedly instrumental, they can hardly command it.[30]

Though they thus approach international law in these terms and acknowledge its failure to restrain decision makers who persist to rely on naked power, the policy-oriented jurists of the New Haven school show great optimism on the observable trends in world public order and the degrees of success achieved by the constitutive process in the transnational shaping and sharing of values. Admitting that international order is possible only when the relevant political elites sharpen and share preferred values, the New Haven school believes that those shared values will lead decision makers to formulate goals based mostly upon authoritative decision in order to provide and defend an international law of "human dignity."[31]

The "Policy-Oriented Theory" of the New Haven school has been criticized at least for two things: its optimistic belief in a "World Public Process" and its concept of legal norms as instruments to frame public policy.[32] Moreover, some critics point to the fact that in McDougal and Reisman's view, raw power seems by definition to be free of international law considerations because it ultimately enables decision makers to treat rules as mere "items of evidence that can be more or less helpful in identifying the act or acquiescence which, in a given encounter between states, will maximize realization of the preferred values of the international community."[33]

From our perspective, this latter line of criticism does not make the policy-oriented framework unusable, though it may reveal some of its limitations. There is a difference between critics who would like the law to be what it ought to be and McDougal who views the law for what it is. However, our assessment of the New Haven school does not focus on the fact that it acknowledges "the failure of the constitutive process to establish enough effective control over the different territorial communities," which to a great extent reflects the present status of international law. What troubles us is the school's indifference to the traditional sources of international law and its extreme reliance on perceptions of human values as sufficient control on and for decision makers. Granted its genuine and important usefulness as an instrument for predicting outcomes and facilitating decision making, these two limitations, as we see them, prevent the New Haven concept of international law from helping us criticize or change state policy.

The New Haven school tends to replace legal restraint--a direct consequence of legal argument and reasoning--with the concept of "control"--a function of decision making linked with human values. Though considerations of value are always important in a decision-making process, the school's extreme focus on sharpening and sharing values tends to overlook the role of legal argument and reasoning within that process. For two reasons, this emphasis on human values unnecessarily widens the scope and difficulty of the "observational standpoint" of the jurist. First, the content of "value categorizations" is more difficult to discern than that of legal knowledge because determining the content of values compels the analyst to look into almost every area of human knowledge and experience.[34] Legal knowledge, however, comprises comparatively concrete standards of conduct which are constantly developed and clarified through procedures specifically designed by the international community for that purpose and that in certain cases may even be authoritatively determined.[35] Second, in particular incidents, the analyst can more readily monitor legal argument than arguments of value. The normative expectations of actors around the principles of nonintervention and self-determination, for example, may be easier to monitor than wider considerations of democratic values and national security. Let us take an even more concrete example. Value categories do not help to explain why in 1989 most of the U.S. Western allies, including those in the region, failed to join the United States in its Central American policy even though the major political goal of the U.S. in Nicaragua was to restore "Western-type democratic values." This development of events may be better examined from the perspective of the impact on actors of the strictures of legal reasoning, both within the International Court of Justice and the Esquipulas Process.[36]

We explain, illustrate, and try to overcome this shortcoming of the policy-oriented framework throughout Chapter II. However, let us suggest at this point that no matter how values are shaped and shared by the actors in the process of decision making, the question arises as to what extent can these values limit the actors' own manipulations on the basis of national interest and other egoistic considerations. To describe a process of World Order by focusing on human values--not to mention just Western-type values--as the major independent variable of the framework may lead to very uncertain conceptions of "control" and "authority." Such is the case because McDougal and Reisman's approach underestimates the exigencies of "legal reasoning" as effective constraining factors over the manipulative or purposive attitudes of actors.[37]

B.2. International Law as Common Body of Authoritative Norms

Recent defenders of the more traditional concept of the law as a body of authoritative rules emphasize the "specific character of international law" as norms that do not necessarily emerge as an instrument of power, but as a body of preexisting common rules with their own sources and means of enforcement. One of the works within this trend is that of Terry Nardin,[38] who clearly distinguishes two major conceptions of international law. On the one hand, Nardin conceives of international law as a set of "authoritative practices," namely rules, principles, ceremonies, manners, and procedures that all members of a particular community are supposed to observe, regardless of whether such observance is favorable or unfavorable to the pursuit of particular ends. On the other hand, he describes international law as a body of "instrumental practices," that is to say rules, maxims, precepts and procedures that prescribe conditions useful for achieving a given end. For Nardin, these two conceptions correspond to two different aspects of the international community itself. "Authoritative practices" operate in "practical associations," he argues, whereas "instrumental practices" work in "purposive associations."[39]

Nardin criticizes McDougal's policy oriented jurisprudence, as being extremely "instrumentalist" since it underestimates the role of rules for the pursuit of shared purposes and ignores the importance of common rules as the only basis for relations between those pursuing different and often incompatible purposes. According to Nardin, the shared beliefs, values, and purposes that constitute McDougal's idea of "authority" provide a basis for association only if they are universally held by all participants. He points out, however, that in a pluralist world, there are potential defectors, or members who may not share perceptions "common" to other participants, and who, according to the conception of international law held by the New Haven school, are free to act out against the law.

He concludes that even though certain rules are the expression of common values or the instruments of desirable ends, the fact is that international law as a whole gives rise to legal obligations because, like all law, it is association on the basis of common rules that constitutes the decisive standards for judging the legal validity of claims.[40] In brief, what Nardin argues is that international law cannot be based on the assumption of shared goals when there is a great variety of purposes in the real world. While the law guarantees the freedom of states to pursue their individual interests, it only intervenes to prevent and solve conflicts.[41]

For explanatory purposes, I have categorized Nardin as "neopositivist" because he, like less traditional positivists, believes that despite the upsurge of new non-state actors in the international arena, the nation-state still constitutes the major international actor within a practical international association.[42] At the same time, he is committed to defend the concept of international law as law irrespective of any lack of centralized legislative, executive, and/or judicial international institutions. Again, he departs from the ranks of traditional positivism in that his analysis of enforcement follows Fitzmaurice's rather unorthodox statement that "the law is not obligatory because it is enforced; it is enforced because it is obligatory; and enforcement would otherwise be illegal."[43] Nardin also attempts to demonstrate the ambiguities of the term "enforcement" and the advantages of focusing on the question of "effectiveness," a concept within which enforcement is certainly an important but not a necessary condition. Most importantly, Nardin aptly points out that "[i]nstead of assuming that, in the absence of the institutions through which law is created and applied in the modern state, international law must be so uncertain as to be virtually nonexistent, we should ask whether and how the society of states have developed alternative methods for increasing the certainty, consistency, and uniformity of its rules."[44] Yet, perhaps because it is not the main purpose of his book, it is not clear whether at answering this question, Terry Nardin endows us also with an explanation of the process by which legal restraint actually makes its way into the minds and motivations of decision makers. This problem, which the New Haven school also does not convincingly address--for its excessive reliance of human values as the main source of expectations of appropriate behavior--and the neopositivists may have only raised, remains the main source of skepticism about international legal methods of inquiry.

Our main theoretical task is then to establish the basis for a framework that would take into account both legal knowledge and process through a selective linkage of some elements of the New Haven and the neopositivist positions.[45] This linkage, which we call "bridging," should also allow us to appraise both the influence of decision making on international law and the impact of legal norms on the process by which actors attempt to resolve their conflicts.

C. Bridging the Theories

C.1. What is "Bridging"?

While any impartial observer of the foregoing debate may appreciate the internal consistency of many of the individual arguments of the theories briefly described above, such an observer will also notice that proponents, on the one hand, of the idea of international law as process and, on the other, of international law as a common body of authoritative norms, do not effectively communicate with each other and do not even seem to try. The two theoretical approaches rather seem distant and incompatible. In fact, however, as I shall argue later, the incompatibility of these approaches is more apparent than real, having been created by commentators and even by the authors themselves.

Thus, it is more constructive to search for ways to bridge the theories in order to link their most compatible and useful features than to disqualify and eliminate either one or both of them.[46] A critical attitude aimed at discarding extant theories by rendering them as "wrong," without first considering differences in *levels of analysis, variables,* and theoretical purposes, can hardly help clarify issues or advance more solid theory.[47] The task here then is not to justify one theory over the other or even eliminate both. I wish rather to highlight the formal structure of the arguments that have led the authors to opposing views about the same problem. Only after their formal argumentative differences are identified, will it be profitable to select their most useful devices in order to address the external conceptual problems to which these theories singly and collectively give rise. Bridging theories, in this sense, endeavor to locate the major gaps between theories, to narrow such gaps by selecting their compatibilities and fleshing out the appropriate links between them, and to surmount the external conceptual inconsistencies of the two former theories. Bridging the theories thus involves finding a way to identify the variables each utilizes and the levels of analysis within which each argument is framed. Examining the variables, the disciplinary embeddedness,[48] and levels of analysis of each theory, may help identify the kind of bridging required.[49]

There are at least two possible ways to link theories.[50] The first, *accumulation*, involves integrating theories in one single whole without necessarily distorting their respective lines of argument.[51] The second approach, *additivity*, entails outlining an eclectic formulation where the full accumulation of variables and disciplinary embeddedness is not possible, but the levels of analysis may be linked because they are not too remotely different and the outcomes of the theories are compatible.[52] Additivity is basically related to integration of levels of analysis, an exercise which is aimed at eradicating conceptual problems between the theories that are mainly due to divergences in focus. *Accumulation,* in contrast, involves a more ambitious task which requires two fully compatible theories that can be "merged" into a single comprehensive whole. In my view, there is a third alternative that does not necessarily mean full additivity or accumulation. This alternative entails an eclectic/selective outline that involves some additivity and some selection of useful elements of theories, elements that are not strictly incompatible though the theories' levels of analysis and outcomes are different.[53]

Adopting the third alternative, which I believe applies to the leading theories sketched above, would produce an outline that does not necessarily entail features identical to those of the *mother theories,* except for those elements that are not incompatible or do not generate "internal or external inconsistencies."[54] This outline is intended to suggest the basis for a framework that could overcome the gap between the neopositivist and the New Haven school. It also seeks to surmount their conceptual difficulties rather than wholly reject any one or both theories. If successful, this approach may contribute to the progress of international legal theory, for external conceptual problems are the primary causes of skepticism about the explanatory capabilities of theories of international law. In the next two Sections I intend to demonstrate that by replacing the New Haven school's value categorizations with international legal knowledge as the decision-makers' main source of normative expectations, it is possible to integrate the concepts of process and legal restraint to explain the dynamics of international law in situations of crisis and, thus, overcome much traditional cynicism toward international law.

C.2. Is Bridging Plausible?

The major discrepancy between the theories here examined is one of focus: while McDougal stresses governing elites' perceptions about normative values in order to isolate variables related to decision-making process, Nardin emphasizes the formal and authoritative practices that emerge from his concept of international society as a systemic "practical association." Borrowing Kenneth Waltz' characterization of John Stuart Mill and Bismarck to illustrate the "second" and the "third" "images," we may say that Nardin keeps his eye on the chessboard (third), while McDougal focuses on the chessmen (second).[55] This divergence in levels of analysis is what leads Nardin to view McDougal's theory as an "extreme claim."[56] Indeed, McDougal's assumption that shared purposes among decision makers determine international legal and moral order seems to gainsay Nardin's whole idea of a systemic normative structure that governs and determines the behavior of actors.[57]

An impartial observer would see that Nardin favors the idea that the international legal system determines the parts (third level/image) whereas McDougal conceives of relevant elites building up the international order with their particular normative perceptions (second level/image). The question arises whether or not one could plausibly accept both conceptions about the law without getting into theoretical inconsistencies.

At first sight, the answer is no. Eminent scholars in the field of international relations already have addressed the question of integrating strictly third-image with strictly second-image theories.[58] In such cases no *linkage* is possible unless a bridging transition is introduced between them. J. David Singer, for example, when discussing the differences between propositions made on both "systemic [third]" and "subsystemic (state) [second]" levels, has concluded as follows:

> Representing different levels of analysis and couched in different frames of reference, they would defy theoretical integration; one may well be a corollary of the other, but they are not immediately combinable. A prior translation from one level to another must take place.[59]

Ernst B. Haas suggests that "this translation" can take only one form:

> [I]f properly fleshed out, the phenomenal [second or state level] approach may be used as a test for the adequacy of systemic propositions. Such fleshing out would call for the inclusion of some kind of decision-making theory in national studies, which could then verify to what extent

> actors have 'internalized' the 'rules' of the system of which they are assumed to be a part.[60]

My opinion is that in the case of Nardin and McDougal the task of building a transition like the one proposed by Haas is possible and, for our purposes, necessary. This opinion derives from the observation that McDougal's policy-oriented jurisprudence is not strictly a second-level discourse. McDougal and Reisman contemplate two different, though related, types of decisions: "constitutive" and "public order." The constitutive decision cumulatively establishes the institutional framework for making authoritative decisions, and the public order decision, which emerges from this framework, "controls and regulates the many different particular value processes transcending state lines."[61] Therefore, any appraisal of the aggregate performance of these decision processes, especially at the level of international governmental organization, finds that a "global constitutive process" is being built."[62] In other words, the "Global Public Order" proposed by the New Haven school is established basically by an "imperfect constitutive process" and not by decisions based on naked power. Supplied by a long history of past constitutive decisions, the authoritative framework for decision making becomes a sort of systemic structure itself. In this sense one may conclude that the New Haven policy-oriented jurisprudence in fact constructs a third image by projecting a second. Such a finding facilitates bridging and provides the basis for a "transition" as suggested by Singer and Haas.

I believe that neither Nardin nor the adherents of the New Haven school would reject this bridging effort. Though Nardin's concept of the law of a "practical association" achieves uniformity, certainty, and consistency from the "customs and procedures maintained by the community of international lawyers,"[63] it does not explicitly refuse McDougal's idea of "process" and the significant role that shared expectations of international policy makers play within the international community. In Nardin's words,

> International law cannot be understood simply as an instrument for furthering the shared purposes of states, nor as an outcome of the transactions arising from the pursuit of shared purposes. More fundamentally, it is a condition of the pursuit of all purposes, and exists only where common procedures for undertaking particular transactions are acknowledged....But the authority of these procedures must be at least implicitly acknowledged in the conduct of states, in much the same way as the authority of linguistic rules is implicitly acknowledged by the users of language.[64]

Moreover, Reisman and Willard are ready to concede that formal sources of law may have significance in shaping expectations and demands of actors. As they recently wrote,

> These expectations [of those who are politically effective in the world community] constitute significant variables in international political behavior, because shared notions of what is right influence perception, reaction, and capacity for mobilization....They are almost entirely derived from the responses of key actors to a critical event. The expectations and demands of those actors themselves may have been shaped, in part, by many of the formal sources of law just mentioned [international judgments, constitutional documents, statutes or treaties]. But whether those formal sources of law have genuine significance or are merely a facade concealing raw and ephemeral political calculations can only be assessed when you have seen how the sources fared in a particular incident.[65]

Thus, what started as two radically opposed conceptions ends up mainly as a difference of focus and emphasis that is determined by certain theoretical factors (independent variables) that are constantly manipulated by the authors.

Nardin's conception of international law resembles Waltz's idea of "social structure" as a set of institutionalized restraints and institutionalized methods of altering and adjusting interests."[66] The systemic approach that Nardin follows leads him to advocate a structural conception of the law by putting greater emphasis on the notion of international legal obligation.[67] In fact, while he does not deny other roles of the law, Nardin is basically committed to defending "the view that the practices of international law and international morality constitute the indispensable foundations of all durable international association."[68] In their recent comments, Reisman and Willard apparently do not deny the validity of this position, but they are more interested in testing the effectiveness of those formal institutions by examining the expectations that are held about them by politically relevant actors.[69] By underlining the different commitments, I show that the compatibilities between the two theories in fact are greater than first appeared, because each of them better explains what the other refuses to address. Likewise, the most crucial limitations imposed by the respective levels of analysis and independent variables can also be surmounted.

Nardin's focus on an international association that is capable of maintaining its common rules and perpetuating itself as a society precludes further investigation of statesman's normative expectations or perceptions about the law. In this context, the role of statesman in the identification and development of international law is not more significant than the ideas and practices of international lawyers.[70] By remaining in the "systemic image," Nardin does not sufficiently explain why the law, being the basis of practical association, does not always compel statesmen to follow widely acknowledged rules when they make policy.[71] Such a shortcoming leaves room for speculation and criticism, for, in the real world, international politics is immediately connected with decision-makers' perceptions about the world and international law as well. The reason Nardin does not fully exhaust this issue is because he is deeply committed to a systemic approach. This commitment contributes to Nardin's strict view of international law as a body of authoritative norms and his only partial description of the way international lawyers and international legal norms influence decision makers. I argue that the rule-emphasis approach finds--to a limited but important extent--its other half in McDougal and Reisman's notion of normative perceptions by relevant elites in a decision-making process. But still, since we have previously ruled out McDougal's sense of process insofar as it involves an "interpenetrating" exchange of values as the basis of control and restraint, a bridging transition is required.

C.3. A Bridging Transition

Our efforts to explicate the possible integration of the different images of both theories have so far indicated what we should take from each of them and what--if we decide to do so--will still be missing. The what-to-take comprises the main variables and levels of analysis on which we want to built our framework. The what-is-lacking reveals the "bridging transition" or the kind of imput we should add in order to arrive at a satisfactory bridging of the theories.

We may take from Nardin the concept of legal norms as the basis of a practical association and the procedures to clarify and apply such norms. However, Nardin does not give us any useful explanation about the actual dynamics of such procedures nor does he indicate how legal norms ultimately affect the minds of decision makers. We may take from McDougal the dynamics of a process by which decision making affects international law through the exchange of perceptions about proper behavior and *vice versa*. However, for the reasons discussed in Section B.1, we can not take from McDougal the concept of human values--nor the New Haven school's value categories--as realistically tractable sources of expectations of proper conduct.

From these fresh associations, we seem to achieve a more comprehensive picture of international law both as legal norms and as process, but still we lack an adequate explanation of "normative restraint" and of the distintictive channels through which the law impinges on actors to shape their decision-making styles.

Indeed, if properly fleshed out, a concept of the law that takes into account both a body of rules and policy makers' many different and often conflicting subjective perceptions and interpretations about that normative body, may reveal much about the way international law works in the modern world. This law certainly does consist of rules, standards, and principles, but these are meaningless except for the way its subjects interpret, argue upon, and advance conflicting perceptions about them within a particular international arena. However, if the linkage stops here, we may come up with a law that may be utilized to justify all kind of anarchical forces, a risk that induces McDougal himself to adopt such vague constraints as "preferred values" and "global order of human dignity,"[72] and most neopositivists to remain attached to the concept of legal norms as "objective" binding standards.[73] It is precisely here, then, that a bridging transition must be introduced.

I suggest that the concept of international law as international legal knowledge provides this bridging transition.

Though international legal norms are not self-defining and self-applying, which means that someone has to interpret and operationalize them, they do not necessarily work in the way actors want them to. Legal norms form part of a wider international legal knowledge, a body of practice, theory, reasoning techniques, and procedures, that constitute a complete frame of reference for users.

True, when resorting to legal argument or bargaining on legal grounds, actors certainly tend to follow the dictates of individual will and interest. However, as soon as the expectations that actors derive from legal knowledge diverge because of normative ambiguity or contrasting interests, a series of constraints that are characteristic of legal argument and reasoning tend to limit the actors' manipulative arguments.

A debate of conflicting normative perceptions among international legal subjects is what in fact provides the means to reveal in particular cases the current--perhaps also contingent and contestable--and prevailing normative expectations of most participants and target audiences. For, successful arguments in political interaction are the ones that adopt the communal view of what a rule means. This collective expectation may always be subject to revision because international interaction in any arena is an open-ended, continuing debate of expectations.

Once the parties' normative expectations are translated through their exchange of arguments into *consensual legal knowledge,*[74] the parties, relevant professional communities, and target audiences tend to use that new-found shared "consciousness" as the "official" collective item of reference for solving the conflict, that is, as "authoritative knowledge." But rarely does the process stop, for long, at least, even there. Epistemic communities--the term we have chosen to refer to professionals sharing a common intellectual interest and method--may play an essential role in having decision makers internalize consensual normative expectations that in turn affect the latter's bargaining styles and goals. To what extent this internalization actually occurs and what effect it may have depend on how influential an epistemic community can be in transnational or domestic policy-making spheres and how vulnerable the decision maker is to the restraining force of the resulting consensual expectations. It is the consensual character of legal knowledge that pressures participants to make up their minds as to what policy is sound and what is destined to failure. I try to demonstrate in Part II how such consensus as engineered through conflict-resolution means, influenced the individual motivations of the main actors in the Central American crisis.

The compromise I suggest between Nardin's determinist system and McDougal's discretionary policy-making calls for an explanation of how key actors (McDougal's decision makers) internalize the prevailing normative expectations about international legal rules and procedures. Since the element of "legal restraint"--the restraint that derives from a process of legal argumentation and legal reasoning--is not satisfactory in McDougal's jurisprudence and "internalization" is not clear in Nardin, the above mentioned "bridging transition" looks most germane. Henkin's descriptive statement of costs and advantages that foreign policy makers face when deciding whether to observe a rule of law or not is useful in this context.[75] Most of the time, policy-makers restrain themselves from violating internationally "recognized" normative expectations about the meaning and purpose of legal rules because they generally believe that departing from these principles will limit the viability of policy decisions in a divided world. Among the factors that help to reveal the international community's normative perceptions and help to account for its restraining character is the existence of an international law to which world participants make frequent and emphatic reference. Nardin himself considers the role of the international legal profession in this regard and the existence of a firm international consensus in many areas of international law as determinative of the "actual and specific character of international law."[76] Equally important as a restraining factor is the extent to which conflicting legal argument itself affects the parties' perceptions about the rule of law and about the possible normative expectations that the international community currently attaches to a norm of law. My attempt to further explain and illustrate the point constitutes the remainder of this discussion.

CHAPTER II

THEORETICAL SKETCH

A. Preliminary Remarks: The Bridging Transition Illustrated: Warning against Skepticism and Delusion

It has been argued that in order to fail, one must be empowered to act autonomously.[77] If this premise holds, then attributing failure to a body of international legal norms which lacks a centralized law-enforcing institution is basically to misuse the term. Without central enforcement, international law cannot truly be said to possess autonomy, a trait which, in the context of international law, may be understood as the power of law to operate irrespective of the actions of diverse legal subjects who allegedly ascribe to the legal and institutional framework. Law cannot fail, but legal subjects can behave in such a way as to impede or promote its effective operation.[78] Putting the problem in this perspective, the question is not whether international law has failed to achieve world order. More appropriate is to ask whether international participants can make effective use of international legal knowledge to solve disputes, and whether their applying clearer and more consensual legal/technical criteria may or may not increase that effectiveness.

I will attempt to answer these questions in Parts II and III. My interest here (in the remainder of Part I), is to propose a fresh way to address the problem, an approach that warns against skepticism toward and delusion about international law. I regard modern skepticism toward and delusion about international legal theory as tied to the assumption that the law is self-activating.[79] Skeptics consider international law to be self-activating insofar as they perceive unresolved conflicts as evidence of the inapplicability or even the disfunctionality of the law. Those who hold the delusion that international law is objectively binding perceive just the contrary, that any settlement of a controversy indicates the existence of a "binding" international order.

I find both the assumption that international law is self-activating and the two contending arguments of skepticism and delusion as extreme generalizations. Neither skepticism nor delusion perceive that international legal knowledge is part of a socially constructed reality.[80] Legal norms and standards are adopted to set forth technical criteria for participants to use to make "appropriate" decisions under conditions of conflict. The usefulness of such knowledge can be tested only by looking at the role key actors allocate to that knowledge as they attempt to manage uncertainty. However, since international legal knowledge is embodied in norms whose content is almost always ambiguous, and since contending parties and interested audiences must therefore derive or process this ambiguity into more consensual and, consequently restraining, normative expectations in order to use it effectively, we see that we cannot judge international law *per se*, but only within the dynamic exchange of normative expectations of actors in concrete situations.

Both skepticism and delusion result from the reluctance of many international legal scholars to test legal usefulness by the level of influence that legal knowledge, among other socio-political variables, may or may not exert on decision making. Richard Falk's treatment of the Iran-Iraq War illustrates the skeptical position. Falk suggests that the mere existence of this tragic war and its endurance for roughly six years indicates that international law has become obsolete.[81] According to Falk if international law were useful, it would have prevented the war from happening or intensifying. Professor Falk is correct if we view the law as a self-activating body of rules that automatically applies itself when there is a violation of any of its rules. He would also be correct if we assume that international organizations, particularly the United Nations, did not act as needed to terminate the conflict, because that would in fact imply that the international community did not feel compelled--or even tempted--to adequately operate the law in the instant case. However, the U.N. Security Council did on several occasions actively tried to restore peace between the contending parties, and the U.N. Secretary General later successfully intervened as a mediator.[82] True, the complexities of the conflict and the mutual merciless and hostile attitudes of the parties did not allow for a rapid end to the war. However, it is fair to believe that international law and institutions helped to solve the conflict, despite the parties' persistent use of forcible means of redress. Thus, the prolongation of a conflict does not necessarily mean that international law had been ineffective or obsolete.

If we were to apply Professor Falk's assumptions to the Central American conflict of the 1980's, we would again have to conclude that international law was ineffective and useless. For a whole decade, international law was unable to solve the various conflicts in the region. However, as I try to demonstrate in Part II of this study, the failure of the Contadora mediation process was due to the inability of the Contadora Group to create more consensual expectations about the principles it selected as normative negotiating criteria, that is, the principles of self-determination and non-intervention, and, more particularly, about the interplay among these principles and their historical links with other characteristic principles of the Inter-American System. The principle of nonintervention has indeed been a very ambiguous concept in the Western Hemisphere and one from which all participants derived different interpretations, especially regarding its application to the hegemonic role of the United States in the region and its effects on the Latin American peoples' right to self-determination.[83] Upon Nicaragua's application against the United States, it was the International Court of Justice who eventually determined how the principles were to apply to the United States' policy for Central America.[84] The Tegucigalpa Bloc (Costa Rica, El Salvador and Honduras) and Guatemala drew from the Court's decision some of the necessary elements to change decision-making styles and set forth the basis for the resumption of negotiations within the framework of the 1987 Esquipulas Accords.[85] In light of domestic political developments substantially motivated by the ICJ judgment, the United States adapted and behaved less aggressively in the course of those negotiations. The greater consensual and authoritative legal knowledge that emerged out of the ICJ judgment on the *Nicaragua Case,* and the strategical impact of Nicaragua's applications against Costa Rica and Honduras at the ICJ,[86] certainly had a great impact in the re-orientation of the negotiations and the decision-making styles of the Central American nations and the United States.

Andrew Willard from the New Haven school once wrote that there are cases where a "set of normative expectations plays no apparent role in an incident that might have been expected to implicate the norm, [and thus] the norm may be considered suspended, rather than denied."[87] In fact, unlike some advanced domestic legal systems where centralized or decentralized law-applying and law-enforcement institutions exercise avid vigilance against violations of the law, the interested parties in international settings bear the major responsibility for legal effectiveness. International law and institutions, as any other law, is there to be invoked by those having sufficient *locus standi* and interest. Clearly, it is much easier to see the possibility of operationalizing international law than to accomplish it. But the need for this type of initiative in conflict resolution is not solely a problem of law; it is also a problem of leadership and decision making.[88] Can we blame international law for what interested actors are not willing to undertake or are unable to clarify? International law has to be translated into concrete, clear, and understandable criteria which participants may use in order to cope with particular uncertainties and find common grounds for achieving agreement, for primary information which is comprised in legal norms is not self-activating or self-defining. As I point out in the following Chapters, negotiation or authoritative determination are plausible methods for clarifying legal criteria. Operationalizing international law may not be the only tool actors have available to resolve conflicts, however, legal uncertainty may be less difficult an obstacle to overcome than broader socio-political ones.

Prolonged wars therefore do not justify Professor Falk's conclusion that to cope with uncertainty and conflict, there is no alternative to a new international consciousness towards an emerging "paradigm" according to which international law will become a populist claim for peace and justice.[89] Though Falk's thesis bears a visionary and inspiring ideal, there is no need to be so skeptical about the current international legal setting. Contemporary international leaders and scholars may continue to focus on the many legal and institutional improvements that new international conditions may require for a more effective international law. But this task can only be undertaken by fully acknowledging the processes through which foreign policy is made and through which the parties may be able to translate international legal conflict-resolution criteria into more similar normative expectations.

At the other side of skepticism is delusion, the pervasive reluctance to realize that the guidelines and constraints that international law and institutions comprise are but a part of the broader social and political machinery that international participants have at their disposal for solving conflicts. Those who see the law as the only way to achieve world order, peace, or the promotion of the welfare of mankind, mainly because they perceive international law as an absolutely binding force to forge international outcomes, are, in a word, deluded by their theoretical commitments about the realities they would describe. In this group, we may also count those who rigorously separate rules and legal acts from socio-economic and political factors.[90] They end up with a narrow and rigid concept of the law as something that is created by "legally relevant acts" of states.[91] This kind of approach becomes circular, shifting from the law as a set of rules to law as a result of legal acts of states. But how can one know when a "legal act" is "legal" and when it is not, or what is first, the "legal act" or the "legal rule?" To find that legality derives from legal relevance, as De Lupis struggles to demonstrate, does not put an end to the legal-political dilemma. This view is useless for solving problems in today's world because it is aimed at presenting a delusionary "perfectionist" impression about the law as a complete, "self-generating," and "self-imposing" normative system.

Equally delusory is the notion that the law, once applied, invariably provides solutions to disputes. This is the idea that states are in all instances constrained to respect and refer to the rules and principles of international law. Advocates of this latter position tend to explain those cases of international actors' mere manipulation of legal norms with the scholar's illusion of an objective imposition of normative commands. That international participants have a limited option to resort or not to legal norms and procedures is a fact of life that one cannot deny. Non-legal as well as legal factors motivate decision makers to behave in the ways they actually do. These factors are linked to or nested in complex networks of issues and goals that decision makers create to advance particular policies. Clearly, several constraints impinge on decision making and some or many of them are normative in character. But we can never rule out the possibility that international actors sometimes overlook international law or even their own normative expectations about the law in their decision-making processes.

Thus, it should be clear by now, that neither delusion nor skepticism have much to offer in our effort to assess the effectiveness as opposed to the "success" or "failure" of international law in conflict resolution. The foregoing comments have been basically intended to illustrate two problematic positions to which laymen and eminent scholars are often exposed when they approach the subject. It is important to note too that neither of these two opposed attitudes toward international law would have been easily uncovered without the analytic help of our bridging transition from the previous sections. The concept of international law as knowledge is the bridging transition that links the notion of international law as common norms with the idea of decision making. As such, this transition suggests that the effectiveness of international legal knowledge--legal rules included--cannot be studied without an understanding of actors' decision-making styles. It assumes, on the one hand, that legal norms, among many other factors of an international association (third image), and, on the other, the will, interests, values, and capabilities of decision makers (second image), affect each other in a recurrent sequence that originates in one system and is reacted to in another. From this perspective, our transition shows that the various criteria of proper behavior that actors use to define specific objectives or to respond to the claims of other actors may derive either from legal commands or from matters of relative power and alliances. It also indicates that such criteria change as actors do. These criteria change through a constant debate of expectations about their meanings and effects. Actors, change in the process of learning from and adapting to the prevailing expectations and the most consensual and authoritative criteria that emerges through the debate. Finally, our transition suggests that legal criteria and knowledge are one principal source of expectations of behavior and may thus induce changes in decision making styles. Our framework as a whole is intended to trace the dynamics of learning and adaptation within a decision-making process and the relationship between those changes and international legal knowledge.

B. Dynamics of International Law: Debate of Expectations

B.1. The Thesis In Brief

International law is ineffective if it lacks "operators," that is, legal subjects entitled to use the law for particular purposes.[92] In this sense too, international participants are both the target subjects and operators of legal and institutional frameworks.[93]

A jurisprudence committed to describing the way the legal system imposes itself on legal subjects without acknowledging that political actors may well behave outside of or against the system is utopian. It overlooks the fact that non- or extra-legal factors also matter in international relations. Indeed, in pursuing their own individual interests, international participants resort to whatever they believe are the most effective means at their disposal. They may well use legal arguments, but they may also use force. Even if one party to a dispute adopts legal means, other parties may respond to a given action in either a legal or a non-legal way. Whether the law remains marginal or assumes an active role in international conflict resolution always depends on the paths the participants choose. The foregoing is meant to emphasize that in approaching the uncertainty of a conflict, an actor will use the means that best suit her or his interests and needs. While some actors resort to the threat or use of force, others utilize less violent means. But at least one international subject must be willing to present claims in a legal way for the likelihood of anything "legal" to happen.

International law is recognized to serve a number of functions. While some point to its problem-solving ability, others emphasize its usefulness for communicating shared values, providing guidelines for authoritative decision-making, and creating expectations about future international behavior.[94] Obviously, but not sufficiently emphasized by current jurisprudence, behind each of these alleged functions lies the assumption of an "operator." In other words, the effectiveness of international law can only be traced if, in addition to the more traditional bases of legal inquiry, we also look at the interaction of what actors believe--or want to believe--the law is. The dynamics of international law are thus to be found in the whole spectrum of legal knowledge, that is, in the normative contents of international rules, decisions, practice, and theory, as well as the normative expectations that legal operators derive from those legal rules, decisions, practice and theory. International operators frame conflicts in legal terms because they concede the existence of a body of norms common to all the parties to a conflict.[95] However, because these operators and their target audiences hold different values, beliefs, purposes, and interests, they project those differences onto their operationalizations of the law and then to derive similar, different, or conflicting interpretations about the meaning, scope, or applicability of the rules. In this sense, as adherents to the New Haven school explain, decisions based on legal knowledge are always "authoritative," since they incorporate perceptions and expectations about lawfulness that at least the interpreting operator regards as authority. This "authority," however, is ephemeral because normative expectations always presuppose that the operators' interpretations are subjective, and thus, subject to change.

In the early stages of any conflict, operators attempt to manipulate legal norms in the same way that they try to manipulate every other variable at their disposal. But still, even when operators seek to restrict normative expectations to their most immediate values and interests, the legal rule is generally not so *elastic* as to allow for extreme arguments reflecting remote calculations of interest. The law might be ambiguous, but it is not devoid of hermeneutic exigencies that almost every user would find her or himself constrained to observe in order to advance relatively credible arguments. How much can actors "squeeze" a legal rule or "expand" it to justify claims? There is no clear-cut answer to this question, but there are certainly limits to such action, as I shall try to explain below.

If operators tend in the early stages of a conflict to manipulate legal norms as much as they can, they tend nonetheless, to limit and decrease their manipulations in the later stages of the bargaining process. Operators need to transmit their particular normative expectations, and they need to do so "successfully." No normative expectation would prevail or survive unless other participants and target audiences accepted it. The operator's successful transmission of normative expectations depends in part on the operator's skillful use of formal and informal methods for settling disputes, at least, if the conflict is approached by the parties through peaceful means and on legal or both legal and non-legal grounds. For example, participant X, and target audiences in general, may become more or less sensitive to Y's normative expectations depending on Y's ability to use the most appropriate transmission methods it has available, such as bilateral or multilateral diplomacy, international public forums, courts and organizations, and even international scholarly debate. Thus Y's manipulation of legal norms and means is not unlimited, because the law can be seen as a frame of reference with characteristic sets of rational or reasonable modes of inquiry, explanation, and argumentation that imposes constraints on the user.[96] Looked at from one vantage, it is the pervasive indeterminacy of legal norms and the operators' need to persuade other parties and target audiences of the "rightfulness" of their own demands and expectations that creates the necessity for operators to reach more authoritative determinations of what the legal norms are really meant to state.[97] Seen from another point of view, the search for negotiated or authoritative determination arises out of the participants' need to make their own normative expectations prevail over the others.

This process of determination requires that procedures exist for settling disputes. These procedures do not necessarily require a differentiated and continuing organization like a court. More consensual normative expectations can also be established through informal diplomatic means. In fact, procedures for settling disputes can involve one or more informal or formal international arenas that are recognized by the parties as suitable for an open and public debate of normative expectations. At the point in a conflict when participants choose to debate expectations that are based on legal or both legal and non-legal grounds, the means for settling disputes involving legal norms tend to prevail over forcible methods of self-help in conflict-resolution efforts.

A peaceful means of determination consolidates when target audiences and operators within a bargaining context envision that a set of common principles, norms, and procedures are available for settling the dispute, and when they collectively accept that set of normative criteria as legitimate, or at least do not contend it as being illegitimate. If skillfully "operated," peaceful methods for settling disputes may serve as arenas for the parties to debate their divergent expectations and for some of their expectations to prevail or survive. If most participants come to share the prevailing and surviving normative expectations as the authoritative meanings of the law, these shared expectations may, in turn, exert sufficient restraint to lead even the most reluctant parties to affirm, modify, or replace their original expectations, that is, those expectations that are opposed in content or scope to those that prevailed. In this sense, prevailing expectations can become the authoritative legal knowledge that serves as the common conflict-resolution criteria upon which the parties may seek agreement.

Under this tenet, normative restraint becomes a matter of degree and can only be measured in terms of the parties' and target audiences' adoption and acceptance of the expectations that prevail in, or simply survive through, the exchange of claims of divergent normative expectations in an international debate.[98]

Where international negotiation unfolds mainly on legal grounds, it is very likely that operators will try to adapt their positions and claims to consensual normative expectations. A foreign policy that does not reflect the preferred expectations of most international participants has little chance to succeed over its rivals.

Bargaining on legal grounds involves both legal knowledge, primarily embodied in legal norms and decision-making processes that are based on the normative expectations that key actors derive from the normative framework. Even when a variety of international participants formally accepts a body of common norms, these operators tend to extract different normative expectations from this set of norms. It seems that everything from the language of the norm to the particular interests of the interpreter give rise to normative ambiguity. To resolve a conflict on legal grounds, almost all major parties must cope with such ambiguity and settle upon common conflict-resolution criteria before this legal knowledge can act as a restraint. The operators' search for such common criteria tends to narrow the general uncertainty of the conflict down to concrete and specific legal issues. The operators then choose the arenas through which their divergent normative expectations can be exchanged and debated. Though the international legal system has no central law-applying institution, it surely provides operators with the means for debating normative expectations and for one or more of them to prevail or survive over the others. The greater the international acceptance of the normative expectations that prevail through a debate, the more effective those expectations are to affect decision making.

In the final analysis, we should be able to observe how legal knowledge does indeed play a role in orienting and restraining decision making, and also how the changing visions by decision-makers of the law affects the authority of legal commands at a particular time and situation.

B.2. Overcoming External Conceptual Problems

Nothing substantial has been achieved through our argument if we are unable to overcome the most important criticisms commentators raise against both the New Haven school and neopositivism. The following remarks are intended to point out these major criticism and suggest how they may be surmounted from an "international legal dynamics" point of view.

I have stressed so far that the international legal dynamics approach permits a bridge between the two theories that, in turn, supports a framework through which one can appraise the impact of legal knowledge on particular efforts to resolve international conflicts. That impact, I have recommended, may well be analyzed by tracing changes in the normative expectations of the relevant actors throughout the bargaining process. I argue that the dynamics of international law, developing within the active exchange of diverging normative expectations, may shed some light on the way legal knowledge in fact helps to provoke changes in the bargaining and decision-making styles of parties and target audiences.

Overlooking several important variables and indicators, the neopositivists' and policy-oriented scientists' appraisals of the central issue of international legal dynamics--the effectiveness of international law in forging (or helping to forge) decision making--has been sketchy at best. Such neglect is one major factor that has pervasively divided international legal theory and subjected it to constant criticism. Policy-oriented scholars have, for instance, been labeled as "apologists" because they are seen to focus narrowly on the way the law is affected by the global process of decision making. Neopositivists are called "utopian" because they advance a "systemic" and "deterministic" vision of the law as a body of norms that imposes itself on international actors of different cultures, interests, and beliefs and that governs their relations irrespective of the motivations underlying their habits and decision-making styles.

B.2.1. Surmounting "Apology" by Incorporating Normative Restraint and Excluding Ideology

i. When complemented with the neopositivist idea of normative restraint[99] McDougal's allocation of discretionary powers to decision-makers appears less problematic. Likewise, when viewed within McDougal's framework of a decision-making process,[100] legal restraint seems less utopian. On the one hand, our bridging effort frees us from the New Haven school's troublesome emphasis of "shared or preferred values" that arise subjectively from the too abstract ideal of "human dignity." Our explanation that increasingly consensual normative expectations may constrain decision making suggest instead that international actors' behavior may change irrespectively of whether these actors share or do not share a set of values. Prevailing normative expectations, in other words, are at least as much the product of an international debate that determines the meaning of a pre-existing base of legal knowledge as they are a result of an underlying set of common values. On the other hand, our bridging effort tempers the neopositivist notion of normative restraint, suggesting that it does not arise exclusively or directly out of a body of international rules. Restraint comes from legal knowledge in general, but it also derives from the participants' debate and their eventual agreement on common normative expectations with respect to that knowledge. Increasing international consensus on the authorized meanings of a determined set of normative expectations generates international pressure and "restraint" on the bargaining and decision-making styles of the parties to a conflict.

Though the "international incidents approach" (IIA)--the most recent development of the New Haven school--is interested in appraising the impact of decision making over international law, the IIA overlooks the role of law in influencing decision. While, in other words, the IIA decreases unfounded faith in international legal norms as fully binding, it nevertheless focuses only on how "expectations of lawfulness" are affirmed, denied, suspended, attenuated, or enhanced and not at all either on the changes such expectations may provoke in the attitudes of the relevant elites or on ways to trace those changes.[101] The IIA remains loyal to the New Haven school's characteristic search for a global world order based mainly on the "discovery" of shared values of "acceptable behavior." A commitment to such an approach may endow the IIA with internal consistency, but it still makes it appear apologetic. As a framework that has produced valuable research, the IIA, however, sheds no light whatsoever on the process by which the law can exert a restraining force on participants, either to predetermine, guide, compel or change particular conduct.

Thus, to surmount the criticism against the New Haven school's oversight of normative restraint, we need to investigate into the exchange of normative expectations within international disputes to find out whether any basic common standards of acceptable behavior have been attained by participants and target audiences. But even more important, in our search for common basic normative expectations, we cannot avoid dealing with the impact, however modest, of these common standards on the bargaining and decision-making attitudes of the relevant actors. Narrowing the menu of expectations recognized by the New Haven school to those deriving from legal knowledge rather than human values, and adding thereon the idea of a gradual and progressive chain of expectations--from plain normative to consensual and authoritative ones--should not distort the idea of process. These adjustments rather add a plausible description of normative restraint that, in contrast with the New Haven school, helps us avoid the risk of being too "apologetic."

ii. Another criticism of the New Haven school is that its interpretation of shared and preferred values "possesses an uncanny ability to justify in pseudo-legal terms whatever course of behavior the U.S. government deems expedient to its national self-interest under the particular historical conditions."[102] This criticism is based on the belief that underlying the value-oriented analysis of the New Haven jurisprudence is precisely the same set of Lockean liberal values as those on which the U.S. government institutions are founded. In this sense, McDougal and his disciples are deemed to be apologetic of United States policy in every single situation.

It is not necessary to duplicate here the debate about the more or less apologetic aims of the New Haven jurisprudence with respect to the foreign policy of the United States.[103] I personally do not view McDougal's classification of values as dogmatic or ideological. McDougal's and his disciples' classification of values seems to set forth a criteria by which observers of transnational developments can clarify the demands new problems create for multinational and international action.[104] To assess the world in terms of power, wealth, well-being, enlightment, skill, affection, respect, and rectitude only introduces a heuristic device; the New Haven school uses this device to help the analyst to explain how the expectations of the various participants in the international community frame policy choices.[105]

I grant some weight, however, to Professor Tunkin's observation that objections "arise from the fact that the values proclaimed by McDougal are actually taken from outside international law and are announced as guidance for the actions of states."[106] By emphasizing human values over legal precepts as the main source of normative expectations, McDougal and his disciples must both exclude legal restraint as an important component of these expectations and engage into the extremely uncertain and overwhelming realm of human subjectivity. As a result, they are forced to search for a "global" multidisciplinary background, covering practically all areas of human knowledge, just to provide some content to their heuristic devices (value categories).

Thus, McDougal and his disciples' concrete applications of their framework tend to reflect mostly the value contents spoused by the authors, who, in turn, mainly happen to share

American-type value contents. But this charge against the New Haven school is certainly more accurate when directed against the specific applications of its framework than to its general theoretical foundations. In other words, one should not confuse the heuristic devices of the New Haven school's framework--neutral from a theoretical point of view--with the concrete application of those devices by their users.

The New Haven school is, thus, ambitious; it goes beyond legal boundaries to explain the global social process of world interactions. We do not need to go that far since our main purpose is to remain well within the confines of the process through which legal knowledge is clarified, affirmed, or recreated in efforts to resolve conflicts. Since we, as observers, do not care so much about human values--as a source of actors' normative expectations--as we do to identify the consensual normative expectations that actors derive from extant legal knowledge, we do not have to take sides to qualify what expectations are more and less "appropriate." Whatever the ideological contents of the consensual normative expectations that result from international interaction, these expectations do not necessarily emerge to justify or advance the observer's particular ideology, for it is a process of legal argumentation and reasoning and not the observer's values that makes some of these expectations prevail and eventually serve as authoritative knowledge.

B.2.2. Surmounting Utopia by Linking Legal Knowledge with Decision Making

The "international legal dynamics" (ILD) approach advanced here does not assume that international actors literally follow legal norms to resolve their disputes. While as a matter of statute, actors are obliged to solve disputes in a legal fashion; as a matter of fact, this obligation does not actually compel these actors to use legal argumentation. Most of the time, however, international actors do try to legitimize behavior;

they often feel attracted to and even constrained to resort to legal norms. This behavior prevails because legal knowledge provides actors idealized notions of what is practical conduct and a convenient frame of reference for justifying their decisions. This holds true particularly in conditions of uncertainty when an actor perceives that a policy that most international participants see as legally untenable may be costly or almost invariably destined to fail. By no means, however, can we believe that actors apply international law in every single conflict situation or that, if they enforce the law against reluctant parties, it would constitute the right prescription to bring about world order. To believe so would be utopian.

Theories of international law that are grounded on the basic argument that states normally comply with the law categorize as legal only those issues over which no international actor is believed to have the power of discretion. Such formulations maintain that states follow the law because they comply with its commands regularly and more often than they violate them. Beyond the basic issue of observance itself, a matter that begs for exhaustive empirical investigations, we also find that theories grounded on the premise that states generally obey the law also generally avoid or fail to answer the important question of how the law influences the motivations of political elites.[107]

Critics of the utopian view of international law have understandably argued that regularities in state behavior are not necessarily due to the actors' obedience of legal rules. Nonlegal factors such as the logic of deterrence, balance of power, and so on, are mentioned as having a greater impact on the way states behave. For Koskenniemi, the utopians' failure to explain the distinct way in which international law is enforced and the way it gets imposed on states' motivations is insurmountable. Even if we could go and ask the State itself why it acts as it does, the state would always claim that its action was motivated by considerations of law. He aptly adds that "there should exist external criteria for determining whether

State's motivations were influenced by law or not."[108] While rejecting the traditional notion that states obey the law for its objective and binding character, the international legal dynamics approach further inquires how a "generally accepted" or consensual legal knowledge--particularly the normative expectations that actors derive from pre-existing legal knowledge in a particular conflict--is built and applied by actors. The ILD attempts to monitor normative restraint by tracing the expectations of proper conduct that actors derive from international legal knowledge and, more importantly, the ways actors translate their own divergent legal expectations about such knowledge into more consensual and authoritative ones. In this sense, the ILD framework imposes upon itself the burden of proving the place of these "perceptions about legal rights" within the constellation of other economic, political, and social factors that also influence decision-making.

If utopian thinking is due to the pervasive commitment to separating law from politics and giving legal restraint excessive credit at solving international conflicts, the kind of propositions involved in this discussion are purported to emphasize a more flexible explanation of legal restraint. It acknowledges the fact that the law is not the only tool that international participants utilize to solve international problems. It also concedes that the effectiveness of international legal norms and procedures has important limits. To be sure, the way I view the dynamics of international law is not to contend that it would explain all the components of a conflict or determine its final outcome, but simply to indicate one possible way in which legal conflict resolution criteria qualifies as the sort of knowledge that international participants are moved--and constrained--to utilize in the midst of controversy and uncertainty.

B.3. Effectiveness Versus Enforcement

Theoretical reflections about enforcement in international law have a lot to do with the misleading perception that international law constitutes sort of a "living" organism, capable of acting and being applied and imposed by itself. However, the law is not capable of imposing itself. That the law is applied implies that someone is trying to impose on others his or her own belief of what the norm commands. Since the international community lacks centralized law-applying institutions, who would coercively impose legal commands on their international subjects, the justification and explanation of international legal enforcement have occupied the minds of scholars throughout the years. As I have already stated, however, focusing on problems of enforcement does not help to clarify the dynamics of international law in the present world. More useful analyses appraise the "effectiveness" or the consequential degree of influence that active international legal dynamics have on the motivations and actions of international participants. The distinction between the effectiveness and the enforcement approaches to understanding international law is the core issue of this section.

Perhaps the discussion of enforcement is so endemic to international legal scholarship because international law has traditionally been studied by comparing it with domestic law. From this perspective, international law is alleged to be "weaker" than domestic orders, because of its lack of enforcement. The comparison seems persuasive, but being inaccurate, has devastating consequences for the discipline. A certain cynicism arises toward international law in the following fashion. Since the international community does not have a supra-government or a centralized law-applying institution, international law does not have the qualities needed for being enforced against a nation. Therefore, for example, who can compel the United States or the Soviet Union to respect the principle of nonintervention in the internal affairs of weaker countries? Who could punish Iranian and Iraqi leaders for engaging in a cruel war, killing their own and each other's people, and violating the principles and goals that constitute the same foundations of international law? In short, what is the use of having international norms if they are to be respected only at the states discretion?

Certainly there is no body in this world who can impose sanctions that would force these nations to obey international law. And in this light, it is difficult for many to see the use of international law. As Brierly has written:

> When the layman thinks of law, he is apt to think first of the policeman, and he is inclined to doubt the value of a system which, so far as he can see, makes no definite provision for the policeman's function.[109]

But not only the layman thinks of law in these terms. Austin believed that law had to be enforceable in order to be legally binding.[110] He added that a law which is not binding is not law. Insofar as the international society lacks a coercive power to enforce its rules, its rules are not binding. As a result, international lawyers have used the best of their imagination and capacities to counter this charge of the "weakness" of their discipline. They have argued that enforcement is not the hallmark of "law".[111] that much of what we call domestic law is also nonenforceable,[112] and that in any case, "almost all nations observe almost all principles of international law and almost all of their obligations almost all of the time."[113] As early as 1931, Professor Brierly addressed the Annual Meeting of the Grotius Society defending international law enforcement as a body of unorganized sanctions emerging from the "strength of public opinion."[114] His argument has been adopted with multiple variants, one of them being Richard Falk's notion of normative restraint as depending on the as yet not fully realized "energies of civil society,"[115] Kelsen, Hart, and others have espoused the idea that coercive sanctions exist in international law, though many have confused the lack of an enforcing agency with lack of enforcement. In the international realm, they maintain, sanctions are applied by the community at large rather than by an agency or agencies specifically authorized to enforce the rules.[116]

That international lawyers are still preoccupied explaining the "binding" character of international law is evidence that they are not yet satisfied with their answers to the criticism that international law lacks enforcement. One of the most recent and celebrated arguments on this matter is D'Amato's theory of tit-for-a-different-tat entitlements.[117] D'Amato maintains that it is possible to show that international law is enforceable in the same way that domestic law is enforceable, though the former is not always enforced. Most usual legal punishment typically provides for "deprivations" or removal of "entitlements," a term that encompasses all legally recognized rights. He writes,

> ...in all cases of law violation, the law responds by depriving you of one or more of your entitlements."[118]

Thus, legal enforcement does not need to use physical force against the violator; more typically it simply deprives the violator of entitlements. In the international sphere, states are bestowed with entitlements by the international legal system, where all states have a collective interest in acquiescing to all the entitlements for any given state in the system. They also have an interest in preserving entitlements *per se,* and to do so, states should act in such a manner as to preserve their own entitlements. In a legal system that does not have a central court of compulsory jurisdiction, world legislature, or world police force, states enforce the law by depriving violators of one or various entitlements in a reciprocal fashion. Thus, if a state breaks the law by depriving another of one or more of its entitlements, the international community accepts (implicitly) that the offended nation repudiate an offense by reciprocally violating an entitlement of the offending nation. Borrowing the idea from game theory in the international relations field, particularly from Axelrod's tit-for-tat strategy, D'Amato calls his enforcement argument the strategy of the "tit-for-a-different-tat pattern."[119]

I cannot completely accept D'Amato's explanation, and he himself acknowledges that such retaliatory deprivations of entitlements may cause a dangerous chain of offenses or escalating violations that could lead to international anarchy and destruction. I perceive D'Amato as viewing the Iran-Iraq war as an example of the reciprocal entitlement model where escalating retaliations were still happening nine years after the first deprivation occurred. Despite his realization of such a probable consequence for the tit-for-tat strategy, what matters to D'Amato is the law being enforceable more than being effective. Enforcement, however, is only one way to achieve effectiveness. No enforcement is needed or wanted if it threatens the preservation of peace or encourages humanity to destroy itself.

Another problem with Professor D'Amato's notion of enforcement is that it is available only to those nations who are capable of retaliating against an offending state, retaliations that are significant enough as to deprive the offending state of one or various entitlements. The United States, and perhaps Iraq, had such power of retaliation vis a vis Iran when hostages were taken from the U.S. Embassy in Tehran, Iran in 1979. But offended-nations that are too weak to deprive an offending-superpower of one of its many entitlements have no such power of enforcement. Though D'Amato was ready to concede from the very outset that there might be times when international law is not enforceable, I fear that international relations too frequently involve weak-strong interaction pairings where the entitlement-retaliation system can only work one way: side by side with the powerful.

What need exists for an international law that can only be enforced on behalf of the strong and where justice is to be administered *manu proprio*. What do we gain by sacrificing "peace" and "order," as opposed to violence and anarchy, for an "enforcement" that is only available to a small number of strong nations? It is unfortunate that Professor D'Amato did not apply his reciprocal-entitlement theory to the Nicaraguan case, though his book devotes a whole chapter to the issue of "Nicaragua and the Academic View of International Law." If he had undertaken the task, he would have run into many difficulties analyzing the kind of retaliatory deprivation that Nicaragua could have implemented in light of the United States' paramilitary and military activities.

The relevant "test" D'amato uses for the reciprocal-entitlement theory, as one of legal enforcement, is the reaction of the world community to the retaliating action. In connection with the Iran-Iraq war, he writes:

> Admittedly, any political realist might object to my theory on the ground that "international law" is not as important as I make it out to be and that certainly Iraq of all countries was not interested in making Iran respect international law. My reply, briefly, is that no one knows exactly how important international law is, but we do know that is has persisted through the centuries and further, that while Iraq may not have had anything in mind about international law and may have attacked Iran simply for irredentist or expansionist purposes, the important point is the reaction of the world community to that attack. If my theory is correct, Iraq's attack would have been condemned by the world community in no uncertain terms but for the Iran's seizure of the hostages.[120]

Legitimacy of legal claims can indeed be measured by the positive reaction of the legal community towards the expectations at stake. Nonetheless, can we judge the legality of an armed attack based upon the inaction or the indifference of the international community? If so, situations like the U.S. invasion of Grenada in October, 1983 would be rendered legitimate simply because there was no perceptible significant reaction from the international community.[121]

The most important observation I derive from Professor D'Amato's theory is that the problem of enforcement has always been an obsession for international lawyers and that it will remain one unless we understand that our objective is to investigate the degree of effectiveness of international law as decision making guiding and constraining device and not the building of a comprehensive theory about its distinct means of enforcement. The efforts of legal inquiry should be addressed to reveal how international law is effective in helping international participants to vindicate expectations about rights. An appraisal of such effectiveness is not only a matter of enforcement or retaliatory strategies; it involves much more than that. It should determine how useful the activation of international legal dynamics has proved to be in disclosing the prevailing expectations of rights the international community is ready to advance and defend, irrespective of the opposing individualistic interests of its members. The problem was aptly posed by Hart when he suggested that one of the essential features of a legal system is that it provides "some generally effective motive for obedience (perhaps a sense of obligation and not necessarily fear) when obedience runs counter to the individual's inclinations or interest."[122] Thus, enforcement is perhaps no more than one way through which the law becomes effective. "This is not to deny that enforcement is an important condition of the effectiveness of many sorts of rules in a wide range of circumstances,...but no simple formula is adequate to summarize the forms, occasions, and degree of enforcement by which the efficacy of law is affected."[123] Effectiveness thus is a matter of degree that international lawyers should be able to measure and monitor and even predict under certain conditions. This is the most valuable advice that legal scholars can give to international clients, when these are confronted with the decision of whether to operate the dynamics of international law or resort to other mechanisms for solving their problems.

CHAPTER III

THE FRAMEWORK:

INDICATORS OF EFFECTIVENESS IN INTERNATIONAL LAW

A. Myth and Operational Systems of International Law

W. Michael Reisman distinguishes between two normative systems: a Myth system is a normative system that is supposed to apply, one, in other words, that enjoys lip service among elites; and an Operational system is a normative system that actually is applied.[124] The effectiveness of international law may be assessed by examining the distinct and varied ways in which these two normative systems function.

Unlike domestic legal systems where centralized law-applying and law-enforcement institutions operate the law on behalf of the society and "victims", international law needs interested participants to assume the role of "initiators" or "operators." In this sense, the effectiveness of the international normative system must be appraised by first tracing the ways actors use that system in their formulation of claims, arguments, and decisions. These ways may be found within a process that, in turn, could be subdivided for analytical purposes into two distinct but sequential phases. The first phase is basically concerned with the "Myth system" whereas the second phase deals only with the "Operational system."

A Myth system comprises all technical legal information available to international actors, including formal and informal sources of law. Moreover, it also incorporates the wide spectrum of actors' interpretations, perceptions, and expectations, which are by no means free of their ideological preferences or self interests. In this connection, a Myth system comprises a form of "knowledge," in the sense that Ernst B. Haas uses the term: as "the sum of technical information and of theories about that information which commands sufficient consensus at a given time among interested actors to serve as a guide to public policy designed to achieve some social goal."[125]. The Myth system, in other words, comprises technical criteria that international actors use while bargaining.

A Myth system becomes effective when policy makers decide to formulate their demands in such technical legal terms and to make use of legal rules according to the appealing and restraining expectations that they derive from them. According to Haas, a knowledge that succeeds in dominating the policy-making process and that implies acceptance by all major actors --and target audiences-- is considered "consensual." It does not matter where this knowledge comes from or who originated it, but "once knowledge escapes the political and economic control of its originators, it becomes a kind of "international public good."[126] The legal knowledge that is contained in the Myth system of international law is presumably "consensual" and "public,"--at least to the parties that have consented to be bound by it--and should fit Haas's conception of "consensual knowledge." However, such presumption is rarely accurate. The language of legal rules is most of the time ambiguous, and as such, the information contained in legal rules--and consequently, the expectations that actors derive from such information--is rarely fully consensual. I propose, however, that when diverging normative expectations become more consensual through the translation of prevailing expectations into the expectations of most parties and target audiences, the legal knowledge of the Myth system becomes more consensual as well. But the mechanics of translating divergent normative expectations into prevailing expectations first and into consensual legal knowledge later, are characteristic features of the "Operational system" that I discuss next. As to the Myth system, it may suffice, in these introductory remarks, to say that it comprises legal knowledge--not necessarily consensual--and that its effectiveness depends on whether international actors utilize or not that knowledge in the settlement of their disputes.

The Operational system is activated when one or more participants resort in fact to the "Myth system" either to advance their legal entitlements or to simply justify their acts. In this sense, when the Operational system enters into the picture, it is because the Myth system has already achieved some degree of effectiveness; namely, most actors evaluate actions and formulate arguments according to their particular understanding of applicable legal standards of conduct. In operational contexts, international actors have already decided to frame a particular demand within the context of technical legal knowledge and to advance their particular normative expectations in support of their demands. To phrase it differently, in the Operational system, legal knowledge, as comprised in a Myth system, is in fact applied to policy-making. The exchange of claims and expectations occurring within the bargaining process, as well as the bargaining styles of participants and their capacity to manage knowledge and achieve consensus makes conceivable an Operational system that affects the motivations of one or all of the parties in the controversy.

The effectiveness of an Operational system can be traced by monitoring the adequacy of the international arenas that participants select, the bargaining styles participants use to link different issues and goals, the international reaction to expectations that prevail or survive,[127] and the degrees of consensual knowledge, learning, adaptation, and restraint that may have motivated participants during and after the bargaining process. A more detailed discussion on these indicators follows in section C below. However, it is useful to point out here that these indicators are inevitably "empirical." Although some of them have been discussed by philosophers of the social sciences in an effort to demonstrate the "rationality" of legal debates,[128] such demonstration is not their purpose here. The empirical devices hereby suggested seek a much less ambitious task. They are only intended to facilitate basic empirical criteria to assist international lawyers and politicians to evaluate international legal dynamics in terms of its probable degrees of effectiveness at influencing decision.

B. The "Appealing" And "Restraining" Character Of The "Myth" System

B.1. "Extrinsic" and "Intrinsic" Indicators

With our interest now focused on the perceptions and expectations that international actors derive both from the body of international legal principles, norms, rules, and procedures and the theories about international law, let us consider how those expectations influence the expectations of other actors and *vice versa*. I am particularly interested in observing the ways in which the consensus that most participants reach on certain legal issues impinges on their behavior so as to promote their learning, restraint, or adaptation.

The first stage in my approach is to focus on the initial contact between the Myth system and its potential operators. The questions that need to be asked here include the following: What makes international actors utilize legal principles, norms, rules, and procedures in their bargaining contexts? What factors determine why actors view existing legal information as tactical or referential guidelines in some cases and as substantive restraining commands in others? These questions focus on the stage at which the international operator is about to decide what "knowledge" and decision making style to use in the bargaining process. In other words, the appealing and restraining features of the Myth system that concern us here are those that impinge on the operator's decision on whether to advance legal arguments and if so, what kind of

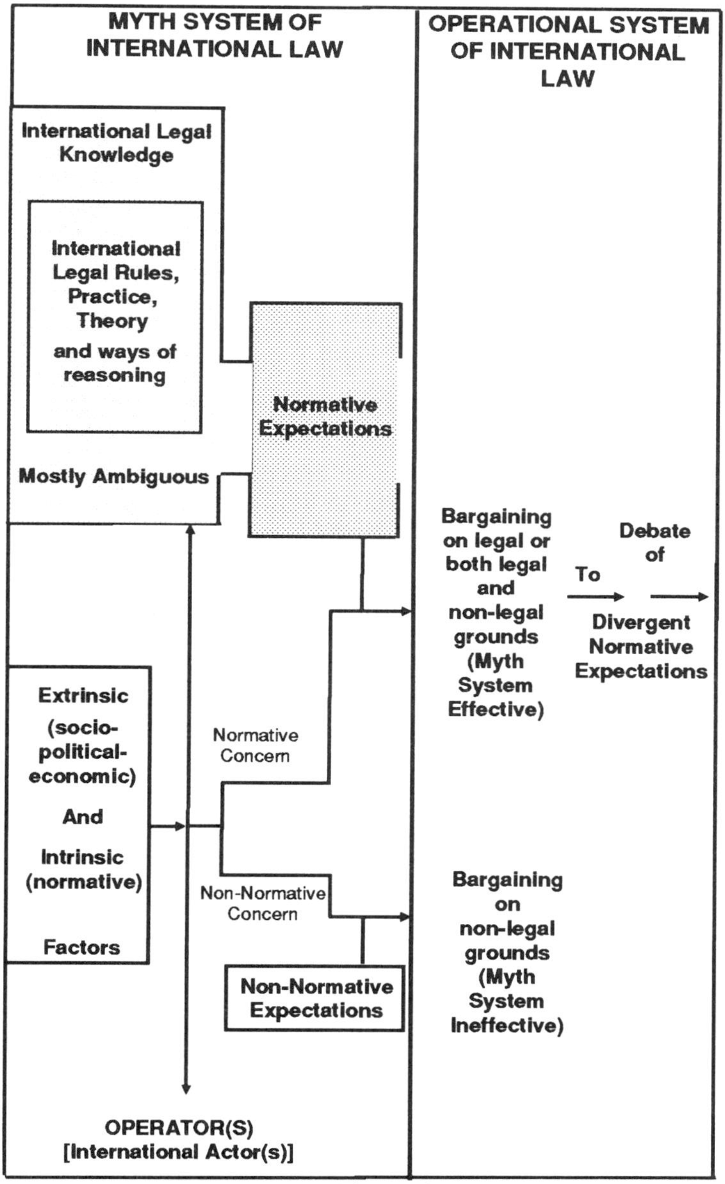
MYTH SYSTEM OF INTERNATIONAL LAW
OPERATIONAL SYSTEM OF INTERNATIONAL LAW
International Legal Knowledge
International Legal Rules, Practice, Theory and ways of reasoning
Mostly Ambiguous
Normative Expectations
Extrinsic (socio-political-economic) And Intrinsic (normative) Factors
Normative Concern
Non-Normative Concern
Non-Normative Expectations
OPERATOR(S) [International Actor(s)]
Bargaining on legal or both legal and non-legal grounds (Myth System Effective)
To
Debate of
Divergent Normative Expectations
Bargaining on non-legal grounds (Myth System Ineffective)

Figure 1

arguments. These features are certainly different from those that influence actors who are already involved in bargaining (Operational system).

Having made this distinction, one may notice that both extrinsic and intrinsic factors affect actors at this early stage. Extrinsic factors are connected with the sociopolitical and economical situation surrounding norms and actors in a particular context; we might also refer to them as "sociopolitical" factors. Intrinsic factors include those features of legal norms and institutions themselves that exert some appealing and restraining effects on actors; these might be called "normative" factors.

Extrinsic factors greatly influence the way participants regard legal rules, norms, principles and procedures. Though some basic principles and norms are transmitted to the public through various media, legal information is not always available or simply utilizable by decision-makers. On many occasions, top policy-makers have not had any substantial contact or exposure to international legal knowledge. This may happen when the foreign affairs office of a nation state may not have adequate professional and technical legal advice.[129] The appealing or the restraining effects of a Myth system have much to do with factors such as participants' exposure to the contents of the system, the financial and educational resources they have allocated to research and training in relevant international legal issues, the degree of influence exerted by legal departments in foreign offices, and the educational and professional orientation and background of decision-makers. Likewise, there seems to be a connection between the appealing or restraining qualities of a Myth system and the relative power of the antagonists, their position in alliances, and the issues that engage them.[130] For example, developing states exhibit a strong affection for legal structures, as indicated by the role of international law in North-South relations, because these countries believe that "the biases of constitutive rules of the sovereignty game today favor the weak."[131] There is much truth, indeed, in the assumption that states in the most marginal parts of the ex-colonial world and particularly Africa, where extreme underdevelopment prevails, have survived as sovereigns primarily by being able to advance their right "not to be interfered". This is what Bedjaoui tries to encapsulate when he asserts that "for the first time in human history, international law is not on the side of force and power"[132]. In fact, Haas demonstrated that even though the United States was the hegemon and leader in United Nations affairs until the middle of the 1960s, no new hegemonic state took its place except when the Non-Aligned Movement voted together and dominated the United Nations General Assembly.[133]

In sum, there are factors, which are external to the legal norms that may determine the attitude of international participants towards such norms. Those factors affect the ways different actors process legal information and formulate their various expectations about that information. These expectations, in turn, determine the degree to which actors feel, if they do, compelled to use that information in their bargaining strategies. External factors also determine the particular forms in which such information is utilized, in order to reflect ideological and individualistic interests of interpreting participants.

The New Haven School recognizes the importance of normative perceptions as forged by external factors, but neglects to address other normative features and constraints that also arise in the pre-bargaining process. These are features and constraints "proper" of pre-existing legal knowledge itself, that may have an effect at shaping the behavior of international participants in a diversified international community. In this connection, the effectiveness of a Myth system is to be sought not only within the extrinsic factors affecting actors' normative expectations, but also in some intrinsic features of that system. We take up this subject in the following section.

B.2. Legitimacy

B.2.1. Legitimacy And Its Major Elements

The intrinsic features of the "Myth System" refer to the particular ways in which the structure of norms and the specific "language" of rules affect decision makers in their applications of international legal knowledge. McDougal and Reisman have pointed out that the "scientific study of the causes and consequences of "rules," without clear relation to decision, is a difficult task, and can scarcely be expected to contribute to the more effective performance of other relevant tasks."[134] But the study of legal knowledge in light of the normative expectations that decision-makers derive from the rule to make-up their minds, is indispensable to assess the effectiveness of international law. While scholars often skip the preliminary question of what intrinsic features of a Myth system make a decision-maker resort to legal considerations in the first place, non-positivists like McDougal and Reisman mainly tend to focus on the "Operational system" to appraise the usefulness of legal norms in solving social problems. In a recent essay, however, Professor Thomas Franck has shed new light on the intrinsic features of legal rules through his theory on the "legitimacy" of international legal norms.[135]

Franck suggests that a legal rule may not necessarily require external means of enforcement as to elicit compliance from international actors. He calls this quality of international rules the norm's "pull to compliance" or legitimacy. Franck focuses on four elements that determine the legitimacy of a norm, namely, determinacy, symbolic validation, coherence, and adherence to a normative hierarchy. Applying this analysis, he finds that some rules exert more pull to compliance on actors than others, and consequently, that legitimacy, as opposed to coercion, seems to be the key to legal order and systematic obedience.[136] Observing the way Franck's categories explain how "rules to varying degrees, contain the determining elements of their own legitimacy" and pull to compliance, enable us with a tenable explanation of why international operators would "seriously" consider resorting to international law in the first instance. Such explanation illustrates, in turn, the intrinsic factors on which international legal effectiveness depends.

The first factor Franck considers is "determinacy," by which he means the "ability of the text [of the norm] to convey a clear message, to appear transparent in the sense that one can see through the language to the meaning."[137] To be determinant, he writes, "a rule must communicate what conduct is permitted and what conduct is out of bounds"[138]. Franck does not contend that all international rules are determinate, but he finds that a "high degree of textual determinacy goes together with a high degree of rule-conforming state behavior."[139] An important ingredient to determinacy is the "clarity" of the norm, which is not, as Franck explains, the same as "simplicity":

> Articles 2(4) and 51 [of the UN Charter] set out a simple rule pertaining to the use of force...nevertheless, despite its superficial clarity, the rule -under certain circumstances --does not satisfy the test of genuine determinacy....The rule would seem to compel a state threatened by a nuclear attack to wait until it had actually been hit [armed attack] before being permitted to use force in self-defence"[140]

Thus, clarity does not preclude complexity. The drafted language of a rule may in fact require several complex constructions in order to avoid *reductio ad absurdum* or ambiguous interpretations. Franck's discussion of determinacy, however, ends up conceding the necessity for some kind of authoritative determination, one that lies beyond the intrinsic features of the norm and that he describes as "a process for resolving ambiguities in its application".[141] This need for a process of authoritative determination is both necessary and inoffensive to the concept of the determinacy of the law itself.

Without some such process, the kind of rules that Franck recognizes as determinant would be so few, that international law would be reduced to a small group of norms that are so precisely worded and structured. Norms that are sufficiently clear to communicate their intent will always require a process through which they are shaped into specific situational commands. The problem for our purposes is not the need for a process of authoritative determination, which we acknowledge as indispensable, but the fact that determinacy in Franck's terms has not true bearing on the Myth system. Because ambiguities in the final analysis need be resolved in some operational way, determinacy, what started as a property of the norm, winds up being dependant on a process that is definitely conducted within the operational system.

Although Franck does not mention this himself, it may happen that a rule that lacked determinacy when created may with time, and in light of substantial past authoritative determination, become so determinant as to convey similar normative expectations to all interpreters without the need for further authoritative determination. This different approach to determinacy may prove more useful for our purposes as an explanation of why some rules attract or restrain potential users. International operators usually seriously evaluate the way a rule has been applied in the past and the consensus previous operators of the rule have reached in their understanding of the technical knowledge expressed by its letter. Indeed, all international legal norms are expected to serve as "items of reference" that restrain to a greater or lesser extent the normative expectations of potential operators. A norm, however, that at the outset is incapable of serving as such a restraining item of reference would be any rule of conventional or customary international law which policy makers rationally perceive--or misperceive--only as an optional alternative of conduct. This happens when the knowledge the rule incorporates is less consensual and therefore, more ambiguous. This might be the case when it is not totally clear whether the international community as a whole expects the norm to prevail in every circumstances at a certain point in time. The prohibition against "us[ing] or encourag[ing] the use of economic, political or any other type of measures to coerce another State in order to obtain from it the subordination of the exercise of its sovereign rights or to secure from it advantages of any kind" falls in this category.[142] While several scholars categorize economic sanctions as a form of pressure that constitutes a threat of force,[143] The International Court of Justice has refused to find such actions to be a breach of Article 2(4) of the United Nations Charter or the customary principle of nonintervention.[144] Thus, Franck's approach to rule determinacy helps us see that clear and determined rules--though not abundant in the Myth system--are more likely than ambiguous rules to appeal to and/or restrain potential operators.

Symbolic validation, the second element Franck discusses, has to do with ritual and pedigree as social strategies to induce compliance with rule systems. Franck mentions as an example of a ritual "the entry of the mace" into the British House of Commons, an act intended to commemorate the Commons' long and successful struggle to capture law-making power from the Crown.[145] It is difficult to ascertain the extent to which a ritual can "pull" participants to respect the rules it is purported to validate. However, the generalized practice of rituals in many areas of human endeavor seems to support the contention that ritual do induce some such influence. Rituals such as the commemoration of "Independence Day" or "National Day" are purported to enhance allegiance to principles and rules of sovereignty, self-determination, and nonintervention. In fact, rituals may not reduce the ambiguity of the norm but affirm specific normative expectations about them. Certain rituals, according to Franck, also endow rules of pedigree. State diplomatic practice, for example, is firmly embedded in rituals and pedigrees: "The sending state, by the rituals of accreditation, endows its diplomats with pedigree."[146] The receiving state, by following rituals of acceptance and *exequatur*, confirms generalized expectations of the sending state. Professor Franck offers numerous examples of these symbolic validations. To mention a few, the form of organization of various transnational agencies such as the "World Bank" is heavily symbolic of the equality of states, though only industrial nations contribute most of its working capital; flags, stamps, and other symbols of the United Nations reinforce the legitimacy of its purposes, institutional jurisdiction, and regulations; "the extension of diplomatic immunity to top UN officials, privileges usually reserved for representatives of states, symbolizes the emergence of the Organization as an autonomous international actor, pedigreed in its own right."[147]

Somewhat more problematic is coherence, the third distinctive element of international legal norms that may induce international operators to use a given norm as a starting point for international debate. Franck bases his treatment of the concept on Dworkin's notion of "integrity."[148] According to Dworkin, "a rule is coherent when like cases are treated alike in application of the rule and when the rule relates in a principled fashion to other rules of the same system."[149] Within this framework, coherence requires that a rule be "applied" consistently in every similar instance. For the purpose of a Myth system we focus on coherence as an element that suggests decision makers the ways a rule has been applied in the past and the ways that rule is to be applied in present and future cases without necessarily disturbing or violating other principles of the system. However, the element of "coherence" as intrinsic to a norm requires that a rule, standard, or validating ritual, gathers force if it is seen to be connected to a network of other rules by an underlying general principle.[150] Such general principle is Dworkin's notion of "integrity", a consistency in action and principle among the acts of a state. As Dworkin indicates, a "state lacks integrity because it must endorse principles to justify part of what it has done that it must reject to justify the rest.[151]" The historic incoherent application of the principles of nonintervention and self-defense in the Western Hemisphere clearly illustrates the degenerative impact of the actors' constant manipulation of principles and rules for different--and often contrasting--purposes. Thus, lack of integrity leads to lack of coherence in the application of rules, and in turn, incoherent practice affects the legitimacy of the rule in question. Unfortunately, this latter phenomena is frequent in the international society where integrity does not seem to be the common force that moves international political action.

Following Franck's notion of coherence is his treatment of adherence. Adherence is used to mean the "vertical nexus between a single primary rule of obligation (cross on the green; stop on the red) and a pyramid of secondary rules about how rules are made, interpreted and applied; rules, in other words, about rules."[152] A secondary rule that lacks adherence to a primary rule has less pull to compliance than another that does. For example, a treaty to commit genocide would be disregarded as a "useful" normative body for the simple reason that it goes against the community's basic public policy, as stated in a norm of *ius cogens*.[153] The same can be said of norms that are *ab initio* or subsequently contradicted by an extensive array of customary practice and lines of consensus in the international community. Franck cites as an example the unfruitful attempt of the United States, in the Nicaragua Case, to maintain arguments based on doubtful considerations of collective self-defense in contradiction with established customary international law.[154] Somewhat harder to demonstrate is to regard adherence to primary rules. In order to find out when a primary rule bears "adherence," we must see how the international community comes to regard such primary rule to adhere to other primary rules or other "more fundamental" rules. Such discussion was precisely the main source of discrepancies between *jus naturalists* and *positivists* various decades ago, and perhaps one of the most controversial issues of general legal theory. However, Franck is correct in assuming that the international community is not merely a playing field on which states are engaged in various, random, or opportunistic exchanges or interactions. He is also right in accepting Dworkin's contention that a true community, as distinguished from a mere rabble, is one in which the members accept that their "political rights and duties are not exhausted by the particular decisions their political institutions have reached, but depend, more generally, on the scheme of principles those decisions presuppose and endorse."[155] We accept this conception with some qualifications that we explain in the following section.

B.2.2. Legitimacy And Consensual Knowledge

Franck's four elements of legitimacy--with the reservations we have highlighted before--serve as indicators that may imply, as Franck suggests, that rules and institutions will necessarily exhibit an intrinsic powerful pull to compliance. Whether that assertion may prove true or false, Franck's indicators at least shed light on why international actors may find it appealing to use, or simply feel constrained to resort to, legal argumentation as a bargaining and problem-solving tool.

An example of the relevance of legitimacy for the effectiveness of a Myth system, is the compelling necessity imposed on decision makers by "precedent," both judicial and diplomatic. The strategy of linking issues through precedent is one of the most common and persuasive methods that actors employ in bargaining contexts. In appealing to precedent, decision-makers almost invariably resort to legal knowledge--in particular judicial or arbitral decisions, and customary international law--to advance expectations they regard as being the most consensual. By more consensual we mean those normative expectations that have succeeded in the past at describing what major actors consider to be appropriate behavior. Decision makers act upon the belief that precedent is persuasive because it shows some degrees of general acceptance. Although they may be opportunistic and unaltruistic, actors seem to be aware that their involvement in a situation of strategic interdependence necessarily entails a "mutual awareness that their moves depend on how they perceive the perceptions of the antagonist, whose array of options depends on the same double calculations."[156] In this sense, we can say that underlying the four elements of legitimacy suggested by Franck is the fact that a Myth system comprises a body of useful guidelines and indicators of constraint on which wise actors may built expectations and support claims in a world of complex interdependence. This property of the Myth system makes it indispensable for decision-making tasks.

To be sure, legal knowledge does not always have to be consensual--it does not have to be shared by major participants--in order for some to use it to advance arguments and shape their decision-making and bargaining styles. But rules the determination of whose meaning has involved several occasions of consensus formation and subsequent acceptance, would be as appealing as those that are clearly written norms or those who show one or more of the qualities suggested above, that is, of certainty, symbolic validation, coherence, and adherence. To illustrate the former kind of rules we can mention the so-called peremptory norms of international law *(jus cogens)* or norms that are defined as having been "accepted and recognized by the international community of states as a whole and from which no derogation is permitted." These rules are deemed as susceptible of being modified only by a subsequent norm of general international law that "has the same character."[157]

B.3. Procedural Indicators

Last but not least, procedural questions also affect the potential operator's assessment of the law. Potential operators need to know whether adequate procedures are available for the efficient transmission of legal claims and arguments, whether, in other words, they can viably initiate and conduct legal argumentation in the first place. While the Myth system provides a series of peaceful methods for settling disputes and in principle prohibits the use of threat of force,[158] self-help is never completely ruled out from the minds of some decision makers. Statute or agreement usually determines the actual limits and mechanics of these various methods,[159] but the operators themselves choose whether or not to use any one or more of these methods, based on their calculated answers to the important procedural questions.

In deciding whether a particular procedure is adequate to transmit legal claims, potential operators most importantly assess the potential of the procedure to favorably or negatively affect the normative expectations and decision-making styles of the adversary and/or target audiences. In this connection, the operator's calculations about the adequacy of a particular procedure seem to indicate about the effectiveness of this procedural aspect of the Myth system. But the operator's calculations are not absolute and their final choice as to what procedure to use is certainly not free from restraint. The power and alliances and other sociopolitical influences on the respective parties as well as the parties' degree of consensus about the legitimacy of the method have all proved to be of great significance in determining the adequacy of a procedure to transmit legal claims. For example, there is a generalized belief that the threat or use of force are not legitimate means to resolve a conflict, thus, it seems unlikely that forcible means are useful and effective methods for transmitting legal expectations. True, the use of force in international relations may be the most direct--and probably an immediately effective--way to impose one's will on someone else, irrespective of the justness and the legitimacy of one's normative expectations. But the threat or use of force can also be the most ineffective way to make one's normative expectations ultimately prevail over the others', simply because our normative expectations--however rightful and consensual--will tend to be judged by the international community according to the community's acceptance of the means that are used to advance them. Perhaps, this is one reason why States will always try to justify the threat or use of force under the protecting umbrella of self-defense in Article 51 of the UN Charter.[160]

At the same time actors are legally restrained against the use or threat of force, they may also feel attracted to use legitimate means for settling their disputes. When facing high levels of uncertainty, decision makers seek information about methods available for action. They find part of that information in extant legal knowledge. Using legal knowledge inevitably introduces legal-reasoning in the decision making process. Legal reasoning, in turn, can only be appropriately conducted through legitimate means for settling disputes. Thus, we can say that decision makers are normally inclined to resort to diplomacy and peaceful means than self-help and force. In this sense, the uncertainty that characterizes conflict and the actors' need for information to cope with such uncertainty favor the use of legal knowledge, legal reasoning, and peaceful methods of conflict-resolution. Legal knowledge attracts the attention of actors not only because it is a tool to legitimize their actions, but also because "legal reasoning helps to limit purely subjective interpretation"[161] and the uncertainty that develops out of manipulative arguments. Using legal knowledge replaces vague criteria such as "common sense" or "reasonableness" as sources of actors's expectations. When legal knowledge prevails as the main source of expectations, actors will necessarily narrow their values and preferences to give room to legal notions of "textual exegesis, original intent, relevant context, evolving purposes, and practice accepted as law."[162]

Therefore, at least in theory, the narrower the conflict-solving criteria that actors apply to the controversy, the narrower their uncertainty. Because legal criteria and reasoning introduce a narrower frame of reference for solving disputes than moral and sociopolitical discourses, a shift in the debate, from moral or political to legal, tends to narrow uncertainty among participants. Military and forcible methods also narrow uncertainty insofar as contending parties focus on logistic considerations to measure their possibilities to succeed in battle. But success in battle does not necessarily mean diplomatic success. We, thus, argue that legal debate is the best alternative to force when it comes to narrowing the uncertainties of a conflict or crisis. For example, Argentina's military occupation of the Falkland Islands on April 2, 1982 was not exactly the best option that President Galtieri had in order "to call attention from the Secretary General of the United Nations or big powers to intervene."[163] Even superpowers have found isolation and failure when using force to communicate claims and expectations. The Soviet invasion of Afghanistan and the United States military actions in Nicaragua are examples in this regard.[164]

However "understandable" the reasons Iraq may have had in attacking Iran, none of them seems to have any relevance today to conceal or justify the means it used to advance such reasons. Within a different context, no matter how voluminous the evidence the U.S. may have had to prove that the Sandinistas were "exporting their revolution," it was the U.S. trade embargo, its laying of mines in the internal and territorial waters of Nicaragua, and its military and paramilitary activities that finally counted for the International Court of Justice and the international public opinion.[165] By exhausting recognized and accepted peaceful procedures and advancing normative expectations, claimants can best reduce uncertainty and prove most capable of distinguishing and transmitting their normative expectations to the other participants and target audiences.

C. Appraising Effectiveness in the Operational System

In the previous section I emphasized the appealing and restraining features of the Myth system and briefly commented upon the uncertainty that characterizes conflict. Indeed, situations of international conflict, especially those that rise to the level of crises, are characterized by high levels of uncertainty. Actors must choose without adequate information about the situation at hand and/or without the general knowledge they need to assess the likely outcomes of different courses of action.[166] As a logical response to uncertainty, international actors search for information, and very often for legal information--as a source of accepted standards of conduct--because international actors generally understand that bargaining on legal grounds and legal reasoning narrows the margins of uncertainty.

When discussing the effectiveness of the Myth system, I emphasized that in coping with uncertainty operators resort to legal argumentation and appropriate procedures for transmitting their expectations, either because they have no other choice or because they find that doing so serves their own interests. But as soon as they start bargaining on legal grounds, operators need to reshape their expectations and claims in order to prevail in the debate. To avoid failure, operators feel constrained to replace old expectations with those prevailing in the negotiated or authoritative determination process.

If "insects cannot transcend stereotyped behavior without genetic change...people can by drawing on experience".[167] Actors, in other words, react to the expectations that major participants recognize as valid and "<u>learn</u>" or "<u>adapt</u>" to change their policies accordingly. Ernst B. Haas writes that "learning occurs when communists, capitalists, totalitarians, and democrats agree that, in some issue-area, new information or knowledge compels the redefinition of past interests."[168] Haas also describes learning in this particular context of bargaining as "a form of persuasion," persuasion that "implies an initial disagreement among the parties, which is gradually resolved or settled by compromise."[169] Applied to conflict resolution, learning is just one possible outcome. Actors may refuse or not be able to learn; they may just adapt--not because of persuasion but because of necessity--or they may simply remain unchanged while the conflict goes unresolved. At "learning" or "adapting," actors find that international legal knowledge exerts degrees of restraint. These degrees are, at least, higher than what they may find in negotiations that are conducted only upon "reasonableness" and "common sense" criteria.

Indeed, legal knowledge comprises normative commands which, if conceded by most parties and target audiences in a dispute, induce participants to follow legal ways of reasoning. From this perspective, legal knowledge, because of its normative character, has an unparalelled importance for settling disputes. The effectiveness of the Operational system can be appraised in terms of the voluntary or constrained changes of the mind and attitude that disputants experience as a direct result of their efforts to apply and clarify legal knowledge; it can also be evaluated by the impact that disputant's increasing consensus over other not strictly legal factors may have on the final solution of the dispute.

The object of this section, is to identify some indicators that may facilitate the task of appraising the impact of legal knowledge over changes in participants' decision-making styles.

C.1. Law And Facts

Among the stronger constraints upon operators in their application of legal knowledge is the requirement that they demonstrate that the rule in question, and the corresponding normative expectations, clearly apply within the given facts of the case. This requirement limits actor's normative expectations to only those allowed by credible and plausible arguments of law and fact. Hence, having to show consistency between their legal claims and the factual context of the situation, pressures international actors to narrow their manipulative attitudes towards the law. The "fattispecie"[170] as denominated by Italian legal scholars, is most relevant within this context. "Fattispecie" is a hypothetical statement of facts that the norm contemplates, whose concrete occurrence in the" real world" justifies the application of the norm's command and its production of legal effects.[171] To advance credible legal arguments, operators must prove that the hypothetical fact provided by the norm actually occurred. Such relationship between the "fattispecie" and the actual fact must thus be supported by adequate "evidence."[172]

In interpreting Article 53 of its Statute, the International Court of Justice has indicated that the Court is obliged to employ "whatever means and resources may enable it to satisfy itself whether the submissions of the applicant State are well-founded in fact and law, and simultaneously to safeguard the sound administration of justice."[173] This way of reasoning complements the application of the principle actori incumbit probatio by which the Court will "formally require the party putting forward a claim to establish the elements of fact and of law on which the decision in its favor might be given."[174] The Court, therefore, is the typical arena where the correlation between law and fact is a major requirement for the sound application of legal knowledge. As a matter of its statute, the Court shall take the major responsibility in matters of evidence, either by producing that which it may consider indispensable or by exercising its discretionary authority to refuse or accept the evidence offered by the parties.[175] In practice however, the Court has constantly interpreted this responsibility as "careful respect for the onus probandi of the Roman and civil law systems,"[176] encouraging the parties to submit the necessary evidence.[177]

A coherent relationship between law and facts in legal argumentation is perhaps the cornerstone of legal practice in all contexts.[178] The previous attempt to stress the way evidence is treated at the International Court of Justice is to indicate that the parties to a dispute are normally responsible to furnish the evidence and relate it to both fact and law. Therefore, actors' claims are required to demonstrate that considerations of fact are undisputed and that they accurately fit the "fattispecie" of current international legal norms.

C.2. Arenas

In a classical course at the Hague Academy of International Law, Derek Bowett opened his remarks by distinguishing between peaceful and legal means for settling disputes.[179] On that occasion Professor Bowett commented that a peaceful technique is "rarely indifferent to the legal rights of the parties." In theory, however, only arbitration and judicial settlement are strictly "legal" means, for this two techniques alone "involve the application of law to the exclusion of political discretion...."[180]

Professor Bowett's view reflects the traditional approach to the study of the methods for the settlement of disputes. Here, "legal means" include all procedures that one or various participants select in order to cope with legal uncertainty. If using legal knowledge narrows sociopolitical uncertainty, remaining uncertainty is supposedly to be mainly one of a legal kind. Professor Bowett aptly reasons that states resort to legal settlement (arbitration and judicial) precisely because the solution dictated by the law is not clear.[181] Different from Professor Bowett's thesis, we believe that all peaceful methods for solving conflict are "legal" to the extent that they involve legal expectations and are intended to reduce uncertainty by way of legal reasoning. The fact that participants resort to arbitration or judicial settlement in search of further reductions of legal uncertainty does not mean that previous negotiation, mediation, or conciliation instances did not touch upon legal expectations.[182]

To monitor the impact of legal knowledge on the resolution of international conflict, then, one should focus on the development of legal argumentation through the various arenas the parties have utilized. Such effort should provide enough empirical data about the legal issues at stake to ascertain whether new legal knowledge has emerged or greater consensus on a particular set of normative expectations has been reached. Full certainty is surely impossible, but increasingly consensual legal knowledge is always a possibility.

As pointed out above, legal knowledge may be processed through two distinct channels:

i. negotiated methods (bilateral or multilateral negotiations, good offices, mediation, conciliation) and,
ii. authoritative determination (arbitration and adjudication).

In negotiating contexts, the international community, acting as target audience, may constrain the actors to re-assess normative expectations. Some constraints upon actors arise out of institutionalized or *ad hoc* requirements that legal arguments be consistent with the facts as broadcast and publicized through the media and other more or less formal channels of information. Also, negotiating contexts process legal knowledge, that is to say, clarifies or diffuse it, through the exchange of claims and through the actors' reassessment of their original expectations. Whether it is arrived at, by negotiation or authoritative determination, a consensus reached by parties formerly in dispute presupposes that some normative expectations have prevailed over others. Consequently, the key to understanding the extent to which negotiations generate consensus is to monitor the parties' normative expectations throughout the bargaining process.[183]

Third-party authoritative determination--including arbitration and adjudication--involves more specialized arenas than do negotiating methods. Within the narrower structural constraints of authoritative determinations, legal knowledge is reflected primarily in the arguments of the parties. Particularly in the sphere of adjudication, the first aim of both the parties and the judges is to reduce the dispute to its major legal issues. These issues are processed within the specialized intellectual framework of international lawyers, professionals who share similar traditions of thought and techniques. The judges and the parties' counsels, on the one hand, are usually members of the same "invisible college" or "epistemic community,"[184] and as such, they tend to emphasize their own frames of reference for the solution of the dispute. Within this context, the disputing parties depend on the advice and counsel of international lawyers, who, in turn, are members of the same epistemic or professional community as the judges, and who accept, in principle, to be bound by the tribunal's decision. Thus, the third-party who arbitrates or adjudicates the dispute is invested with authority not only by the parties in dispute but also by their counsels, advisers and by other members of the international legal community throughout the world. That means that actors themselves may be influenced by the advice of professionals who belong to the same community or to compatible or equivalent ones. Though decision makers are not necessarily vulnerable to epistemic communities (transnational or domestic communities of international lawyers and other associated professionals), these communities, may in turn, help confer meaning on events, and hence predetermine the variety of policy alternatives that will be invoked in response to such events.

Thus, two distinct sets of indicators of the impact of arenas on legal knowledge and participants' attitude need to be highlighted. First, one may watch the influence of epistemic communities on the parties decision-making styles, that is, the role of national and transnational scholars, experts, advisers, and professionals, who share the normative expectations that prevail through negotiation or that are determined by arbitration or adjudication. Second, one may monitor the translation of prevailing expectations into "consensual knowledge" and its effects on the bargaining styles and goals of decision-makers by tracing the ways the parties either reaffirm beliefs or change their minds as to means and goals, by learning or adaptation.

The categorization of arenas as indicators has to do not only with the methods through which knowledge is processed, but also with the interaction and sometimes interdependence between those arenas. Complex international conflicts, particularly those that amount to crises, are usually worked out at various arenas. The way in which these arenas are interconnected and affect each other depends on the kind of predominant knowledge orienting the various debates and the prevailing expectations at either one of those arenas. Without a clear distinction and delineation of arenas, it is more difficult to assess changes in the goals and bargaining styles of participants. A further discussion of this interconnectedness between arenas is attempted when discussing the impact of the ICJ's judgments on Central America over the Contadora and the Esquipulas Processes and the different coalitions of participants themselves.

C.3. Bargaining Styles

The most relevant aspect of our bridging effort is our attempt to highlight the variables that make possible that international actors "internalize" the prevailing expectations about legal norms. Evaluating the ways by which these actors make-up their minds and change their bargaining styles should illustrate the impact that normative expectations have had on the conflict-resolution process.

Our framework assumes that the actors' bargaining styles intimately relate with the knowledge these actors are using to resolve uncertainty. Thus, changes on bargaining styles are themselves indicators of the effectiveness of legal knowledge. The more consensual the knowledge the greater its impact on the actors ways of bargaining, that is, on their goals and their linkages of issues. Perhaps the ideal case for testing our assumptions is one where all international participants and target audiences fully agree on the applicable knowledge, their expectations from such knowledge, and the resulting criteria for settlement. But, has a conflict ever existed under these conditions? Such a "well-founded consensus" would imply an absolute order of a kind hardly ever seen in actual international affairs and logically possible only within an "ideal speech situation," where "communication...is hampered neither by external contingent factors, nor by constraints which are internal to the structure of communication itself."[185] Situations, however, do exist in which decision makers rely on greater "consensual knowledge" and agree, though just temporarily, to pursue common goals. In this situation, actors who do not share the common conception may well be constrained to learn or adapt, or simply be excluded from the game.

Ernst B. Haas has developed a comprehensive model to explain the relation between "consensual knowledge" and decision-making styles in international relations.[186] In this discussion I adopt his four main bargaining styles and knowledge interconnections.[187] These include, first, the *analytic* decision-making style, where participants link issues and goals in a "substantive" manner. This bargaining style presupposes a "more consensual knowledge" base and usually results in "learning." Second, there is the *pragmatic* mode, where participants raise issues that are "fragmented," some being substantive and some not, and when a significant though not definitely "consensual knowledge" base is present. Learning is less likely to occur under these conditions, but adaptation is still possible. Third, is the *skeptic* mode. Here, non-substantive issues predominate and the knowledge base is less consensual. If changes result, they are through adaptation, not learning. Finally, there is the *eclectic* style where no consensual knowledge exists and thus, issues are linked in purely tactical fashion, if at all. To Haas, bargaining may occur intragovernmentally (between domestic epistemic communities, constituencies, bureaucracies and decision-makers), intracoalitionally (among members of coalitions) or intercoalitionally (among international groups of participants). Within each of these settings, bargaining may be similar (consensus on issues and goals) or dissimilar (no consensus on issues and goals).

Actors in one specific dispute may adopt one or more of the above bargaining styles. Changes in actors' bargaining styles occur to the extent that their claims and arguments are based on a "consensual knowledge" base because the degree of consensual knowledge tends to determine the ways actors link issues to advance their goals. Thus, whether it is reached by negotiation or through authoritative determination, a newly arrived-at consensual knowledge should alter the bargaining styles of participants under the formulae that the stronger the consensus on the relevant knowledge the greater the changes on bargaining styles. I shall further describe Haas's models when using them in Part II to analyze the impact of legal knowledge on the Central American peace negotiations in the 1980s. The sketchy description of Haas's model that precedes, should serve only to indicate that as applied to international legal dynamics, our main concern is the impact of consensual international legal knowledge in the decision-making process. To trace such impact, we must look both at the actors' ability to build a greater consensual knowledge from their legal expectations and the corresponding changes that knowledge produces in their bargaining styles throughout the conflict-resolution process.

PART II

FROM ADAPTATION TO LEARNING: A DECADE OF PEACE NEGOTIATIONS IN CENTRAL AMERICA

INTRODUCTION

This discussion is not intended to provide a comprehensive explanation of the Central American crisis. The purpose is to monitor the influence of legal knowledge in the various arenas in which the parties to the Central American conflict--the so-called Contra War--chose to settle their major disputes between the years of 1979 and 1989. Part II is thus limited in scope to trace the actors' use of legal knowledge to resolve the regional crisis of the 1980's as just one of many variables at play in that historical chain of events.[188]

Legal knowledge certainly cannot be expected to explain failure or success of efforts to resolve conflict through bargaining. It is not the only factor impinging on decision making and cannot be deemed to override social, economic, political and technological factors. True, at specific times and places, the parties in dispute may attribute more relevance to one variable than to another, but the more complex and diverse the issues involved, the less likely that one single variable would prevail distinctly over many others.

I assume that in times of conflict, parties may attempt to settle disputes or to behave in ways that aggravate the problem. However, whenever the intention is to solve conflicts peacefully, legal knowledge is normally expected to provide the basic technical criteria on which negotiations are to be conducted. Though participants may or may not feel compelled to utilize such criteria in the early stages of the problem, there is always a trend in the international community to evaluate demands and counter-demands in terms of legal principles. In other words, legal knowledge is brought into the picture sooner or later in the debate, either as a response to other parties' normative expectations or as a frame of reference within which to support one's own demands and methods for transmitting expectations.

To be sure, technical legal criteria for conflict resolution usually does not permit absolute determinacy. Most of the time, participants' normative expectations diverge even when they derive from a common set of legal norms. But prevailing expectations may be attained from diverging perceptions by "negotiation" or "authoritative determination." In negotiations, either good offices, mediation, conciliation, or any other kind of direct diplomatic bargaining may provide prevailing expectations. In "authoritative determination" the parties delegate to a third decision-maker--arbitrator or adjudicator--the task of coping with ambiguity.

In the past decade, the various attempts to negotiate and adjudicate between the Central American countries constituted a significant effort to use legal expectations to resolve a complex crisis. For this, this period of Central American history that goes from 1979 to 1989 can be used to study the dynamics of legal knowledge. To undertake this task, it is particularly relevant to monitor the influence that increasingly consensual normative expectations exerted on participants' decision-making styles and bargaining strategies.

Tracing the application of legal knowledge in this way has a double advantage. On the one hand, as mentioned, it helps clarify the role of legal knowledge in influencing international decision-making. On the other hand, it allows an evaluation of the methods the parties have chosen to settle their disputes, either for their knowledge-producing or knowledge-disseminating capabilities. This latter advantage requires further qualification. If, as I hope to demonstrate here, consensual knowledge provides clearer, authoritative, or simply more compelling criteria for settling a conflict, then the method that best achieves consensual legal expectations is the most useful for resolving conflict.

In this discussion, I identify four different arenas that the main participants utilized in attempting to resolve conflicts in Central America. The first is *ad-hoc* in nature, namely, the Contadora Process (Contadora). The second is also informal, the Esquipulas II negotiations. The third has a strong institutional component: The United Nations (UN) and the Organizations of American States (OAS). These international organizations are considered here as one type of arena though they clearly have features that are unique to each one of them. The fourth arena, the International Court of Justice (ICJ or the Court), is also formal in character but differs from the UN and the OAS because it provides more than a negotiating context. Although the ICJ is an organ of the United Nations, it is classified separately for expository convenience. However, whatever merits are allocated to the ICJ apply as well for the UN.

In the following pages, I try to demonstrate that the Contadora Group failed as mediator and, as such, it failed to generate consensual legal criteria according to which the parties would be able to accommodate decision-making and bargaining strategies in more similar and meaningful ways. Contadora's failure to produce a consensual legal knowledge resulted mainly from its symbolic use of a few abstract and indeterminate legal principles. This rigid attachment to a few abstract principles artificially connected with other more concrete issues and the lack of a coherent interplay between those principles themselves, prevented all parties from coping with uncertainty. As a result, the parties could not identify and negotiate decisive trade-offs.

Contadora negatively affected other negotiating arenas as well, particularly those within the UN and the OAS, who gave Contadora *de facto* exclusivity to handle Central American problems by persistently sidestepping debate on Central American matters. The ICJ, as I also describe, was much more effective in forging similar normative expectations and thus, shared technical legal criteria for decision-making and bargaining tasks.

Finally, I try next to map out the channels through which this consensual base of legal knowledge impinged on the parties' attitudes. As I have argued before, the effectiveness of legal knowledge in solving international disputes can be measured in terms of its impact on decision makers and by monitoring the extent to which these actors change their bargaining attitudes and decision-making styles.

CHAPTER IV

THE CONTADORA YEARS: 1979-1986

A. An Overview

The June 10, 1986 Contadora Act on Peace and Co-operation in Central America[189] purports to achieve a variety of goals. It seeks national reconciliation, pluralistic democratic systems with free and open elections, and human rights. The Contadora Act also attempts to promote regional detente and confidence building, general security, and other economic and social ideals. Moreover, the 1986 Contadora Act strives to control foreign military intervention, transborder aggression by irregular forces, arms traffic, and internal strife. The final Contadora Act embodied a complex agenda to confirm the fact that "Central America is small but not simple"[190] Summing up the events leading to the drafting of the final Contadora Act provides enough information to suggest the kind of role that international legal knowledge should and should not play in the complex crisis. This section is intended to provide such summary.

With a heritage of social injustice, military governments, fraudulent elections, constant armed conflicts within and across national borders, and violations of basic rights, Central America has undergone increased civil strife and regional military and political tension, particularly, since open insurrection broke out in Nicaragua after the assassination of Pedro Joaquin Chamorro in the late 1970's.[191] The involvement of the United States and the ascent to power of a communist regime in Nicaragua marked the path for regional tensions of great international import.

While its involvement in 1979 was only marginal, the United States by 1985 became the "principal architect, financier, and strategist for the Salvadoran government in general and the armed forces in particular."[192] Washington's efforts were also clearly aimed at preventing a leftist government from consolidating in Nicaragua and spreading throughout the rest of the Central American isthmus. Though the Carter administration made a few efforts in 1979 to communicate with the Sandinistas, President Reagan "proved less tolerant and launched a covert war in Nicaragua with the hope of ousting the Sandinistas and restoring a regime more congenial to the interests and influence of the United States."[193] Costa Rica, El Salvador, and Honduras joined the U.S. in responding negatively to Soviet and Cuban influence in Nicaragua. U.S. Central American allies perceived the Sandinista government as a threat, as capable of both aiding internal insurrection and "exporting its revolution."

The Sandinistas claimed that this fear was unjustified but did little to appease it. Frequently, various Comandantes within the Sandinista army publicly upheld Marxist-Leninist commitments and firm intentions to "export their revolution."[194] Comandante Tomas Borge, for example, told a North Korean audience in June 1980 that "the Nicaraguan revolutionaries will not be content until the imperialists have been overthrown in all parts of the world."[195] Statements like this and evidence that the Sandinistas were supporting the Salvadorean guerrillas (FMLN) and terrorist activities in Costa Rica, Nicaraguas's claim undermined it was not a threat to other countries in the region.[196] International tensions were heightened by the Sandinistas's adoption of intimate political, economic, and military ties with the Soviet Union. Encountering a growing hostility in their relations with the United States and increasing organized insurrection, the Sandinistas declared a state of emergency and established strict internal political and military controls. Local measures in Nicaragua, in turn, gave rise to frequent reports by international organizations of human rights violations.[197]

In 1981, the US and Nicaragua made a few attempts to establish bilateral and multilateral negotiations. In March

1982, during a Meeting of the Nassau Group (Mexico, Venezuela, Canada and the United States), the U.S. proposed an eight-point dialogue with Nicaragua.[198] This was the first of a series of formal proposals that culminated in aggravated tensions between the two governments. The U.S. proposed to subscribe reciprocal promises of non-aggression, to suspend aid to Somoza's insurrectional forces, and renew U.S. economic aid to the Sandinistas, provided that Nicaragua would stop importing arms and supporting the FMLN guerrillas in El Salvador. Nicaragua responded with a ten-point plan that called upon the U.S. to renounce Central America as its strategic frontier.[199]

In January 1982, at roughly the same time that these first bilateral negotiations between the U.S. and Nicaragua took place, the Presidents of El Salvador, Honduras, and Costa Rica formed the so called Central American Democratic Community (CDC). This was an effort t to limit the emerging military power of the Sandinistas. The CDC's strategy was to pressure the Sandinistas into compliance with the promises of representative and democratic institutions they have made to the OAS. The CDC also adopted various resolutions concerning regional economic matters, human rights violations in Nicaragua, and the need to stop incidents of terrorism and sabotage in Costa Rica. Most importantly, the CDC firmly expressed its commitment to resort, if necessary, to the Inter-american Treaty of Reciprocal Assistance (The Rio Treaty), a collective security hemispheric agreement, to implement and enforce all CDC's resolutions.[200]

Mexico strongly oppossed the CDC at meeting on February 12, 1982. Mexican President López Portillo submitted a three-point peace plan that sought to establish of negotiations between the United States, Nicaragua, and Cuba. Reaffirming Mexico's belief that U.S. involvement in the region was a major source of conflict, López Portillo wished to prevent the U.S. from intervening in Nicaraguan internal affairs.[201] Having accomplished little at this meeting, Mexico joined with Venezuela on September 7, 1982 and called for direct negotiations between Nicaragua, Honduras, and the United States. This new diplomatic initiative aimed to stop increasing armed conflicts along the Honduran-Nicaraguan border.[202]

Neither Mexico or Venezuela participated in a subsequent October 1982 meeting in San José, Costa Rica, where the CDC bloc adopted the "Declaration of San José" and a proposal to create the Pro-Peace and Democracy Forum.[203] The Pro Peace and Democracy Forum was intended to verify and coordinate the various peace proposals so far submitted for a negotiated peace in Central America. Mexico and Venezuela feared that the forum would be dominated by the United States and biased against Nicaragua.[204]

By the end of 1982, the diplomatic approaches to solve the regional conflict in Central America were clearly headed in two distinct directions. On the one hand, the United States and its closest Central American allies persisted in pressuring the Sandinistas towards a more pluralistic and representative government. On the other hand, Mexico and Venezuela, sought to prevent further U.S.-sponsored military activities against Nicaragua.

The tension between these two diplomatic approaches was the most immediate cause for the creation of the Contadora Group. Of these two rival coalitions, the Mexican-Venezuelan group managed to prevail. This happened when Mexico, Venezuela, Colombia, and Panama joined forces around their mutual and "unanimous distaste for previous unilateral U.S. interventions in the region" and created the Contadora Group (Contadora or the Group).[205]

Nicaragua supported Contadora from its inception. The Sandinistas clearly disliked the CDC's enforcement means based on the collective-security mechanisms of the Rio Treaty. They also feared resorting to the OAS on the belief that this forum would be dominated by the United States and the CDC bloc. This latter perception explains Nicaragua's preference in seeking relief at the United Nations and not at regional forums.[206] Nicaragua supported the Contadora approach because it represented an informal regional alternative to the OAS and it could defend her more effectively than the UN.

The Contadora Group was officially created in January 1983. During the first months of its existence, Contadora developed a multiple and complex agenda of issues with no substantive connection among themselves. The first meeting of the Group declared the intensification of dialogue in Latin America as a firm step to find effective solutions to the political, economic, and social problems of the Western Hemisphere. It also discussed South-South economic aid for development and the importance of the Non-Aligned Nations Movement to developing nations. It stressed the recessive tendency of the world economy and its negative effects in Latin America. Some emphasis was also given to the need of periodic consultations at the ministerial level in order to discuss economic matters of interest to Latin America. The discussions highlighted the Group's desire to effectively contribute to "fulfill the purpose of coordinating and setting forth a joint negotiating posture for the developing nations at the VI [United Nations Conference on Trade and Development] UNCTAD to be held in Belgrade."[207] A few other issues ranged from the bicentennial of the birth of Simon Bolivar to the faithful compliance of the Panama Canal Treaties. In sum, Contadora had evinced since its inception a paramount lack of definition as to sub-regional objectives. Four months later, the Group was only able to identify a few Central American problems. On April 21, the Group made public its "diagnosis" of "the principal matters of dispute,"

> Among the matters which, in the view of the Contadora Ministers, require the most attention, the following should be mentioned: the arms race, arms control and reduction, the transfer of armaments, the presence of military ad-

> visers and other forms of outside military assistance, actions aimed at disruping internal order of other countries, threats and verbal aggression, warlike incidents and border tensions, the violation of human rights and individual and social guarantees, and the grave economic and social problems which are at the heart of the region's present crisis".[208]

This "diagnosis" served as the basis for the next Contadora discussions of July 17, 1983 in Cancun, where the "diagnosed" issues were incorporated in the so-called "Cancun Declaration."

As a result of both the diagnosis and the Cancun Declaration, the Central American countries redefined their positions and expanded their demands. On July 19, Nicaragua declared its acceptance of multilateral negotiations and its willingness to further discuss the points of the Cancun Declaration. In addition to Contadora's new agenda, Nicaragua proposed to discuss six additional matters: 1) cease-fire and non-aggression agreement with Honduras; 2) cessation of military aid to El Salvador; 3) cessation of support to insurrectional forces; 4) clear compromise and absolute respect for the principles of self-determination and non-intervention; 5) cease of economic aggression and discrimination against any country in Central America; 6) prohibition of foreign military bases in Central America. On July 20, the CDC countries made public their revised agenda to include the following points: 1) complete suspension of armament acquisitions and foreign military advisers; 2) establishment of international verification mechanisms on arms traffic control; 3) revival of regional economic relations; 4) promotion of free and democratic institutions through pluralistic and representative elections; 5) national reconciliation; 6) protection of human rights and refugees; and 7) adequate verification of the agreements.[209]

By September 1983, the Contadora Group, encouraged by the strong will of the Central American countries to negotiate under the auspices of such an innovative mechanism, brought the parties to the negotiation table. This apparent positive step, which the larger international community overwhelmingly supported, contributed to make of Contadora the de facto exclusive mediator for the whole of Central America. Participants in the negotiations verbally rejected both the Organization of American States and the United Nations as suitable mediators. All parties except Nicaragua viewed the United Nations as a forum through which East-West differences could be introduced into the Central American conflict. Enthusiasm about Contadora also permeated the United Nations and the Organization of American States, whom later excluded themselves from the conflict not to jeopardize the Contadora Process.[210]

The Contadora declaration that emerged from this first meeting with the Central American nations, "The Document of Objectives" of September 1983, encompassed the claims of all parties and further expanded issues, now to twenty-one points. Additional matters not previously proposed concerned economic and social development programs. They also included the achievement of "better and full access to the international market in order to enlarge the flow of trade between the Central American countries and the rest of the world."[211] To pursue these objectives Contadora approved, in January 1984, a document entitled "Norms for the Implementation of the Commitments of the Document of Objectives."[212] Curiously, this document subdivided the various objectives into less concrete tasks. For instance, the promotion of national reconciliation was to be pursued "on the basis of justice, freedom and democracy...to establish the necessary mechanisms that would facilitate the dialogue among the countries of the region." The means (justice, freedom, and democracy) gained in generality over the goal they were seeking to implement (national reconciliation). Likewise, the norms for the fulfillment of "Security Issues" were vaguely drafted and revealed that Contadora was just acquainting itself with the problems of the region. All six points on security matters were connected with the collection of information on issues such as control and reduction of armament, foreign military advisors, and aid to insurrectional forces, to mention a few.

Due to the slowing of negotiations within Contadora, regional governments initiated a series of trial-and-error incursions into other regional and international arenas. Honduras and Costa Rica fruitlessly persisted in bringing their bilateral problems with Nicaragua to the OAS. At the same time, Nicaragua, continued searching for other solutions at the United Nations. On April 9, 1984, Nicaragua submitted its application against the United States at the International Court of Justice. Under the shadow of failure, Contadora rushed to submit to the parties its first draft. The goals that were set forth in the "Document of Objectives" and the "Norms for the Implementation of the Commitments of the Document of Objectives" were incorporated into the later known "September 7, 1984 Contadora Act for Peace and Cooperation in Central America."[213]

Nicaragua immediately accepted the draft of the Act. This unexpected announcement may have caught the Reagan administration "completely off guard."[214] However, the U.S. refused to accept the "draft document" arguing that it was just "a vague statement of goals without concrete limits on Nicaraguan Action."[215]

In October 1984, the foreign ministers of Costa Rica, Honduras, and El Salvador--in full agreement with the U.S.--met at Tegucigalpa, Honduras, to reject the September 1984 Contadora Act and propose a counterdraft. The U.S. and its Central American allies, later the "Tegucigalpa Bloc" (named after the Tegucigalpa meeting), advocated a series of amendments to the draft agreement, particularly on the criteria for limiting arms and troop levels. A formula of parity among all the countries of the region was intended to replace a criteria based on the defensive needs of each country.

Another amendment sought to exclude all provisions that would have required the elimination of U.S. military bases and the cessation of U.S. military maneuvers in the region. In a similar fashion, "the Tegucigalpa Draft" (the counterdraft) purported to eliminate a protocol to the Act that would have required the United States to agree in writing to observe the draft Act and cease funding of the Contras.[216]

In its desperate efforts to avoid deadlock in the negotiations, the Contadora Group sought to expand its membership to other Latin American nations. In July 1985, the Group convened to create the Contadora Support Group with Peru, Brazil, Argentina, and Uruguay as members. The Support Group was conceived to demonstrate that the Latin American countries were united under the Contadora perspective of Central America. The participation of the Support Group was more than symbolic. On various occasions, the Support Group raised the idea of establishing a "military security cordon" in Central America. The idea was only abandoned when Mexico and Brazil refused to participate.[217]

On September 12, 1985, the Contadora Group circulated among the Central American countries a revised version of the 1984 Act, which incorporated practically all of the Tegucigalpa Bloc amendments. Nicaragua, naturally, refused to sign it. This facilitated another stalemate in the negotiations. The Support Group; Peru and Argentina in particular, later played a significant role in bringing the parties back to the negotiation table. The parties met in Caraballeda, Venezuela on January 11-12, 1986. The aftermath of the meeting was the "Caraballeda Message for Peace, Security, and Democracy in Central America," in which the Contadora and the Support Group reaffirmed its commitment to peace negotiations and called for renewed efforts to resolve the outstanding issues. The Caraballeda message also called for a halt to Contra-aid and a renewal of the Manzanillo talks.[218] The negotiations resumed by the Central American countries on April 5, 1986, but did not last. Managua insisted that Contadora condemn U.S. aid to the Contras, a request that the Tegucigalpa Bloc refused to grant. The shadow of a final stalemate spread further over the negotiations. Indeed, the lack of progress moved the parties to unrealistically establish June 6, 1986 as the final deadline for the approval of the treaty. This approval, of course, did not happen. The Sandinistas were impatiently awaiting the ICJ judgment on the merits of their case against the United States and would not make further concessions until a judgment was rendered. Even with Guatemala's decision to join the Tegucigalpa Bloc to put additional pressure on Managua to resume the talks, the positions of the parties hardened.[219]

A formula was introduced by Contadora that would combine Nicaragua's "reasonable" military balance with a weighted point system for calculating force-level equivalencies.[220] But what the parties were now pursuing was a decomposition of Contadora's main issues. The "Declaration of Panama," the last significant declaration of Contadora contained only a small part of the several issues of the original Act. Contadora had no further hope.[221]

On June 6, 1986, Contadora submitted its final revised draft act.[222] The revision incorporated the agreement on arms and troop level reduction that was reached in Panama. It also decomposed and postponed all controversial issues concerning U.S. military activities for future negotiations. However, decomposition of issue-areas could not be complete. The Group had to give Nicaragua its portion of the issues. The second point of the Preamble listed aspects related with: frontier incidents, arms build-up, arms traffic, the presence of foreign military advisers, the holding of international military maneuvers in the territory of states of the region, the presence of military bases, schools and installations, other forms of foreign military presence, and the use by irregular forces of the territories of certain states to carry out disrupting operations against states in the region. Except for arms build-up, all other matters in point two were to the exclusive interest of Managua. The Tegucigalpa Bloc's requirements for democratization and national reconciliation in Nicaragua were not mentioned anywhere in the Act. Only section 2 of the 1986 Contadora Act included a brief reference to "national reconciliation," and Section 4 mentioned the commitments of the parties "with regard to electoral processes and parliamentary cooperation." Not surprisingly, the Tegucigalpa Bloc petitioned for the reopening of negotiations, precisely on these two issues. "They argued that the requirements were not stringent enough to force Nicaragua to negotiate seriously with its internal opponents."[223] In addition, Costa Rica and El Salvador denounced the agreement's lack of adequate verification. Honduras criticized the treaty's failure to include concrete reciprocal obligations sufficient to guarantee its security. In the end, the Tegucigalpa Bloc simply refused to sign the 1986 Act and Contadora, for all practical purposes, was made defunct.

B. Uncertainty

B.1. The Clash of Substantive Expectations

B.1.1. In General

The Contadora Group (The Contadora Four or The Group) resembled in many aspects the Group of 77 (G-77) of the 1970's.[224] This similarity is ascertainable from the continuity not only of membership--the members of the Contadora Four and of the Support Group were also members of the Group of 77--but also of negotiation and decision-making styles. Robert Rothstein (1984) has demonstrated that the failure of the Group of 77 to build up a new commodities regime in the mid 1970's was basically due to the Group's persistent development of "broad or abstract discussion of causal variables."[225] According to Rothstein, the Group of 77 should have moved beyond such highly uncertain questions to make an "effort to link particular configurations of the causal variables with appropriate bargaining strategies."[226] The Contadora Group did not escape the inclusion of broad issues that marked its very inception.

Such principles as self-determination and nonintervention provided the weak links that kept the Group together. Had those principles not been introduced, Contadora would have been based solely on Mexico's vague statement that the solution of the crisis could only be attained by attacking its social and economic roots. But not even that delusive goal reflected the main intentions of the Group. Abstract principles of law served to conceal the premises of the Group's more concrete commonality: a shared disapproval of U.S. intervention in the Central American region.[227] In fact, the main goal of Contadora was to avoid direct U.S. military intervention in Nicaragua. In light of growing U.S. hostility towards Nicaragua and U.S.-sponsored military build-ups in Honduras and El Salvador, Mexico and Venezuela, who joined forces with Colombia and Panama to form the Contadora coalition in January 1983, particularly feared that a spillover of the intensifying conflict into the larger region would lead to an East-West confrontation.[228] Thus Contadora needed a few "abstract" principles, an expanded agenda, and a great deal of rhetoric on which to base itself. Without the highly principled environment such terms as nonintervention and self-determination provide, the Group would probably have failed to persuade actors to gather around a common table.

A breaking up of the Central American problem into its component parts--as happened later within Esquipulas--would have brought serious doubts about the effectiveness and the neutrality of Contadora's mediation efforts. A series of stalemates that occurred between 1984 and 1986 evinced the Group's lack of conceptual consensus on the basic expectations it needed to transmit to direct actors and coalitions. Without such consensus, the contending parties felt free to interpret the leading normative principles in their own ways.

As a result, actors misinterpreted the normative expectations of their opponents, the intentions of the mediator, and the direction of the process. The Group did little to clarify its "causal variables" and the relation of those variables to the issues involved. The Group seemed again and again only to bury important conceptual disagreements within a vague agenda of legally drafted obligations--mostly recitations of already existing Inter-American treaties and conventions--. Even within the Group itself, disagreement as to specific issues was patently evident. For example, Venezuela did not agree with Mexico's views on the status of revolutionary forces in El Salvador.[229] Venezuela, Panama, and Colombia never enthusiastically supported--as did Mexico--the course of the Sandinista revolution in Nicaragua. Venezuelan and Mexican evaluations of the Sandinistas differed because "Venezuela seemed more willing and able to cooperate on military and security dimensions with the United States than did Mexico."[230] Unlike Mexican goodwill towards the Sandinistas, Panamanian relations with the Sandinistas turned sour in 1979 when General Omar Torrijos, head of the Panamanian National Guard, expressed concern over the level of Cuban activities in Nicaragua and ordered a withdrawal of the Panamanian advisers sent to Nicaragua after the overthrow of Somoza.[231] Finally, Colombia's attempt to "Mexicanize" its foreign policy responded mainly to a strategic effort by Colombian President Betancur to support his own domestic negotiations with the Colombian guerrillas.[232]

Thus, union within the Contadora Group was possible only around a few abstract and controversial principles extracted from the "Panamericanism."[233] The Group had to institutionalize these principles--ambiguous as they were--and make them invulnerable to change or compromise. To do so, the Contadora Group accepted the wholesale Latin American notion of nonintervention and its interplay with other principles basically as a matter of faith. The principle of nonintervention and its various connotations, were simply transcribed into the various Contadora Acts from the basic related articles of the OAS Charter. In fact, in none of its documents did the Contadora Four ever attempt to link the principle and the specific demands of the parties. As a result, the parties drew very different normative expectations from the principle. Costa Rica, Honduras and El Salvador, as well as the United States, interpreted nonintervention as intrinsically connected with such notions as "collective security," "self-defense," and the Inter-American requirement for "democratic and plural democracies." Nicaragua and the Group advocated a more literal and less flexible interpretation.

On the important but uncertain and ambiguous issue of nonintervention and self-determination, the Group neither sought nor achieved any new negotiating knowledge in the course of its negotiations. Consensual normative expectations about these principles among the parties could have provided substantive agreement among the Group and the Central American countries for determining a unified stance, not only on the desirability but also on the legitimacy of U.S. military pressure against Nicaragua. In other words, though the main object of the Contadora Group was to prevent the development of a new hegemonic intervention in the region, it could not even persuade the parties of its goal. The Group hid this goal from the participants, who needed to clarify the emotional notions of "good" or "bad" intervention in general and reach a consensual categorization of current and potential U.S. interference in Nicaragua. Contadora's rhetoric of abstraction hid its own goal even from itself.

All this is to be explained in more detail below. With respect to our comparison of the bargaining styles of the Contadora Group and the Group of 77, Rothstein has this to say:

> In a large coalition such as the Group of 77, with great diversity in interests and perspectives, the capacity to build a genuine consensus (that is, something more than rhetorical support for grand principles) is limited"[234].

Though not a large coalition, the Contadora Group, as Rothstein points out for the G-77, encompassed a great diversity of interests and perspectives, especially when contrasted with the direct participants in the Central American conflict. What holds here for the Group of 77 applies also to Contadora. Rothstein has shown that the interest of maintaining cohesion compelled the Group of 77 to avoid contentious issues in its ranks and to rest on lowest common denominators--often at the level of aspiration, principle, and rhetoric--rather than to grapple with the hard issues that might have divided members.[235] To be sure, the Contadora Group, like the G-77, also concealed the hard issues. Contadora never made any attempt to build a genuine consensus on the basic knowledge base of the selected conflict-resolution criteria among the contending coalitions.

In fairness, one must admit that there was a contextual difference between the Contadora negotiations and those in which the Group of 77 were engaged during the 1970's. The G-77 was a direct party within a North-South confrontation. The Contadora Group was acting in Central America as a mediator, though sometimes its role was perceived by the Tegucigalpa Bloc to trespass the boundaries of mediation.[236] As a mediator, the Contadora Group had the burdens of maintaining both its own unity and the cooperation between the parties at the negotiation table. This double role was difficult to balance because, on the one hand, a clear definition of conflict-solving criteria was necessary to successful negotiations, and, on the other hand, a clearer definition of criteria might have endangered the unity of the Group. Apparently, the Group chose to protect its unity at any cost. Thus, a minimum trend towards division between the parties

Change in Contadora	
Contadora as of	Negotiation Status
Early 1984	Incremental Growth
From Mid-1984 to 1986	Non-Growth Deadlock
After 1986	Decay Termination

Diagram 1

Decision Making and Bargaining Styles
Contadora
1984-1987

Actors	Legal knowledge	Political Goals	D.M/Bargaining	Change
Contadora Group	Not consensual between coalitions but consensual within coalitions	Interconnected Expanding by aggregation	Skeptical issues linked some tactical some fragmented	Adapt
Nicaragua	Same as above	Specific/Static Means to accomplish goals fexible.	Eclectic Issues linked tactically	Adapt or No Change
U.S. Bloc	Same as above	Specific/Static Means to accomplish goals rigid	Eclectic Issues linked tactically	No Change

Diagram 2

made decomposition of issues inevitable, and the Group's potential to identify agreeable substantive trade-offs unfeasible. The negotiations ended up promoting tactical concessions which the parties sporadically offered in view of the other's reluctance to accept their own extreme demands. Throughout the various stages of negotiation within the Contadora process, trade-offs were made but not on the basis of similar expectations. The contending parties fell into the practice of appraising military trade-offs and conducting their dialogue under the shadow of continuing and potentially increasing U.S. military actions in the region.[237]

The unresolved ambiguity of abstract legal principles--purported to become the common conflict-resolution criteria--within the Contadora process became so pervasive that issues could not be strongly linked in a cohesive package. The parties started to "decompose" issues, that is, decided to deal with separate questions in detail rather. This "decomposition" of issue areas undermined the whole negotiation process. Diagrams 1 and 2 try to capture the various decision-making and bargaining styles in Contadora, and the status of negotiations from 1984 to 1987. We shall now detail the divergent normative expectations that actors derived from the abstract principles supporting the Contadora negotiations. The following insights are intended to illustrate the intimate connection between the ambiguity of legal knowledge and deception within a conflict-resolution process.

B.1.2. In Specific: Nonintervention And Related Conflict Resolution Criteria

"The Latin American nations have, in practice, a profound ambivalence about the concept of intervention. The record indicates that the issue is not whether to intervene, but who is to intervene."[238] This observation seems true if one considers only the instances in which Latin Americans have--with great impunity--intervened on each other's internal affairs. The overthrow of Somoza in Nicaragua in 1979 is perhaps the classic example that illustrates the ambivalence with which Latin Americans treat the concept of nonintervention. With regard to this case, R. Scheman explains,

> Everyone intervened...(t)he Mexicans and the Venezuelans sent arms; the Panamanians transported them; the Costa Ricans delivered them."[239]

The same commentator adds that "the Cubans and the Sandinistas maintained one of the most extensive systems of intervention in the history of the hemisphere in the early 1980s."[240]

Confusion about the principle of nonintervention permeated institutionalized levels as well. On June 23, 1979, the XVIIth Meeting of Foreign Affairs Ministers of the Organization of American States practically legitimized all interventionist activities against the Somoza regime. While denouncing the "inhumane conduct of the dictatorial regime" governing Nicaragua, this high organ also declared that,

> [T]he spirit of solidarity that guides Hemisphere relations places an unavoidable obligation on the American countries to exert every effort within their power, to put an end to the bloodshed and to avoid the prolongation of this conflict which is disrupting the peace of the Hemisphere.[241]

Within the same resolution, the XVIIth Meeting of Consultation urged for

> the immediate and definitive replacement of the Somoza regime...the installation in Nicaraguan territory of a democratic government.

Even though the resolution also called for the "solution of the serious problem" to be "exclusively within the jurisdiction of the people of Nicaragua," it went further to indicate the method through which a future Nicaraguan "democratic government" should be composed as to reflect the "free will of the people of Nicaragua." The most immediate observation one may extract from this resolution is that at least when they act collectively, the principle of nonintervention permits some states to dictate the type and composition of another American state's government.

Although the principle of nonintervention is defined in clear and strong language in Articles 18 and 19 of the Organization of American States Charter (OAS Charter), one encounters some problems with the analogical interpretation of the principle.[242] By analogical interpretation, we mean reading the norm in light of other principles of similar or equal value, such as collective security, threat or use of force, protection of human rights, and self-determination. Analogical interpretation also describes the process of looking at the norm in relation to the habitual practice of states and organizations. Analogical methods are very attractive to decision makers who search for legal excuses, particularly in the presence of hardly self-defining terms such as "intervention" and "interference in any form."[243] In the final analysis, a persistent pattern of conduct inconsistent with the norm "would undermine at least to some extent the hypothesis that states consider themselves under a legal obligation to comply with it."[244] The legal obligation does not completely fade in such cases, but a higher degree of uncertainty gets incorporated in the norm to preclude a state's literal obedience. Such has been the case with the principle of nonintervention in Latin America.

B.1.2.1. Nonintervention And Collective Security

As early as 1979, the Sandinistas were involved in multiple border conflicts with Honduras and Costa Rica. On most occasions, Honduras and Costa Rica claimed that Nicaraguan forces were indiscriminately violating their territorial sovereignty. The Sandinistas did not always deny those protests, but they alleged that the "Contras"--the U.S. financed guerrillas fighting in the Northern part of Nicaragua--and Pastora's guerrillas were respectively using Honduras's and Costa Rica's territory to launch armed attacks against Nicaragua. For its part, El Salvador contended that the Sandinistas were giving military assistance to the Salvadoran guerrilla in its attempt to overthrow Duarte's legitimate government and install another communist regime in the region. Thus, Costa Rica, El Salvador, and Honduras all viewed Nicaragua's military build-up and border operations as a threat of aggression.

Based on their own assessments of the various incidents, the three countries signed an agreement in January 1982 by which they constituted the Central American Democratic Community (CDC). The clear purpose of the pact was to warn the Sandinistas. Nicaragua had to stop its increasing military build up and promote democratic, pluralized, and representative institutions.[245] Otherwise, the CDC was to invoke the Rio Treaty and resort to the "measures of collective security within the framework of existing treaties."[246]

The CDC's reference to "collective security" were partly based on Article 3(1) of the Rio Treaty and its notion that, "an armed attack by any State against an American State shall be considered as an attack against all the American States," which seems to contradict Article 18 of the OAS Charter which prohibits intervention. But a conceptual problem of this kind is not too insurmountable considering that an armed attack against a state constitutes sufficient basis for such a state to resort either to collective or individual self-defense. The reason why Article 3(1) explicitly provides for collective self-defence on the basis of an "armed attack" is the intention of the drafters at the 1947 Conference in Rio de Janeiro to implement through such article the notion of "solidarity." The principle of "solidarity" was originally adopted in Buenos Aires at the 1936 Inter-American Conference for the Maintenance of Peace and conveys the understanding that every act susceptible of disturbing the peace of America affects each and every one of the American nations.[247] The CDC maintained that the conduct of the Sandinistas was compromising the peace of the region and, thus, the peace of America.

It might have been clear to the CDC that collective self-defense implies that all the countermeasures to an armed attack against an American state can only be taken through the OAS and specifically through its Organ of Consultation.[248] Article 3(1) should be no source of confusion in this regard, except in the wake of procedural uncertainty of the kind I explain in section III(b). When the parties believe that access to the OAS is legally and politically blocked by the action and de facto exclusivity of an informal procedure like the Contadora Process, the question of collective self-defense gives way to divergent and certainly confusing normative expectations on the principle of nonintervention.[249] Despite how controversial the assertion that collective security may still be rendered legitimate when decided upon and pursued outside of OAS organs, the fact is that the United States and the CDC made indeed such a claim.[250]

The issue of collective counter-intervention, under the facade of collective self-defense, was even more complex in Central America because the core of CDC's normative expectations was based as much on Article 3(1) as on Articles 6 and 7 of the Rio Treaty.[251] Under the implicit expectations to which Articles 6 and 7 gave rise, the Sandinistas' constant trans-border aggressions and support to irregular forces were viewed as but a few of many external effects of a "dangerous" internal division within Nicaraguan politics that posed a significant threat to the CDC nations' national securities and to "the peace of America" as a whole.[252] To the CDC, therefore, Nicaragua could not be regarded as the only master of its internal political processes. The CDC countries viewed themselves in the privileged position of deciding and adopting the measures which should be taken for the common defense and for the maintenance of peace and security of the Continent.[253]

Article 6 contemplates some forms of aggression besides armed attacks.[254] According to Article 6 of the Rio Treaty and Article 28 of the OAS Charter, the collective security defense could be invoked in the presence of "any other fact or situation that might endanger the peace of America." Within such same tenet, Article 6 was applied against the "subversive activities of international communism" during the X Inter-American Conference of Caracas in 1954.[255]

Interpreting the Rio Treaty in this light shows enough ambiguity as to promote many diverging normative expectations. As I mentioned before, the U.S. bloc defended the extreme claim that a military 'collective' action against the Sandinistas was justified as a matter of collective self-defence even if no resort was made to the Organ of Consultation at the OAS.[256] In fact, to the CDC the Sandinistas were threatening the peace of the Americas not only because of their "transborder aggressions," but also by the mere fact that their regime was communist. It was thus clear that the existence of a communist government in Nicaragua was the main cause of local and regional conflicts and that something had to be done about it, within or without the OAS.[257] The CDC countries were originally joined by Colombia and Panama--later members of the Contadora Group--at the "Declaration of San José" and the "Pro-Peace and Democracy Forum" of October 1982.[258] These initiatives were intended to revive the classical fight against "international communism" that characterized the Inter-American system in the 1950's and 1960's and to incorporate in its essence the CDC's normative expectations on collective security and nonintervention.[259] Nicaragua and the Contadora Group, of course, did not derive the same expectations from the various articles in question, but rather advocated radically different ones.

B.1.2.2. Nonintervention And Human Rights

Since the XVIIth Meeting of Ministers of Foreign Affairs adopted its resolution of June 23, 1979 condemning Somoza--the Nicaraguan regime that the Sandinistas helped to overthrow a few months later--for the "horrors of a fierce armed conflict" and the "inhumane conduct" of the dictatorial regime, the protection of human rights in the region has functioned as an additional element of uncertainty undermining consensual expectations on the principle of nonintervention in the Western Hemisphere. The OAS's resolution condemning Somoza was extensively based upon a report of the Inter-American Commission on Human Rights that named massive human rights violations as the "fundamental cause of the dramatic situation faced by the Nicaraguan people."[260] The Contadora agreement to include the concerns of the U.S. bloc for human rights violations and refugees in the negotiating drafts helped affirm the U.S. bloc's position that it is both a right and a duty of every nation to uphold human rights.

Costa Rica and Honduras had both long complained about the massive immigration into their countries by Nicaraguan refugees and displaced persons. They also complained about the negative effects of Nicaraguan refugees and immigrants on their countries' public health and social and political stability. Thus, Nicaragua's neighbors rendered the Nicaraguan internal civil war and the Sandinistas' pervasive violation of human rights--major causes of refugee migration--a matter of concern for all of Central America and another ground to demand internal political changes in Nicaragua.

Once again, normative expectations differed, at least with regard to the extent that the protection of human rights would justify some forms of intervention by one or more states in the domestic affairs of the state who allegedly violates those rights. That interpretations and expectations diverge in this matter is perfectly understandable because the 1980's have witnessed an emerging international trend towards the more effective protection of human rights. New developments have gone far enough to make some legal scholars affirm that, in Lori Fisler Damrosch's words,

> (I)t is the State that has the right to political independence, not a particular regime and certainly not a regime that denies to the state's people the opportunity to make political choices.[261]

The clash between a more decisive protection of international human rights and respect for the principle of nonintervention brings further ambiguity to the phrase "interference in all forms." The Latin American countries have contributed to widen this ambiguity, as demonstrated by the OAS resolution against the Somoza regime. The Tegucigalpa Bloc also routinely insisted that human freedoms and the democratization of Nicaragua were basic values that the Sandinistas owed both to the Nicaraguan people and to the other Central American countries.

B.1.2.3. Nonintervention and Self-Determination

During the Contadora process, the CDC's position on self-determination brought further ambiguity to the principle of nonintervention. As enshrined in the Charter of the United Nations, the right to self-determination provides that "all peoples have the right freely to determine, without external interference, their political status and to pursue their economic, social and cultural development." The U.N. Declaration of Principles further stipulates that "every state has the duty to respect this right in accordance with the provisions of the Charter."[262]

Clearly, if self-determination is interpreted as the right to political independence and territorial integrity, there is a strong link between self-determination and nonintervention. The latter is a pre-condition for the former. The duty of nonintervention is the main guarantor of both self-determination and the sovereign equality of states. But the question arises whether this notion of nonintervention as "guarantor" also applies to a wider interpretation of the principle of self-determination, one that embraces the right to internal democracy for all peoples irrespective of the status of the territory.[263]

In Latin America, where classical colonialism ended more than a century ago but neocolonialism is still highly feared and criticized, it is not clear whether self-determination has acquired this additional connotation of "majority rule," "one man, one vote," and/or "effective exercise of a representative democracy."[264] To be sure, the United States is the American state that has most enthusiastically identified the notion of self-determination with the existence of a representative democracy.[265]

An indirect link between this provision of the OAS Charter and the principle of self-determination has been introduced and advanced in Resolution 78 of the OAS General Assembly.[266] The problem with this expanded notion of self-determination as self-government is that, if accepted, achieving or properly safeguarding this principle involves controversial expectations and actions from states. If "external interference" should be avoided in order to assure the right to self-determination understood as political independence, should external interference also be avoided when the right to self-determination is understood as the right to "self-government" and that latter right of the people is endangered or excluded? Furthermore, under the UN Declaration on

Principles every state has "the duty to promote through joint and separate action universal respect for and observance of human rights and fundamental freedoms," in what light should we interpret Article 18 of the OAS Charter which prohibits intervention, "directly or indirectly, for any reason whatsoever...?" Does this mean that the other American states must not interfere in another American state where a non-elected, dictatorial, and oppressive ruler annihilates the right of their own people to choose their own form of government and to exercise their basic human rights? or does it mean the opposite?

Answers to these questions varied significantly from one interpreter to the next in the Central American conflict. The U.S. bloc considered that the Sandinista regime was depriving the Nicaraguan people of their right to effectively exercise a representative democracy. Therefore, the U.S. bloc's normative expectations on intervention, were based on the wider interpretation of self-determination, and assumed that every American country had the duty to promote, through joint or separate action, the realization of the principle of self-government of the people of Nicaragua.[267] This radical formulation was defended by the U.S. and the Tegucigalpa Bloc during the Contadora Process, and was later incorporated in the Esquipulas II Accords to the extent that the Sandinistas ended up committing themselves to hold presidential elections on February 1990.

The Contadora Group and Nicaragua, however, viewed self-determination in the more restrictive sense. To them, the political independence of Nicaragua precluded other nations from intervening in that country's internal affairs, irrespective of the latter's current form of government. True, Contadora placed some relevance on the duty of the Central American States to hold free and democratic elections, but the incorporation of such an objective into the various Contadora Acts was not necessarily connected with the adoption of a particular notion of self-determination. The inclusion of representative and democratic elections in the Contadora Act responded to a simple accumulation of demands from the parties, which Contadora perceived as necessary to retain actors at the negotiating table. Nothing else but tactical reasons can explain Contadora's willingness to discuss the need for more democratic electoral processes in Nicaragua at the same time that it was advocating the strongest notion of *nonintervention of noninterference in internal matters for any reason whatsoever*. If nonintervention is to be read with genuine fondness for the letter of Article 18 of the OAS Charter, as the Contadora Group and Nicaragua maintained, then not even the slightest consideration to internal matters, like electoral processes and national reconciliation, could have properly been included within the Contadora's drafts.

B.1.2.4. From 'Good' to 'Bad' Intervention

A commentator has maintained that "[a]dvocates of democracy in Latin America are consistently urging the United States to use its power to intervene against dictatorships, which they consider *good* intervention"[268]. True, when it comes to legal justification of international behavior, actors find it very convenient to use such broad and emotional terms as *good intervention*. Users of this term generally perceive that since intervention in the internal affairs of a foreign sovereign is in principle prohibited, any exception to the rule must be distinguished as a special, *good*, and therefore justified kind of intervention.

In its alleged effort to safeguard the peace of the Americas, for instance, the U.S. bloc advocated the inclusion into the Contadora process of issues connected with *democratization and national reconciliation*. But the problem with such use of the idea of good intervention, however, is not that the U.S. bloc would have a say in Nicaraguan internal elections or national reconciliation. Contadora entertained those issues because Nicaragua accepted to include them in the negotiating agenda, and because an eventual agreement within Contadora would have committed all the parties--not only Nicaragua--both to democratization and national reconciliation. The real problem with the notion of good intervention, is that it is already too pervasive in Western Hemisphere's affairs. In order to make this concept useful, we must at least define a border line between *good* and *bad* intervention. I suggest that such a dividing line has to do mainly with the means by which one or more states intend to affect the domestic policies and decisions of another state. While agreement and negotiation are generally considered as appropriate contexts for influencing other state's national affairs, the threat or use of force are definitely not. No matter how simple, this is a distinction that has not always been drawn in the presence of such a wide and risky term as *good* intervention within the Americas. The U.S. bloc did not make the differentiation during the Contadora process, and the Contadora Group lacked the capability to clarify and eradicate the confusion.

When the basic normative distinctions are not properly spelled out, an international commitment to effect internal political change is likely to raise several difficulties. Indeed, the differing normative expectations of the parties in question become reflected not only in the eventual agreement per se, but also in its implementation. Take, for example, the relationship between nonintervention and the issues of free elections and national reconciliation. Suppose that the Contadora draft was signed in 1986. The persisting confusion surrounding the basic conflict-resolution criteria--nonintervention--would have undermined the eventual implementation of the agreement and the value of the agreement would have been that of plain paper. Suppose moreover, that after the Contadora Draft was signed in 1986, the Sandinistas and the Contras failed to reach agreement to end Nicaragua's internal strife after extensive negotiation and that the elections in Nicaragua were negatively affected by that outcome or not finally held. The war would continue in absolute violation of the Contadora agreement. How and by whom was it to be determined whether that failure constituted a violation of the Sandinistas' previous commitments to democratization and national reconciliation as per the Contadora agreement? The U.S. bloc would have eventually accused the Sandinistas for not achieving national reconciliation with the contras. The U.S. bloc would have considered a military invasion of Nicaragua among the available mechanisms to enforce the Sandinistas' commitments to democratize. Such an expectation would have been pursued by the U.S. bloc as *legitimate* because of its unique idea of *good* intervention. Nicaragua's neglect could have been interpreted as the intention of the "Comandantes" to maintain a totalitarian regime in Nicaragua. The prolongation of the civil war in Nicaragua could have been regarded as a threat to the peace of the Americas. A U.S. invasion of Nicaragua would not have been out of question and nothing would have been gained from signing the Contadora draft.

These hypothetical possibilities may be imaginary but surely not absurd. As indicated above, the Contadora Group's strategy was to cumulate the demands of the parties without previously providing for a set of prevailing normative expectations that would become more consensual among the parties to the process. Existing knowledge, not being consensual, could not serve as the necessary link between the aggregated demands and the guiding principles of negotiation. The need for a linkage between *good* intervention and national reconciliation or free elections, though concealed under outstanding pieces of rhetoric, had to reappear sooner or later in the peace negotiations. In fact, it was brought up when the Court rendered its order indicating provisional measures in the Nicaragua Case on May 1984. Just one month before the 1984 Contadora Act was released, the U.S. bloc anticipated that the Court would condemn U.S. military activities against Nicaragua as illegitimate under the collective security argument. Under these circumstances, the U.S. bloc decided not to sign the 1984 Contadora Act and refocused the negotiations on verification and implementation matters, in particular on democratization measures.

The Tegucigalpa Bloc,[269] however, never ruled out the possibility that the United States would eventually have to interfere militarily in order to secure compliance by Nicaragua. Most of the amendments proposed in the "Tegucigalpa Draft"--the Tegucigalpa Bloc's counterproposal to the 1984 Contadora Act--can be read in this light. The Tegucigalpa Draft responds to a series of consultations between the U.S. Secretary of State George Shultz and Costa Rican, Salvadoran and Honduran leaders that took place immediately before the proposal was drafted on September 1984. The key amendments of the counterdraft sought a further reduction of Nicaragua's arms and troops to a parity level with the other Central American nations. Most drastically, it proposed to exclude the provisions of the 1984 Contadora Act that would have required the elimination of U.S. military bases and cessation of U.S. military maneuvers in the region. The amendments also excluded the final protocol that would have required the United States to agree in writing to observe the provisions of the treaty and immediately cease funding of the contras.[270] In this sense, of all the explanations about Contadora's stalemates it is the lack of a common conflict-resolution criteria that appears to us to be the most persuasive.

The Contadora Group's pattern of aggregating demands in the midst of substantial uncertainty shows up again during the subsequent 1985 and 1986 Contadora Acts. On these occasions, the Contadora Group simply incorporated the new exigencies of either the Tegucigalpa Bloc or Nicaragua just to keep actors at the negotiation table. But the main question on the kind of intervention that was "permissible"--and the U.S. role that would chiefly pursue it--remained unanswered and uncertain. Compromise, if ever achieved, would have been artificial for not really touching on the questions from which tension was authentically emerging. Contadora's strategy was to keep the negotiations alive by sidestepping the most controversial issues or concealing them with questions that were substantially decomposable. This approach slowed down the negotiations, under the aegis of a system of "passive consensus," which not only blocked the negotiations but also precluded the acquisition by the parties of a common conflict-resolution criteria.[271]

C. The Clash of Procedural Expectations

Beyond the substantive uncertainty discussed in the previous pages, there is a procedural confusion that the Contadora Group's involvement in Central American tensions only helped to aggravate. The Contadora Group did not realize that some form of institutional support from an international governmental organization (IGO) could have provided both useful knowledge and assistance in the implementation of an eventual agreement. Moreover, as a Latin American *ad hoc* procedure, Contadora lacked the necessary financial and institutional resources to verify and secure compliance to a very complex accord. The lack of institutional links with an IGO can be explained in many ways, but the ambitious negotiating style of the Group was a decisive factor.

Contadora's agenda was founded on the misconception that everything involved in securing peace had to be decided through a single document and at one specific point in time.[272] Thus, the Group grew up from a simple declaration of rhetorical aims in early 1983 to an overwhelming mechanism for settling every single regional dispute in 1984. Indeed, the Contadora Group's original intent was to serve as a "good offices" mechanism. On January 9, 1983--the Group's first meeting--the Contadora Four expressed their intention to "increase communication among Latin American nations" and to "make an appeal to all Central American countries to reduce tensions...."[273] But perhaps encouraged by a positive international reaction to their preliminary calls for negotiations in Central America, the Group later proclaimed itself as the regional "mediator" and announced that it had achieved "the general guidelines" of a peace program.[274] By 1984, the Contadora Group was in full charge of settling every single Central American issue, including all technical investigative and fact finding operations.[275]

Despite the complex bureaucratic machinery they presupposed, the verification mechanisms set forth in the various Contadora Acts did not impress the parties or the United States as feasible or realistic. A major shortcoming of Contadora's verification and implementation machinery was certainly the exclusion of international organizations. This exclusion deserves further discussion.

Contadora applied a double standard concerning both the Organization of American States (OAS) and the United Nations (UN). First, Contadora sought to keep the regional conflict out of the OAS. Second, it took advantage of the Group of 77 allies to achieve majority voting in condemning U.S. foreign policy in Central America at the United Nations. That is to say, on the one hand, Contadora refused to establish a strong connection with IGOs, but, on the other hand, it used them in a very tactical fashion.

Contadora was originated as a diplomatic response to the United States and Nicaragua's direct neighbors. Its conception and establishment may fairly be interpreted as the Mexican and Venezuelan response to the October 1982 "Declaration of San José" and the "Pro-Peace and Democracy Forum." These two countries, together with Panama and Colombia, created the Contadora Group just two months after the Declaration of San José, as a preemptive effort to ensure that the mediation process in Central America would not be controlled by the United States and its closest Central American allies.[276] Since the U.S. bloc was considering resorting to the Rio Treaty, Contadora and Nicaragua felt that the OAS was not a safe forum for their diplomatic interests.[277] Nicaragua openly aired its concern that the United States would dominate this forum. Nicaragua and the Contadora coalition then blocked each of several attempts by Costa Rica and Honduras to engage the OAS in their bilateral tensions with Nicaragua. But contrary to what Nicaragua originally believed, it was the Contadora Group who controlled the voting majority both at the OAS General Assembly and the Permanent Council. Indeed, the Contadora Group and the Support Group--not the United States--were the ones who actually dominated OAS decision making through the operationalization of a majority voting structure.

In this connection, Contadora was able to secure from the early stages of the process the full support of the OAS. Thus, the General Assembly resolved on November 18, 1983 to give full support to the Contadora Group in its efforts to achieve peaceful relations in the region.[278] Though no formal exclusivity was granted to Contadora,[279] the OAS managed to delegate most of the Central American issues in favor of the Group on every subsequent occasion. The records show that as a matter of statute, the OAS General Assembly always viewed Contadora's mediation as efforts for peace not governed by the inter-American treaties and conventions in force.[280] But as a matter of fact, these records rather suggest that the Contadora's peace efforts were the major de facto cause that prevented the parties from resorting to the OAS Charter, the Pact of Bogota, and the Rio Treaty mechanisms. The confusion arises out of this "tacit" trend at the OAS towards granting exclusivity to Contadora, a trend that might have been obvious to the countries comprising the Tegucigalpa Bloc. As mentioned above, Costa Rica and Honduras unsuccessfully submitted to the OAS's Permanent Council various claims against Nicaragua. One salient instance was the Costa Rican invocation of Article 82 of the OAS Charter on June 28, 1985. The incident, commonly known as "Las Crucitas," concerned the killing of two and the wounding of another nine Costa Rican civil guards by the Nicaraguan army on Costa Rican soil. After a brief fact finding operation conducted *in situ* by an investigative commission, the Permanent Council simply resolved to "repudiate the incident...and recommend[ed] both governments to negotiate within the framework of the Contadora process."[281] Various other regional border incidents were handled in similar fashion by the OAS.[282]

The second Contadora's procedural standard can be traced by following Nicaragua's experience at the United Nations. Despite the Sandinistas' vociferous opposition to the OAS as "the screen behind which Costa Rica and Honduras sought to undermine the Contadora process,"[283] the Sandinistas never really felt obliged not to resort to other forums. Indeed, Nicaragua unhesitatingly exhausted every available resource under the United Nations Charter, including the Security Council. Between March and April 1982 alone, the Security Council held a total of eight meetings to discuss Nicaragua's complaints against the U.S..[284] In 1983, in a letter to the President of the Security Council of March 22, Nicaragua requested an urgent Council meeting "to analyze [the grave increase in acts of aggression] which endangers international peace"[285] and petitioned the Council once again on May 5 "to review the situation and consider possible measures to be taken" in view of the launching of a new stage of counter-revolutionary armed attacks.[286] The Security Council met again on September 13 to discuss Nicaragua's complaint that new acts of aggression had been committed against it "by mercenary counter-revolutionary forces trained and financed by the present Administration of the United States of America." Because the U.S. vetoed every potentially definitive action by the Security Council, the Council's response to Nicaragua's complaints never resulted in a direct resolution but rather just conveyed verbal support for Contadora.[287] Instead of staying within the confines of Contadora,

Nicaragua also sought the support of the Non-aligned Nations and the utilization of majority voting at the UN General Assembly. The Contadora countries not only voted in favor of Nicaraguan initiatives but also worked out a decisive support from the G-77 and the Non-Aligned countries in general.[288]

Contadora did not block Nicaragua's frequent initiatives at United Nations forums. In contrast with its attitude at the OAS regarding claims by other Central American countries, Contadora supported, when possible, Nicaragua's moves at the General Assembly. This double standard brought further uncertainty to the already controversial procedural expectations of the parties. Contadora's inconsistent diplomacy at IGOs created very devastating results for the peace process itself. The Tegucigalpa Bloc countries got the impression that the Contadora Four were not the impartial mediators they claimed to be. Costa Rica, El Salvador, and Honduras ended up looking at the Contadora Group as protective of Nicaraguan interests and "as increasingly obstructionist" to theirs.[289]

Participants experienced procedural uncertainty especially when seeking a best alternative to Contadora's mediation. While Nicaragua resorted to the International Court of Justice in April 1984, the Tegucigalpa countries were still dreaming either of a Rio Treaty application or of a militarily forged "democratization" of Nicaragua.

A general evaluation of procedural expectations in Central America before 1987, shows that not one participant in the Contadora process, except perhaps for the mediators themselves, ever believed that Contadora alone would successfully implement and monitor an eventual agreement. Indeed, during the best years of Contadora, the parties continually resorted to the IGOs of their choice, including the ICJ. Every time they dropped the various Contadora Acts, they manifested disagreement with implementation and verification matters. Distrust on the capability of the Group to handle implementation and compliance stemmed from the fact that Contadora lacked the necessary institutional means and support for such an end. Moreover, no IGO was acceptable to the parties unless Contadora would have made clear that one thing was to appreciate the advantages of informal mediation and another to extend such informality to matters related with implementation. An *ad hoc* multilateral approach is a reasonable option when no IGO is acceptable as mediator or conciliator to one or more of the disputing parties."[290] However, the Contadora Group took this advice to the extreme of ruling out any further IGOs' participation in the implementation and verification of the prospective accords.

Whether Contadora's total informality was premeditated or not, the fact is that the Group did not help the parties to agree on the necessary intervention of one or more IGOs in implementation and verification matters. This omission helped to raise distrust from the U.S. and the Tegucigalpa Bloc as to the mediator's alleged impartiality. Moreover, Contadora's double standard of support to Nicaragua at the UN and of reluctance towards Honduras and Costa Rica's initiatives at the OAS, further separated the parties. In sum, Contadora's negotiating style did not contribute to clarifying procedural uncertainty, but rather aggravated it to a very dangerous level.

CHAPTER V

THE STRUGGLE AGAINST UNCERTAINTY

Nicaragua's resort to the International Court of Justice (ICJ) on April 9, 1984, provided the consensual normative expectations and the authoritative knowledge that the parties needed to resolve the conflict.[291] The ICJ proceedings contributed to putting an end to the Contadora's negotiations because it ultimately provided the prevailing normative expectations and, later, the more consensual knowledge--the guiding legal criteria for solving conflict--that Contadora was unable to achieve. Our overall purpose here is to explain change in the attitude of participants during the negotiations that followed the Contadora process and the role of the ICJ and legal knowledge in promoting change.

A. The Effects of Judicial Proceedings On Contadora's Negotiations

The Contadora Process might have decayed even without Nicaragua's judicial initiatives at the International Court of Justice.[292] But if judicial procedures were not the only factor causing Contadora to decay, it surely was a precipitating element. Nicaragua's resort to the ICJ against the United States in June 1984, is one important indicator evincing that, for Nicaragua, the Contadora process was just one method to obtain its neighbors' cooperation in preventing the use of their territory by the contras.[293] Nicaragua had a marginal interest in most of the complex issues included in the Contadora's acts. That interest was wholly contingent on the Sandinista's expectation that the mediation process could significantly constrain U.S.-sponsored military maneuvers in and against Nicaragua.

Nicaragua's filing of the apllication at the ICJ on April 9, was that country's most significant diplomatic move before the Contadora Group submitted the first Contadora Act on June 9, 1984. It certainly gave the United States and the Tegucigalpa Bloc countries the impression that Nicaragua was not seriously interested in making major concessions within Contadora's negotiations. Furthermore, the U.S. bloc realized that Nicaragua's almost static goal prevented it from complying with most of its obligations under an eventual Contadora treaty. Thus, stronger efforts were pursued by the U.S. and its Central American allies on matters connected with verification and control. After several months of negotiations, the U.S. bloc also found out that Contadora's *ad hoc* multilateral negotiations would not constrain the Sandinistas to "democratize."[294]

Moreover, the ICJ proceedings clearly constituted the Sandinistas' better alternative to a Contadora's negotiated settlement and consequently facilitated Nicaragua's hardening of its negotiating positions.[295] No other variable would explain Nicaragua's intransigence not to change "one single comma" of the 1984 Contadora Act.[296] Thus, the demands of the parties within Contadora became more rigid, and this, in turn, strengthened the likelihood of failure in the negotiations and the escalation of U.S.-backed military operations in Nicaragua.[297] These events occurred between 1984 and 1986, the same period of time within which Nicaragua filed its application before the ICJ and the Court rendered its decision on the "merits" of the case.

The judicial proceedings Nicaragua instituted before the ICJ against the United States constituted a "rival" procedure to the Contadora's mediation. This was so even though the United States was a direct party in the case and, formally speaking, only an indirect participant in the Contadora negotiations. Also, the ICJ was not entrusted with the Contadora's set of expanded issues. The *Nicaraguan Case* nevertheless helped identify the main issues truly at stake,

Proceedings, Orders, and Judgments International Court of Justice
Impact on Legal Knowledge During Peace Negotiations in Central America
1984-1988

Development of Events at the International Court of Justice	Legal knowledge
1984-1986:	
Order Indicating Provisional Measures (Nicar. v. U.S.) Rejection of Salvadoran Intervention in Proceedings (Nicar. v. U.S.) 1984 Judgment on Jurisdiction and Admissibility of Nicaraguan Application (Nicar. v. U.S.)	Though not consensual parties realize why not consensual. Normative expectations and demands hardened
1986-1988:	
1986 Judgment on the Merits (Nicar. v. U.S.) 1986 Nicaraguan Applications (Nicar. v. Hond.) (Nicar. v. Costa Rica)	Becomes more consensual on the basic norms parties are willing to use as conflict-resolution criteria. Nicaraguan applications against Costa Rica and Honduras serve as constraint and catalyst for changes within alliances and decision making styles.
1988-1989:	
1988 Judgment on Jurisdiction and Admissibility of Nicaraguan Application (Nicar. v Hond.)	Becomes more authoritative both on substantive and procedural grounds. International Organizations assume greater role

Diagram 3

something that became evident only by treating the bilateral Nicaragua-U.S. conflict in isolation. In other words, if Contadora preferred to approach the regional conflict as a "single sweeping whole," concealing hard and soft issues in artificially nested sets of issue-areas, the Court was requested to deal concretely with very specific questions, including the toughest demands of the most salient disputing parties. If legal knowledge could not become more consensual through negotiations, it was now to the judicial method of authoritative determination to decide which of the contending expectations would prevail or survive. The Court thus assisted in the search for consensual legal knowledge, but it could not do so without harming the Contadora process. In the remainder of this section I attempt a step-by-step analysis of the ICJ proceedings, orders, and judgments to explain the Court's knowledge-determination process in Central America. A synthesis of this process is offered in Diagram 3.

The first task of the Court was to decide whether to indicate provisional measures, as provided by Article 41 of its Statute, in order to preserve the rights claimed by Nicaragua.[298] The Court granted the provisional measures that Nicaragua requested, despite the United States' contentions that the indication of such measures "could irreparably prejudice the interests of a number of states and seriously interfere with the negotiations being conducted pursuant to the Contadora process."[299] Nicaragua, on the contrary, insisted that the Court's proceedings dealt only with "claims against the United States [which] cannot be resolved, or even addressed, through [the Contadora] process."[300]

Though the order of the Court that indicated provisional measures made clear that it did not prejudge the question of the jurisdiction of the Court to deal with the case or any questions relating to the merits themselves, the language of the order made the Court's future judgments on jurisdiction, admissibility, and the merits most predictable. *The Court inter alia* held at this early stage in the proceedings that "[t]he United States of America should immediately cease and refrain from any action restricting, blocking or endangering access to or from Nicaraguan ports, and in particular, the laying of mines."[301] But most importantly, by fourteen votes to one, the Court went on to indicate that the "right to sovereignty and to political independence possessed by the Republic of Nicaragua...should be fully respected and should not in any way be jeopardized by any military and paramilitary activities which are prohibited by the principles of international law."[302] An express reference was made by the Court to the principle that States should refrain in their international relations from the threat or use of force against the territorial integrity or the political independence of any State. That they must also remember their duty not to intervene in matters within the domestic jurisdiction of a State, as embodied in the UN and the OAS Charters.[303]

From the wording of this Order, the following consequences might have been anticipated: first, Nicaragua succeeded in involving the Court in Central American issues and engaging the U.S. in a face-to-face confrontation, at least in a very preliminary phase, and second, the Court seemed ready to reject any alleged waiver to the application of the principles of territorial integrity, political independence, and nonintervention, at least in the light of facts such as those mentioned in the Nicaraguan application. The readiness of the Court to reject arguments in favor of unorthodox applications of these principles in "current Central American political developments" are evident in the rationale of the Court and in Judges Mosler, Jennings, and Schwebel's emphatic warnings against such attitude of the Court. Indeed, in their separate opinion, Judges Mosler and Jennings emphasized that "the duties...to refrain...from the threat or use of force against the territorial integrity or the political independence of any State, and to refrain from intervention in matters within the domestic jurisdiction of a State, are duties which apply to the Applicant

State [Nicaragua] as well as to the Respondent State [U.S.].[304] An even stronger cautionary message in the same direction was Judge Schwebel's only negative vote in this matter, as compared to the unanimous vote on the other issues, and his own separate opinion. Judge Schwebel was more concerned with the indifference of the Court to the principles of equality of States and "collective security."[305] Judge Schwebel wrote:

> [t]hese fundamental rights of a State to live in peace, free of the threat or use of force against its territorial integrity or political independence, are rights of every State, erga omnes... They do not depend upon narrow considerations of privity to a dispute before the Court... *They depend upon the broad considerations of collective security.*[306]

The May 10, 1984 Court Order on provisional measures and the simultaneous development of events within the Contadora process prompted the April 30-May 1 meeting of the Contadora Group and the Central American Ministers of Foreign Affairs. The meeting was convened just three months after the signing of the Contadora's procedural norms; its purpose was to discuss the recommendations of the three working commissions (dealing with regional security issues, political matters, and economic and social cooperation) that were created in accordance with those procedural norms. At that time, the Contadora Group was very confident that an agreement around the Contadora draft act was very likely to occur.

To the surprise of the Contadora Group, Costa Rica, El Salvador and Honduras abruptly announced a collective hardening of positions. The three U.S. allies proposed reducing Nicaraguan troop levels, foreign military advisors, and weaponry to agreed levels, "...prohibiting the importation of advanced weapons systems and eliminat[ing] trafficking in arms and the exportation of subversion to antigovernment guerrillas."[307] They also charged Nicaragua with refusing to accept arms limits. The United States joined the accusations and characterized the Sandinistas as "playing the aggrieved party and proclaiming peaceful intentions before international audiences,"[308] with a clear reference to the ICJ. The move was intended to pressure Nicaragua, despite its preliminary success at the ICJ, to remain within the negotiating context, rather than seek alternative arenas.

If judicial proceedings were to follow the same trend of this preliminary Order, they would strengthen the Sandinista's determination to hold out for their most important trade-offs. Moreover, because the decision of the Court undermined the legitimacy of the U.S. and the Central American Allies' most important negotiating asset, namely, collective pressure against Nicaragua, this preliminary court order further diminished Nicaragua's incentive to negotiate within Contadora. Commentators credit the Kissinger Commission Report for this first disruption of Contadora's apparent consensus,[309] but in truth this report actually considered Contadora as a "constructive" process that "the United States should actively encourage...."[310] The impetus of the new U.S. and Allies' claims and accusations against Nicaragua, along with a new aid package to the contras, and the renewed US-Nicaraguan Manzanillo talks, substantially contrasted the U.S. bloc's cooperative attitude of just a few months before. Nicaragua did remain in the negotiations, but it also continued the judicial proceedings before the ICJ. The Contadora Group reasonably felt that it was losing control over the situation and, on June 9, submitted its first draft treaty--the 1984 Contadora Act for Peace and Cooperation in Central America--for comments and amendments.

Disruption in Contadora meant even more than just lack of consensus. It revealed that among the many divergent expectations that the actors derived from the abstract common conflict resolution criteria, none of them had in fact prevailed and made had become more consensual among most participants. The almost predictable position of the Court to uphold the strong and traditional interpretations of nonintervention, political independence, and territorial sovereignty served to emphasize the parties' main diverging normative expectations. As described before, these expectations had been concealed by Contadora within complex sets of issues in order to forge some form of superficial consensus among the parties.

An important additional effect of the ICJ order was to encourage the United States and the Tegucigalpa Bloc to further clarify their main competing demands and the relation of these demands to the guiding notions of nonintervention and political independence. The subsequent submission by El Salvador of its "Declaration of Intervention" before the ICJ must be seen within this context. Indeed, the second task of the Court was to decide on the Salvadoran "Declaration of Intervention" pursuant to Article 63 of the Statute of the Court.[311] This initiative was specifically directed to challenge the Court's jurisdiction over the case and the admissibility of Nicaragua's Application.[312] El Salvador contended that it considered itself under the pressure of an affective armed attack by Nicaragua and felt itself along with the other Central American countries threatened in its territorial integrity, sovereignty, and independence. The claim alleged that Nicaragua was providing military support to the Farabundo Martí National Liberation Front (FMLN) and allowed installation of training sites in Nicaraguan territory by the Salvadoran guerrillas.

In the opinion of El Salvador, it was not possible for the Court to adjudicate Nicaragua's claims against the United States without determining the rights of El Salvador and the United States to engage in collective actions of legitimate defense. A final argument by El Salvador was the "political character" of the Central American conflict, which the Court could not deal with, for it would fundamentally undermine the negotiations currently being carried out within the Contadora process. This latter contention emphasized that the Central American conflict had "moved beyond the scope of simple bilateral treatment and become a regional issue entailing the participation of multilateral interests.[313] The Court decided not to hold a hearing on the Declaration of Intervention of El Salvador, and found it inadmissible inasmuch as it related to the jurisdictional phase of the proceedings.[314] To the Court, the Salvadorean Declaration involved questions that presupposed that it had jurisdiction to entertain the dispute between Nicaragua and the United States.[315]

The Salvadoran petition to intervene in the case clearly purported to strategically strengthen the collective-security and self-defense arguments advanced by the United States and its Central American allies. The litigation strategy consisted in having a Central American nation and direct participant in the Contadora negotiations--El Salvador--backing and seconding the United States' legal arguments. Moreover, the Salvadoran declaration to intervene was intended to weaken Nicaragua's contention that its application concerned solely its bilateral relations with the U.S. and not its collective negotiations with the other Central American countries. The most important objective of the Salvadoran application was to obtain a more specific decision from the Court on the soundness of the various US expectations about collective and individual self-defense. More specifically, the Court was expected to detail a collective-security justification of the US's military and paramilitary activities in Nicaragua. This strategy failed when the Court avoided substantive legal elaborations and rejected the Salvadoran initiative on merely procedural grounds. The immediate consequence of the failed Salvadoran request for the Contadora negotiations was the realization by the United States and the Tegucigalpa Bloc that in view of Nicaragua's recourse to the ICJ, no realistic implementation of the Act was predictable unless the hard issues were directly addressed and the main trade-offs were consciously achieved.

The Court's almost predictable position regarding the principles of nonintervention, collective security, and political independence, forced the United States to strongly oppose both the Court's jurisdictional basis in the case and the admissibility of Nicaragua's demands. But these efforts proved fruitless. By fifteen votes to one, the Court ruled that it had jurisdiction to entertain the application filed by Nicaragua, and unanimously, that the application was admissible.[316] Relevant to our present discussion is the opinion of the Court regarding the U.S. contention that the rights of the other Central American states were directly implicated and that these states were indispensable parties to the proceedings. The Court held, *inter alia*, that it had no power to direct that a third State be made a party to the proceedings, and that in any case, none of the three states had communicated their intention to intervene in the proceedings before the Court.[317]

As a direct consequence of this opinion, the United States became isolated from its Central American allies in the proceedings, a circumstance that made an appropriate defense of the collective security argument even more difficult.[318] Furthermore, the Court reiterated its views that the existence of the Contadora process did not constitute in this case an obstacle to the examination by the Court of the Nicaraguan application.[319] Thus, from a procedural standpoint, these holdings reiterated the separation of Nicaragua's major demands against the U.S. from the Contadora process and the other Central American countries, assuaging the Sandinista's needs to give up further negotiated concessions to the Tegucigalpa Bloc. The U.S. and its allies, on the other hand, were required to be more explicit in terms of verification and compliance at Contadora and more emphatic of a "collective" forcible pressure against the Sandinistas. Not surprisingly, Contadora became an agonizing process, especially in light of the United States' termination of its acceptance of the compulsory jurisdiction of the ICJ[320] and its unilateral suspension of the Manzanillo talks with

Nicaragua.[321] Clearly, the signing of 1984 Contadora Act would have meant just a ritual that the parties were not ready to execute in realistic terms. The 1984 ICJ's judgment on jurisdiction made negotiations more difficult for Contadora, although it helped the parties to avoid an agreement that was condemned to be nothing but dead letter.

B. Towards Consensual Knowledge: Further Developments at the ICJ

On June 27, 1986, upon the U.S. failure to appear in Court, the International Court of Justice handed down its decision on the merits of the Nicaragua case.[322] Out of the sixteen issues resolved by the Court, perhaps the most relevant to our discussion is decision (3) where the Court, by 12 votes to 3 (Oda, Schwebel and Jennings),

> Decides that the United States of America, by training, arming, equipping, financing and supplying the contra forces or otherwise encouraging, supporting and aiding military and paramilitary activities in and against Nicaragua, has acted, against the Republic of Nicaragua, in breach of its obligation under customary international law not to intervene in the affairs of another State.[323]

By comparable votes, the Court decided that the United States had violated other important rules of customary international law that prohibit the use of force against another state. The Court ruled that by directing and authorizing overflights of Nicaraguan territory and by other acts, the United States was in breach of its obligation under customary international law not to violate the sovereignty of another state. It also ruled that by laying mines and failing to make known their location, the United States had violated its obligations under customary international law not to use force, not to intervene, and not to violate the sovereignty of another state.[324] Other decisions were connected with the Court's finding that the United States was in breach of its obligations under the 1956 Treaty of Friendship, Commerce and Navigation between the United States and Nicaragua.[325] In view of the previous findings, the Court decided that

> the United States of America is under a duty immediately to cease and to refrain from all such acts as may constitute breaches of the foregoing legal obligations...and...that the United States is under an obligation to make reparation to the Republic of Nicaragua for all injury caused to Nicaragua by the breaches of obligations under customary international law."[326]

These findings are especially remarkable because in light of its inability to apply accepted multilateral treaty law, the Court relied on its own assessment of customary international law to make these decisions.[327] The Court's primary reliance on customary international law would appear to have been more convenient for the legal position advanced by the United States. As I pointed out earlier, the practice of the Inter-American States and the analogical interpretation of relevant treaty rules generated most of the uncertainty about the content of the main guiding principles in this dispute. The United States and the Tegucigalpa Bloc's normative expectations about the complex interplay among concepts of nonintervention, collective security, use of force, political independence, self-determination, and human rights, were founded upon alleged rules of customary international law. However, it was very unfortunate for the United States not to appear to defend its points of view. The Court, while recognizing the inconvenience caused by the United States non-appearance did not uphold the most of the U.S. interpretations of nonintervention and collective and individual self-defense.[328] In a generous fashion, even without the U.S. appearing during the merits phase of the proceedings, the Court approached the determination of customary law by itself raising the probable arguments of the U.S.. Concurrently with its analysis of the principles of customary international law governing the non use of force, nonintervention, and political independence, the Court gave exhaustive consideration to the argument of collective self-defense and its relation to those other principles.

The Court defined "armed attack" and categorized Nicaragua's conduct towards El Salvador as not constituting armed attack.[329] The Court observed that

> It is also clear that it is the State which is the victim of an 'armed attack' which must inform and declare the view that it has been so attacked. There is no rule in customary international law permitting another State to exercise the right of collective self-defence on the basis of its own assessment of the situation.[330]

To test its rationale under the usage given to collective self-defence in the Western Hemisphere, the Court referred to Articles 27 and 28 of the OAS Charter and Article 3 of the Rio Treaty. The purpose of the Court was not to apply these provisions, but to draw from them some confirmatory inferences for its reasoning. In doing so, it made the following observation about the Rio Treaty:

> [The treaty] provides that measures of collective self-defence taken by each State are decided on the request of the State or States directly attacked. It is significant that this requirement of a request on the part of the attacked State appears in the treaty particularly devoted to these matters of mutual assistance.[331]

Both the arguments of individual and collective self-defence were rejected by the Court on the basis that Nicaragua's conduct was not alleged to constitute an armed attack and that the directly affected nations made no request for collective self-defense.[332]

The Court then considered the right of the United States to take counter-measures in response to that conduct of Nicaragua which did not constitute an armed attack. This matter was examined in connection with an analysis of the principle of nonintervention in customary international law. The Court noted that the principle "has since [the Corfu Channel Case in 1949] been reflected in numerous declarations adopted by international organizations and conferences in which the United States and Nicaragua have participated." The ICJ further defined the content and the character of the principle. As to its content, the Court held as follows:

> the principle forbids all States or groups of States to intervene directly or indirectly in the internal or external affairs of other States. A prohibited intervention must accordingly be one bearing on matters in which each State is permitted, by the principle of sovereignty, to decide freely....[I]ntervention is wrongful when it uses methods of coercion in regard to such choices, which must remain free ones. The element of coercion, which defines, and indeed forms the very essence of, prohibited intervention, is particularly obvious in the case of an intervention which uses force, either in the direct form of military action, or in the indirect form of support for subversive or terrorist armed activities within another State.[333]

Furthermore, the Court categorically excluded as a rule of customary international law, any exception to the application of the prohibition to interfere in the internal matters of another state,

> Reliance by a State on a novel right or an unprecedented exception to the principle might, if shared in principle by other States, tend towards a modification of customary international law....The United States authorities have on some occasions clearly stated their grounds for intervening in the affairs of a foreign State for reasons connected with, for example, the domestic policies of that country,

> its ideology, the level of its armaments, or the direction of its foreign policy. But these were statements of international policy, and not an assertion of rules of existing international law.[334]

The ICJ's judgment bestowed further precision on its ruling that exceptions to the principle of nonintervention are unlawful, by establishing that the only occasion on which a forcible intervention could be rendered lawful is when it is made in response to an armed attack:

> States do not have a right of collective armed response to acts which do not constitute an 'armed attack'."[335]

In this connection, a wrongful act which does not qualify as an "armed attack," even if wrongful, does not justify an armed response. The Court acknowledged that Nicaragua's help to the insurgency in El Salvador might constitute an "intervention" but refused to accept the view that counter-intervention in such a situation can legally include uses of force against the political independence and territorial integrity of the intervening state.[336] The Court also ruled out the possibility that a provision such as "the maintenance or restoration of international peace and security" could apply to the "eventuality of the exercise of the right of individual or collective self-defense" or as a justification to interfere in the internal affairs of a state.[337]

Having thus dealt with the prohibition of the use of force and nonintervention, the Court next considered the "closely linked" principle of respect for State sovereignty.[338] In this respect it found that U.S. assistance to the contras, as well as the direct attacks on Nicaraguan ports, oil installations, etc., not only amounted to an unlawful use of force, but also infringed upon of the territorial sovereignty of Nicaragua.[339] Perhaps more significantly to this discussion, the Court refused to regard the 1979 resolution of the OAS Meeting of Consultation and the breaches of the Government of

Nicaragua of its commitments to the OAS as a justification for collective counter measures or intervention against Nicaragua. For the Court, Nicaragua's "commitment" to the OAS was a question of domestic policy, falling within the exclusive jurisdiction of a State.[340] The Court stated that even if such a commitment were to be examined in light of the early international events before the OAS in 1979, it must, however, conclude as follows:

> [T]he Court is unable to find anything in these documents, whether the resolution or the communication accompanied by the "Plan to Secure Peace," from which it can be inferred that any legal undertaking was intended to exist. Moreover, the Junta made it plain in one of these documents that its invitation to the Organization of American States to supervise Nicaragua's political life should not be allowed to obscure the fact that it was the Nicaraguans themselves who were to decide upon the conduct the country's domestic policy. The resolution of 23 June 1979 also declares that the solution of their problems is a matter "exclusively" for the Nicaraguan people, while stating that solution was to be based [in Spanish, *debería inspirarse*] on certain foundations which were put forward merely as recommendations to the future government....This was an essentially political pledge, made not only to the Organization, but also to the people of Nicaragua, intended to be its first beneficiaries.[341]

Even if considered to be a legal commitment, the Court added, such a political pledge could only be fulfilled towards the OAS, "the latter being alone empowered to monitor its implementation."[342] More explicitly, the Court held that:

> [H]owever the regime in Nicaragua be defined...adherence by a State to any particular doctrine does not constitute a violation of customary international law; to hold otherwise would make nonsense of the fundamental principle of State sovereignty, on which the whole of

> international law rests, and the freedom of choice of the political, social, economic and cultural system of a State....The Court cannot contemplate the creation of a new rule opening up a right of intervention by one State against another on the ground that the latter has opted for some particular ideology or political system.[343]

The Court noted the fact that none of the arguments concerning "ideological intervention" were advanced by the United States. However, it found itself not solely dependent for its decision on the probable arguments of the parties, but rather felt compelled to consider on its own initiative all rules of international law "which may be relevant to the settlement of the dispute even if these rules have not been invoked by a party."[344]

Not every holding of the Court in the Nicaragua Case can possibly be mentioned in this section. However, one final point relevant to our discussion is that concerning Nicaragua's violations of human rights. The Court's analysis of the 1985 finding of the United States Congress accusing Nicaragua of violating human rights, goes as follows:

> Where human rights are protected by international conventions, that protection takes the form of such arrangement for monitoring or ensuring respect for human rights as are provided for in the conventions themselves....In any event, the use of force could not be the appropriate method to monitor or ensure such respect....The Court concludes that the argument derived from the preservation of human rights in Nicaragua cannot afford a legal justification for the conduct of the United States and cannot be reconciled with the legal strategy of the respondent State, which is based on the right of collective self-defence.[345]

The Court thus, did not accept the contention that the protection of human rights legitimizes unilateral forcible measures against the violator of such rights, particularly when the protective measures are not taken under the arrangements of existent international human rights conventions. In addition, the Court highlighted that the argument of forcible counter-intervention based on the right of collective self-defence contradicted the allegation that intervention was needed to protect human rights.

In summary, the most evident observation one can make of the ICJ judgment in the Nicaragua case is that the Court disposed of and rejected all of the U.S. bloc's normative expectations. The Court precluded most of the analogical interpretations on the principle of nonintervention that we pointed out before as the sources of uncertainty in Contadora. Whether rightly or wrongly, the Court left no further doubts on the basic conflict resolution criteria that was applicable to the Central American conflict.

This being the case, the question arises as to how to appraise a judgment that, like this, cannot realistically be enforced. As we pointed out before, the traditional idea that international law must be enforceable to be effective is very problematic. Our appraisal of the judgment will be more useful if it is directed to elucidate the judgment's impact on the goals and negotiating styles of main participants within the post- Contadora Central American peace process (1987-1989).

CHAPTER VI

THE WORLD COURT: EXCURSUS ON THE ANATOMY OF A TRANSNATIONAL AUTHORITATIVE DETERMINATION PROCESS

The *Nicaragua case* was one of very few instances in which the ICJ has substantially entertained a situation involving an armed conflict.[346] In other occasions, when the court was asked to adjudicate cases of armed force, respondent governments denied or revoked jurisdiction, refused to appear, and balked at complying with court orders.[347] Thus, force cases have been used as an indicator of the failure of the international compulsory adjudication of the ICJ.[348]

There are many weaknesses one can mention about the ICJ, though most of them are subject to significant debate. The sole aspect that its jurisdiction is only optional and consensual, so that States must agree to bring their disputes to the Court, precludes the possibility that many important and salient controversies are submitted to international adjudication. This problem is clearly aggravated by the fact that just 29 percent of United Nations members have declared acceptance of the Court's jurisdiction, as opposed to 55 percent in 1955.[349] Moreover, from the forty six adherences to the Optional Clause, only nineteen are not expressly subject either to unilateral termination by the declarant state at any time or to modification at any time.[350] The only Permanent Member of the UN Security Council who currently adheres to the Optional Clause is the United Kingdom.[351] Many other leading states such as Algeria, Argentina, Brazil, the Federal Republic of Germany, Italy, Senegal, and Syria, Poland and the other states of Eastern Europe, do not adhere.[352] But even among those who have accepted the jurisdiction of the

Court as compulsory, there have already been cases in which the relevant states have declined to participate.

Another problem of the Court is the occasional but nevertheless significant failure of states to comply with its judgments, a problem linked to enforcement.[353] On top of these and other problems is the existence of many and different constraints that make international participants distrustful and reluctant to submit their disputes to the Court. They believe that negotiated alternatives would work better to keep their options open and that the law to be applied by the Court--or even the impartiality of the Court--be open to question.

Supporters of the ICJ argue that despite such weaknesses, newer states seem increasingly to bring their disputes to the Court. Thus, new technical problems are being presented to the Court, which is now dealing with new and old issues, arguably in a more sophisticated and comprehensive manner. Among the more complex technical questions ICJ supporters mention are issues related to delimitation of maritime boundaries,[354] intervention in the proceedings by a third state,[355] and the constitution of chambers.[356]

But the main interest guiding these pages is not to revive or duplicate the debate about the pros and cons of the World Court. The above is just to acknowledge the current debate about the utility of the Court. My interest rather is to highlight the concepts and indicators that may help understand whether decision makers care about and are influenced by the Court's proceedings and particularly by the normative expectations which have prevailed and survived ICJ litigation. The weaknesses that the existing literature has identified about the Court may help to slowdown the final political impact of the technical knowledge contained in a judgment of the Court, but certainly does not prevent that such legal knowledge would grow and prove an effective factor constraining and changing decision.[357]

The disparity between commentators' analytical assumptions and the reality of the ICJ rests on the deeper assumption that the ICJ should resemble domestic courts in every aspect. Thus, we would want the ICJ, most of the time, to exert incontestable compulsory jurisdiction and provide for the unavoidable enforcement of its judgments. But the role of the ICJ since 1922 as the "universal" international adjudicator has developed in such a unique and particular fashion that its effectiveness cannot be measured by the same standard that is commonly applicable to national courts. The accomplishment and influence of the Court must rather be assessed in full accordance with the degree of consensus that its judgments have generated, not only among the parties to a controversy but also within the international community in general. In this sense, it is the notion of the World Court as "source of legal knowledge" or a developer of international law[358] that deserves attention.

When we regard the ICJ as a producer and disseminator of new and increasingly consensual legal knowledge, we may perceive its role similar to that of some "international scientific and professional associations" (ISPAs) in other areas of human knowledge.[359] But as a Court of "universal" scope, the ICJ's role goes beyond the mere production and dissemination of knowledge. Its institutional character and legitimacy endows it with a series of features that make the knowledge it produces even more likely, than the knowledge produced by other ISPAs, to have an impact on the behavior of international actors.

It has been said, for instance, that a factor in the failure to integrate knowledge with power on behalf of a "global society" is the absence of an infrastructure of scientific and technological research institutes with a mandate to study of global problems.[360] Yet the ICJ, unlike most ISPAs, has much of that infrastructure and mandate. The ICJ is the principal judicial organ of the United Nations and its judgments are deemed by the UN Charter and its Statute as binding upon the parties. This legal connection is reflected in the practice of the United Nations, particularly at the General Assembly. The advisory opinions of the Court--and even, exceptionally, a judgment in a contentious case which binds only the parties[361]--are generally confirmed and usually supported by the United Nations as a whole. When this does not seem to be the case, as, for instance, when the Security Council refuses to enforce an ICJ judgment or decision, the discussion and reaction of the Council members, nevertheless, tend to confirm that the Court's decisions are, at least in principle, considered to be authoritative.

This is not to say that the relevant parties will always comply with all aspects of an ICJ decision as soon as it is adopted. The normative expectations of participants, however, normally do tend to conform to the principles articulated and the guidelines introduced by such decisions, at any rate if they are seen as internationally sound by target audiences. This tendency is reasonably inferred from the fact that most of the U.N.-member states have generally agreed that ICJ judgments and opinions state what international law really is.[362] This "official" reception of the product of the ICJ results not only from the perceptions of states, but also to the indisputable fact that the ICJ is a permanent and stable tribunal "that when deciding individual disputes, could at the same time determine and establish general principles and rules, thus completing and developing the existing body of law."[363] This is what Jiménez de Aréchaga calls "the elaboration of a consistent jurisprudence" that only institutional continuity and permanency are capable of providing, maintaining, and developing. Possibly with this perception in mind, it has been said that when the World Court speaks, the community of international lawyers and states listens.[364]

Because of its almost seventy years of existence and highly systematized work, the ICJ and its immediate predecessor, the PCIJ,--together, the *World Court*--have been able by prescription and interpretation to develop a body of legal knowledge that is significantly comprehensive and that has influenced the way legal scholars and political decision makers view the content and sources of international law. True, the independence of the judges of the ICJ is severely evaluated. But the variety of nationalities, ideologies, cultures, and traditions represented in the Court, together with the selection process, ethical rules of the judiciary itself, and the assurance of a minimum of representation for all parties in a controversy,[365] have served to endow the Court's decisions with great international legitimacy and authority.[366]

The voting trend of the judges themselves (or at any rate, certain of them) has served to assuage the strongest criticisms about the partiality of the World Court's judges. The judges, for instance, from what until lately was known as the People's Republic of Poland voted in ways not evincing a national or socialist bias. Also, Judge Schwebel, the member of the Court of United States nationality, has nine times since his appointment in 1981 voted against the position of the United States.[367] Such examples certainly do not guarantee the Court's impartiality as a whole and in all cases. That depends above all on the subjective predispositions of each judge.[368] But further evidence has been collected to indicate that the voting record of the Court "does not reveal significant alignments, either on a regional, political, or economic basis"[369] A more significant finding is that "there is a high degree of consensus among the judges on most decisions."[370] Evidence of this sort, though not overwhelmingly, or invariably convincing, nevertheless enhances the Court's reputation as a reliable mechanism for authoritatively resolving current legal disputes and giving the resultant legal knowledge--or legal holdings--an important place in the minds of statesmen.[371]

A measure of the influence of the ICJ on public policy decisions of nation-states and international bodies is suggested by the fact that once a decision is rendered by the Court on a particular case, scholars, private and public organizations and the international public invariably discuss and comment on the legal and political consequences of the Court's judgment and the rationale that supports it.[372]

An equally persuasive argument about the effect of ICJ's decisions on decision making considers the Court's intergovernmental character and its organic relationship with the United Nations. In October and November 1986, for example, when Nicaragua sought enforcement of the Court's decision on the merits under Article 94 of the UN Charter and political condemnation of the U.S. at the U.N. Headquarters, it became clear that the United States stood in an isolated position both at the Security Council and at the General Assembly.[373] Though the US has vetoed at the Council every draft resolution intended to enforce the Court's judgment on the merits of the Nicaragua case, the US representative to the UN Security Council has never questioned the judgment itself, rather, he has essentially confined himself to restating the U.S. position that the Court lacked jurisdiction to render the judgment.[374]

The historic role played by the Court's advisory opinions provides further examples on how the ICJ influences intergovernmental organizations (IGOs) and governments. In its 1980 advisory opinion on "Interpretations of the Agreement of 25 March 1951 between the World Health Organization (WHO) and Egypt," the Court stated that IGOs "are subjects of international law and, as such, are bound by any obligations incumbent upon them under general rules of international law, under their constitutions or under international agreements to which they are parties."[375] The practical effect of the opinion was to frustrate the attempt of the Arab League to punish Egypt for its Peace Treaty with Israel by removing the WHO regional Office from Cairo. In its 1962 advisory opinion on "Certain Expenses of the United Nations" the Court safeguarded the legal validity of peace-keeping operations by UN forces.[376] In 1950 the Court held that the UN

General Assembly was not intervening in domestic matters when dealing with treaty questions of human rights and fundamental freedoms.[377]

Other important advisory opinions, fully upheld by the United Nations, have dealt with decolonization[378] and protection of the rights of staff members.[379] In general, one may assert that, although in practice the United Nations has not invariably applied the legal advice of those opinions, the Court, through its advisory opinions has indisputably contributed to the clarification and development of international law so as to facilitate problem-solving tasks within international organizations.

The same can be said about the Court's handling of contentious cases and the impact of its decisions on the disputing parties. Though not clear in cases involving the use of force, most ICJ decisions have in some measure provided prevailing expectations that have affected the ultimate outcome of the controversy. This is particularly true in settlement of territorial disputes and maritime delimitations.[380]

As a possible consequence of the significant influence that the Court's judgments are accorded at the United Nations and other regional and specialized organizations,[381] national governments normally find it difficult not to take the Court's legal interpretations and prescriptions into consideration when they frame or justify their foreign policy. ICJ judgments have less direct but nevertheless significant influence on decision makers who must respond to the national affiliates of invisible international colleges and ISPAs who themselves feed in part or in whole on the knowledge that is produced in ICJ quarters.[382] For example, on July 3, 1986, just a few days after the ICJ's June 27 decision on the merits of the Nicaragua case, Reuters published a series of interviews in order to survey the reaction of American legal experts to the World Court ruling. The news report concluded as follows:

> [E]xperts from around the country told Reuters that last week's finding [of the ICJ] that Washington broke international law by aiding anti-government rebels, known as contras, was a credible judgment by distinguished jurists.[383]

The US Department of State reacted indicating that the Administration certainly rejected the decision but said that it was "the facts, and not issues of international law, which were in dispute."[384] Moreover, in countries where international law is considered to be part of the "law of the land," national courts may keep "attentive eyes" on major legal developments at the ICJ.[385] Though not a "binding" authority, ICJ-produced knowledge certainly inspires domestic pressure against that foreign policy which would contravene against it.

When discussing the lack of enforcement of ICJ decisions, judge H. Dillard explained the special function of the Court:

> A court is not as such peace-keeping organ. Rather, it is an adjudicative organ whose contributions to peace flow from its resolution of a particular dispute through the interpretation, application, and monitoring of legal norms. It...has a *guidance function.*[386]

By "guidance function" judge Dillard meant that, as in the case of the United States case against Iran,[387] while the Court may not always resolve a particular dispute, it may ultimately affect its resolution. "It may do so by fortifying the legal authority and possibly even the moral force of the diplomatic effort."[388]

Judge Dillard thus emphasized some of the features that make the ICJ much more than a knowledge-producer or an ISPA. It is indeed a source of authoritative criteria that not only help decision makers cope with uncertainty, but also constrains them to frame policies within the confines of such knowledge. However, none of the foregoing arguments in favor of the ICJ's role as a knowledge-producer underestimates the fact that the Court has been significantly underutilized, or that, in a few important cases--*Icelandic Fisheries, Hostages in Iran, Military and Paramilitary Activities in and against Nicaragua*--, its judgments have been ignored by the losing party.[389] But neither of these points invalidates the assumption that ICJ-produced legal knowledge and criteria do have a significant impact on international conflict resolution and decision-making. Certainly the issue deserves further study. Legal scholars' realization of the extent to which ICJ judgments set forth more common and consensual legal criteria for conflict resolution may ultimately help them pursue more meaningful efforts to improve the effectiveness of international law in forging peace and minimum world order.

CHAPTER VII

COPING WITH UNCERTAINTY THROUGH CONSENSUAL KNOWLEDGE AND NORMATIVE RESTRAINT

The events in Central America that followed the June 27, 1986 ICJ judgment on the Nicaragua case took a remarkably different direction from that of the Contadora years. Between July 1986 and August 1987 all participants and the international community focused their attention on the International Court of Justice and the possible impact of its rulings.

Encouraged by their overall success in Court, the Sandinistas took immediate action to publicize the judgment at every relevant forum and audience.[390] On July 28, 1986, Nicaragua filed simultaneous applications to the Court against Costa Rica and Honduras.[391] This move was most unexpected because it contradicted Nicaragua's argument that its resorting to the ICJ was intended only to isolate Nicaragua's and the United States' bilateral problems from the larger Contadora agenda. These two new applications deserve some attention for they significantly contributed to a change of attitude in Central America.

The complaints were based upon Article XXXI of the American Treaty on Pacific Settlement, otherwise known as the Pact of Bogota.[392] Both applications shared the same legal grounds but referred to different facts. The application against Costa Rica focused on a series of border incidents allegedly evincing Costa Rica's support and complicity with Pastora's rebels (the guerrilla group active in Nicaragua's southern territory). Nicaragua emphasized that despite its efforts "towards a peaceful solution by means of bilateral conversations," Costa Rican authorities were not taking any specific measures to stop Contra's activities inside Costa

Rican territory. The application against Honduras listed a series of incidents along the Nicaraguan-Honduran border but, unlike the application against Costa Rica, it also claimed involvement of the Honduran army in direct armed attacks against Nicaragua. Nicaragua categorized Honduras' behavior as constituting a threat or use of force against the territorial sovereignty of Nicaragua. Both applications complained about Costa Rican and Honduran intervention in the internal or external affairs of another state, violation of another State's sovereignty, and injury (killing, wounding, and kidnapping) of another state's citizens.

In addition to these new applications before the ICJ, Nicaragua engaged in a diplomatic campaign to take advantage of the 1986 judgment against the United States.[393] President Daniel Ortega traveled extensively to request support for "law and peace," with express reference to the June 27 ruling of the ICJ.[394] In an attempt to persuade the U.S. Congress to withhold President Reagan's $100 million proposal for aid to the Contras, Nicaragua managed to submit a draft resolution to the Security Council calling for full compliance with the Court's judgment.[395] The United States casted the only negative vote and vetoed the resolution on grounds that "the measure could not, and would not, contribute to a peaceful settlement of the situation in Central America."[396] In October 1986, just a few days after President Reagan signed into law the $100 million for aid appropriation to the Contras, a "CIA-Contra supply plane" was "shot down" by the Nicaraguan Army over southern Nicaragua. The Sandinistas submitted through the non-aligned members of the Council a new draft resolution calling for the enforcement of the Court's judgment.[397] Another U.S. veto at the Security Council prevented the draft from being approved. Nicaragua resorted to the UN General Assembly where a resolution "calling on the United States to stop aiding Nicaraguan rebels" was overwhelmingly approved. The U.S. allies such as Great Britain, France, West Germany, and more significantly, Costa Rica and Honduras, surprisingly abstained from voting.[398]

Nicaragua's initiatives based on the merits of the 1986 ICJ judgment were directed to make the judgment relevant in Central American issues and to attract the support of the international community. The applications against Honduras and Costa Rica may be seen from the same perspective. The convergence of these moves by the Sandinistas seem to have facilitated that even the closest U.S. allies in Western Europe and Central America not only accepted the Court's rationale and conclusions, but also were ready to adapt or change their own attitudes more in consonance with the legal precisions advanced by the Court.

A. From Adaptation to Learning: The Case of the Five Central American Presidents

The impact of the ICJ's judgment on the Tegucigalpa Bloc countries was certainly strengthened by Nicaragua's subsequent applications against Costa Rica and Honduras. Losing their cases before the ICJ would have meant for Costa Rica and Honduras more than mere "isolation." In contrast to the United States, neither one of these two countries was willing to face an unfavorable judgment. Thus, the Tegucigalpa Bloc was to be the first coalition of governments to show signs of change.

On July 29, one month after the 1986 judgment against the U.S. and one day after the filing of Nicaraguan applications against Costa Rica and Honduras, Costa Rican President Oscar Arias, announced that he was considering sanctions against Nicaraguan rebel groups who violated his country's neutrality by building a hospital within Costa Rican territory.[399] Although months before taking office President Arias was very critical of Contra military activities against Nicaragua,[400] he aimed his July 29 declarations at confirming to the international community--the World Court included--

that Costa Rica was acting with due diligence and in full compliance with its international obligations towards Nicaragua.[401] This reaction acquired full meaning in light of the convulsion that Nicaragua's application generated within the Costa Rican public. It also matched President Arias concerns for the critics' statements that the previous government of President Luis Alberto Monge did not adequately enforce the ban on rebel military activities.[402]

The importance of the Nicaraguan application for what later became the Arias administration policy in Central America was indeed paramount. Costa Rica, a country that itself possesses a sophisticated judicial system, grants courts of law a significant place in daily life. Since the Costa Rican constitution places international law above ordinary legislation, Costa Ricans naturally view the ICJ with great respect. Thus, the Nicaraguan application impacted greatly on Costa Ricans. The Arias administration could not afford to get entangled in international litigation without being assured of a favorable decision. Such assurance, however, was not clearly available, especially in the light of the rumored double standard assumed by the previous Monge administration toward the Contras.[403] Moreover, in contrast to Honduras who was ready to reject the Nicaraguan application on jurisdictional grounds, Costa Rica expressly accepted the ICJ's jurisdiction over the case under the previous Costa Rican recognitions of such jurisdiction both through the Pact of Bogota and unilateral declarations, and could not possibly question the Nicaraguan application on the same jurisdictional excuses as Honduras.

In brief, the Arias administration saw negotiation as the only way out. But for diplomacy to constitute a realistic alternative, it would have to be initiated and developed in full commitment to sound and consensual criteria, of the kind set forth by the ICJ. More importantly, to entertain new negotiations outside the Contadora context needed a complete redefinition of issues and bargaining strategies. All these domestic and diplomatic constraints may have had some impact on President Arias when, in early 1987, he submitted to the Presidents of Guatemala, El Salvador, and Honduras his document "A Time for Peace." The document contained the basis for the Esquipulas Accords of August 1987.[404] After the signing of these accords, Arias' move proved most appropriate. On the same day, Nicaragua announced its withdrawal of the application against Costa Rica.

Honduras and El Salvador followed Costa Rica's proposal for reopening the negotiations, though for more tactical reasons. Honduras verbally accepted the ICJ's prohibition against further U.S. assistance to the Contras, but it did so to demonstrate consistency between actions and legal arguments in its own case before the Court. Honduras called the jurisdiction of the Court and the admissibility of the Nicaraguan application into question. At the same time, Honduras joined negotiations under the Arias peace plan to persuade Nicaragua not to ask the Court for an indication of provisional measures.

As a litigation strategy, provisional measures would have meant disbanding the Contras' operations in Honduran territory, something Honduras had neither the will nor the resources to comply with. Thus, when President Reagan signed for further Contra-aid in October 1986, the Honduran Government reiterated that they "would not allow contra military aid to be dispensed through its territory...and the U.S. would not be permitted to use Honduran territory to train Contras."[405] Honduras later signed the Esquipulas Accords in 1987, officially committing itself to discontinue aid to irregular forces and to restrict the use of its territory. Nicaragua never believed Honduras's public statements and maintained its application against Honduras. By keeping its application against Honduras, Nicaragua clearly intended to secure the latter's respect for its commitments under the Esquipulas process.

The changes in the attitude of the members of the Tegucigalpa bloc after the 1986 ICJ's judgment against the United States and Nicaragua's submission of its application against Costa Rica and Honduras, can also be traced by looking at the developments within Contadora since late 1986. The OAS meeting in Antigua, Guatemala on November 1986 constituted the first of three symbolic events suggesting the death of Contadora as a mediation process for Central America. While Costa Rica, El Salvador, and Honduras reiterated their open intention to boycott any future meeting of the Contadora Group,[406] the OAS Secretary General Joao Baena Soares acknowledged that the crisis could not be solved except by the decision of the countries directly involved.[407] What was termed as a last-ditch bid by the Contadora Group to pull together another meeting of the Central American countries failed when the OAS refused to reiterate its support for the Group in the Antigua meeting of November 14.[408]

The second event signaling the failure and termination of the Contadora process was the Contadora-sponsored tour for the Secretaries General of both the UN and the OAS after of Central America in December 1986. They concluded that the conflict was far from being solved and that negotiations were not really bringing new hopes in that regard.[409] The third and most important indicator of Contadora's end was the meeting of the U.S. Central American allies and Guatemala--Nicaragua being deliberately excluded--in San Jose, Costa Rica on February 15, 1987, where the Arias Plan ("A Time for Peace") was formally discussed and accepted in principle.

The meeting in San José was especially important because of the detail and precision with which it challenged the authority of Contadora. It focused on the discussion of the Guatemalan proposal for the creation of a Central American Parliament. It also achieved the four countries' full consensus on the legal and procedural bases demanded by further dealings with Nicaragua. In the course of the meeting, the relevant parties realized that remaining within Contadora did not offer any possibility to pressure the "leftist" Sandinista Government to relax restrictions on domestic opposition.[410] Moreover, since the U.S.-sponsored Contras were not a significant--or a legitimate--mechanism, the Presidents agreed that Nicaragua had to be democratized by diplomatic rather than military means. The Guatemalan proposal for a Central American Parliament also played an important role in this respect. On the one hand, it secured Guatemala's adherence to the Arias' plan mainly because Guatemalan President Vinicio Cerezo was the most enthusiastic sponsor of the idea. The Parliament was also conceived to serve as a Central American forum which could rightly claim to represent the peoples of Central America. To achieve such purpose, direct elections under fully democratic and representative conditions were established as pre-requisite for the constitution of the Parliament. If Nicaragua signed the agreement for the creation of the Parliament, then the whole of Central America would have a legitimate stake in pressuring Nicaragua toward *representative and pluralized elections*.

Whatever the strategic objectives at the San José Meeting, the fact is that it opened new avenues for more substantive negotiations. The inclusion of the Central American Parliament in the peace negotiations secured Guatemala's adherence to the larger agenda of the Arias plan. Thus, Honduras, Costa Rica, El Salvador, and Guatemala emerged from the February 1987 meeting more united in their purpose than at any time before. The inclusion of the Central American Parliament also facilitated the agreement between the Presidents of these four Central American countries around the premise that the Contras were not an effective nor legal method to democratize Nicaragua. In turn, the adoption of this agreement as common conflict resolution criteria set forth the basis for Nicaragua's renewed interest in the negotiations. Likewise, Nicaragua realized at this time that it needed full cooperation from its neighbors if it wanted to get rid of the Contras. From a Sandinistan point of view, the "incomplete" sincerity of Honduras and El Salvador's promise to collaborate was not a big problem since at least they were willing to sign on such commitment.

On August 7, 1987, the five Presidents signed in Esquipulas, Guatemala, an "Agreement on a Procedure for Establishing a Firm and Lasting Peace in Central America," (Esquipulas II).[411] They thus entered into a distinctly different stage of negotiations. The main difference between Esquipulas II and Contadora is that negotiations within Esquipulas initially reduced the number of issues to those considered as essentially urgent. Those issues included "national reconciliation," "cease of fire," "democratization" and "free elections." All other Contadora security matters--except for the cease of aid to irregular forces and restriction to use territory to attack other states--were excluded. A general reference was still made to some more decomposable issues such as economic and social affairs, but the obvious intention of the five Presidents was to delay discussion of these latter issues in order to focus on the less decomposable ones. All the protocols that were annexed to the Contadora Act were eliminated, though some timing provisions were added.

The negotiations within Esquipulas II developed on the basis of an increasingly consensual base of legal knowledge and, thus, with less skeptic decision-making styles. Still, the learning process was not free of disappointments. The negotiations suffered a first stalemate after the January 15-16, 1988 meeting in Alajuela, Costa Rica. On that occasion, the five Presidents met to discuss the future of the peace process and to receive the conclusions of the International Verification and Follow-up Commission (CIV). When the conclusions of the CIV were disclosed some of the Presidents had understandable reservations about the actual compliance of the Accords. They found that the obligations assumed in Esquipulas II "have not yet totally been met."[412]

Change in Esquipulas II
1986-1989

Time Range	**Negotiation Status**
1986-1987 Before Esquipulas but after Contadora	End of Contadora. Five Central American Presidents reexamine means to accomplish their political goals. and adapt. Some incremental growth is experienced around the Arias Peace Plan in early 1987.

August 1987

Esquipulas replaces Contadora

Esquipulas as of:

1987-early 1988 From Esquipulas to Alajuela	Incremental Growth
early 1988-early 1989 From Alajuela to Costa del Sol	Turbulent Non-Growth
early 1989-December 1989 From Costa del Sol to Tela and thereafter	**Attempted managed interdependence (aftermath unknown as of Dec. 1989)**

Diagram 4

According to the Final Report of the Lasa Commission on Compliance with the Central America Peace Accord, all governments had taken the formal steps envisioned by the agreements to varying degrees--appointing national commissions of reconciliation and opening dialogues with internal opposition groups. Formal amnesty had been declared in Guatemala, El Salvador, Honduras, and Nicaragua (the CIV exempted Costa Rica from this obligation).

The report also indicated that the call to pursue negotiations for a cease-fire had led to irregular but continuing discussions in the case of Nicaragua but that no lasting cease-fires had been achieved in Nicaragua, Guatemala, and El Salvador. As to democratization, the report mentioned that Nicaragua had taken some steps, the most significant being the reopening of Radio Católica and La Prensa. On the proposed treaty for establishing a Central American Parliament, the report found that so far only Guatemala and Nicaragua had ratified the treaty. Likewise, since the signing of Esquipulas II, the CIV found that while Honduras still served as a major channel for U.S. aid to the Nicaraguan Resistance Forces (Contras), there was little consistent evidence that any Central American country was providing material aid to armed opposition groups operating in neighboring countries. And while the CIV found that the number of Contras operating from Honduras had substantially decreased, they also found that the armed Nicaraguan opposition still continued to use Honduran territory. The report also indicated that even though Contadora continued to be willing to supervise and mediate talks on security issues, such tasks had been covered by Esquipulas II and the need for Contadora's supervision was not realistically envisaged. Finally, on the calendar for the fulfillment of the Accord, the report informed that the five countries had not met the ambitious timetable they had set.[413]

Pessimism arouse from the Alajuela meeting.[414] No significant progress was achieved on the implementation of most points of the accords. Though the original uncertainty regarding the common criteria for reaching agreement was surmounted when political attitudes changed and the Esquipulas II Accords were signed in 1987, uncertainty as to the implementation of the agreement was still unresolved. The sequence of events that occurred in Central America from late-1988 through 1989 reveals a renewed effort by the five Presidents to manage their newly acquired interdependence and to implement the 1987 agreement with the help of international organizations.

The CIV was replaced by the Executive Commission, consisting of the Central American foreign ministers. The new Commission was entrusted with the determination of mechanisms for further verification. The Presidents' dissatisfaction with the CIV as originally formulated was based on the fact that much of the inherited procedural uncertainty from the Contadora years had yet to be overcome. The persistence on intraregional verification, this time through the Commission, seemed to follow the same path of the Contadora Group as to excluding any direct link with an international organization. The Lasa Report, for example, stated that "whether extraregional verification will be sought in the future is unclear, sources indicated that Honduras and El Salvador appeared particularly hostile to verification by parties from outside the region."[415] The matter had to be once again resolved through strong leadership and new legal knowledge. On December 20, 1988, the ICJ handed down its judgment on jurisdiction and admissibility in the case brought by Nicaragua against Honduras.[416]

The Court determined that, in light of the events of June/July 1986, the Contadora process was "concluded" both for the purposes of Article IV of the Pact of Bogota and of any other obligation to exhaust that procedure which might have existed independently of the Pact.[417] Article IV of the Pact of Bogota, upon which Honduras relied, reads as follows:

> Once any pacific procedure has been initiated, whether by agreement between the parties or in fulfillment of the present Treaty or a previous pact, no other procedure may be commenced until that procedure is concluded.[418]

The Court also interpreted the preambular paragraph 35 of the Final 1986 Contadora Act to indicate that the dispute settlement procedures under that instrument were not intended to exclude "the right of recourse to other competent international forums."[419] Before the judgment, it was not clear whether any other procedure could be commenced before Contadora was officially declared as terminated and Esquipulas II was still ongoing.

Although the judgment is not clear on what was to be expected from the letter of Article IV, the final interpretation of the parties after the Court's decision was that both Contadora and Esquipulas II were procedures not falling within the scope of the Pact of Bogota. The finding of the Court and the new expectations of the parties implied that any further mechanism could be commenced even before negotiations were concluded. The probable impact of this judgment on the decision-making and bargaining styles of the Central American Presidents converged with a contemporaneous letter from UN Secretary General Javier Pérez de Cuellar to the Central American foreign ministers of January 5, 1989.[420]

The letter explained in detail the necessary steps towards establishing a UN peace-keeping mechanism in the region. To be sure, the ICJ's ruling cleared the way for the five Presidents' decision to search for newer and consensual formulas for the implementation of the Esquipulas accords. Without this new ingredient, no more substantive negotiations could have been expected from Honduras and Nicaragua. Thus, in early 1989 new knowledge was introduced into Esquipulas II under the following premises: a) the Central American countries were free to resort to the most appropriate international organizations for the implementation of the Esquipulas II accords, and b) some possible procedures for the verification and implementation of the accords were available at the United Nations and the OAS, i.e., the notion of peacekeeping and verification activities as presented by the UN Secretary General in January 5, 1989. In fact, on February 13-14, 1989, just two months after issuance of the ICJ's judgment and the letter from Mr. Pérez de Cuellar, the Central American Presidents agreed in Costa Del Sol, Province of La Paz, El Salvador, to make a "special invitation" to the Secretaries General of the United Nations and the Organizations of American States to exercise verification and technical roles on the meeting's major commitments.

The "Costa del Sol" meeting established a turning point in substance and process in the Esquipulas II negotiations. Two basic commitments were adopted at this meeting. On the one hand, Nicaragua was to develop a process of democratization and national reconciliation. Elections for President, Vice-President, and Representatives to the National Assembly, Municipalities, and Central American Parliament were to take place after the Sandinistas were able to conclude major electoral and media legislative reforms but no later than February 25, 1990. The interim was needed to guarantee political organization and action "in the broadest sense for political parties" and at least a six month period of political activity. On the other hand, the five Presidents committed themselves to "formulate, within a period of no more than 90 days, a Joint Plan for the voluntary demobilization, repatriation or relocation in Nicaragua and in third countries of Nicaraguan Resistance members and their families."

In order to comply with the commitments on verification of security, the Central American Presidents were now commissioning the Executive Committee to hold talks in New York with the Secretary General of the United Nations. They were also contemplating a substantial intervention by the United Nations and the OAS in "certifying" the integrity of the electoral process in Nicaragua and providing technical assistance in repatriating and relocating the members of the Nicaraguan Resistance.[421] In this connection, increasingly consensual knowledge on substantive principles seems to have been achieved. Regional intervention aimed at Nicaragua's democratization was now possible, though the parties realized that it could not be possible without the acquiescence of the Sandinistas. Moreover, collective military or armed pressure was ruled out as a legitimate means to attain such purpose. On procedural questions, the Presidents shared the knowledge that verification, compliance, and implementation of the new commitments were only possible through the active involvement of one or more international organizations. The United Nations was perceived to play a predominant role in this context.

On a subsequent meeting at Tela, Honduras, on August 5, 6 and 7, 1989, the five Presidents seemed actually to have learned the main legal and procedural criteria for conflict resolution. Thereby, the five Presidents adopted three key documents: a) the Tela Declaration, which endorsed and ratified the Esquipulas II Plan and the Alajuela and Costa del Sol Declarations; b) the Joint Plan for the voluntary demobilitization, repatriation or relocation to and in Nicaragua or third countries of the members of the Nicaraguan Resistance and their families, a plan that also envisaged demobilization assistance for all involved in armed actions in the countries of the region who voluntarily sought that assistance and provided for the creation, by the UN and the OAS Secretaries General, of an International Support and Verification Commission (CIAV); and c) the Agreement between Honduras and Nicaragua, a bilateral instrument whereby the Government of Nicaragua committed itself to postpone and eventually withdraw the application filed against Honduras before the International Court of Justice once conditions regarding implementation of the Joint Plan and prevention of the use of the Honduran territory by irregular forces have been met.[422]

For the first time in ten years, the Central American countries were able to agree on the hardest issues. Most significantly, they were able to take concrete steps toward the implementation of the agreements. The Tela Agreements cleared the way for the Secretary General to send of a reconnaissance mission to the region to prepare a formal proposal to the Security Council for the establishment of ONUCA.[423] The participants ceased relying on their own assessments of the guiding principles. At the same time, the guiding principles were consensually interpreted as barring any forcible intervention in the internal affairs of any of the Central America countries. Consensual knowledge has been achieved as to clarify procedural questions, such as the role of international organizations in the implementation of the accords.

B. The United States: Adaptation?

Change occurred in Central America after the 1986 judgment not only within the Central American countries themselves, but also in the ways the United States actually behaved in the region. True, the U.S.'s public verbal support for the Contras and its political goals on Nicaragua and El Salvador remained invariable. However, though gradual and by no means implying a complete change, there was a drift in the U.S. policy towards Central America since the signing of the Esquipulas II Accords that suggests a less skeptical standpoint on peaceful alternatives for settling disputes in the region. The United States maintained the same set of political goals since 1981 but adjusted, at the same time, the means for its achievement to the newer development of events within the Esquipulas process. The causes and extend of change in U.S. policy is the subject matter of this section.

Since 1979, both before and after the 1986 judgment on the Nicaragua case, the decision-making style of the United States in Central America had been "eclectic." This means that in view of its specific and static goal to prevent a "second Cuba" from developing in Nicaragua, the U.S. managed issues and demands in a tactical fashion. The guiding concepts on which the U.S. grounded its policy toward Nicaragua have been widely commented upon elsewhere and do not need to be detailed here.[424] In general, however, the U.S. has from time to time and according to the circumstances advanced the ideas *of vital national interest and security, the security of the Americas, and democratization.*[425]

Though military pressure in the name of the collective security of the Western Hemisphere was consensual between the Tegucigalpa Bloc and the United States during the Contadora years, that consensus vanished since late 1986. The U.S.'s coalition in Central America lost substantial cohesion because the U.S., unlike its allies, was unable to accept the new prevailing normative expectations as reflected in 1986 ICJ judgment.

Since early 1987, the U.S. notions of national and collective security gradually yielded to the concept of *democratization,* which then became the Reagan Administration's most preferred slogan.[426] But a significant disagreement arose between the U.S. and its Central American allies as to the most appropriate means to achieve democracy in Nicaragua. Washington's insistence on maintaining military pressure against the Sandinistas as the only strategy to achieve democracy in Nicaragua isolated the Administration's policy in Central America. The U.S.' *eclectic* policy became particularly secluded when its most loyal Central American allies struggled hard to accommodate their policies and bargaining approaches more consistently with the rationale of the 1986 ICJ's decision. On October 30, 1986, for example, a *L.A. Times* editorial reported that:

> At the United Nations, the United States stood alone to veto a Security Council resolution urging this nation to comply with a World Court decision....It was revealed that

> the Administration is looking for places in the United States to train the Contras because its Central American allies refuse to have anything to do with them....Rarely has the Administration's isolated position on Nicaragua been illustrated so starkly....At [the] UN, even close allies England and France chose to abstain rather than support a U.S. position that is not just stubborn and arrogant, but in violation of international law.[427]

The different response of the United States' Central American allies was perceivable not only at the United Nations. The Nicaraguan Application against Honduras and Costa Rica also significantly affected U.S. alliances in Central America as to undermine most of Washington's policy in the region.[428] The signing of the Esquipulas II accords further deepened the gap. On several occasions during 1988, the Administration was unable--U.S. Secretary of State George Shultz himself failed twice--to persuade Costa Rica and Guatemala either to isolate or condemn the Sandinistas.[429] Costa Rica and Guatemala refused to follow U.S. proposals because they would have meant continued support for military pressure against the Sandinistas, in violation of the ICJ's holdings in the Nicaragua case.[430] The changes in alliances in Central America may have had as well a great effect in dividing the [U.S.] Congress and public opinion from the Administration policy as well."[431]

However, U.S. decision-makers did not learned from legal defeat at the World Court nor failure to maintain a cohesive coalition in Central America. A classical study on government learning has demonstrated that for the U.S., much more than simple failure or disappointment is required.[432] ICJ-produced legal knowledge may, however, have impacted on Washington and induced some adaptation of U.S. decision-making style. Yet, adaptation by the United States can only derive from the confluence of international and domestic constraints.

Within the United States, the Reagan administration managed to keep general support until late 1986. After George Shultz' appointment as Secretary of State in 1982, the Administration was able to "calm [previous] rhetoric, maneuver around symbolic sensitivities, and neutralize its critics in the media and Congress."[433] In dealing with the public, the Reagan administration "skillfully outmaneuvered potential congressional opposition to effect a major U.S. troop buildup in Honduras under the guise of training exercises."[434] But the situation changed for President Reagan four years later when, despite the approval by Congress of further contra aid in October 1986, a scandal connected with certain U.S. covert actions gave rise to strong domestic criticism against the Administration in Central American affairs. The discovery of the illegal sale of arms to Iran and the deviation of funds to support the Contras polarized the Executive branch and the Congress.[435]

To be sure, the legal criteria supplied by the ICJ and the conduct of the administration towards the Court deepened the domestic division, particularly within Congress.[436] The ICJ provided newly-determined legal criteria against which the American policy in Central America could be evaluated and criticized. That knowledge became significantly shared by epistemic communities of legal experts and academicians both inside and outside the government.[437] Beyond congressional and academical quarters, the new knowledge was also accepted by individuals and non-governmental organizations whose potential to influence administration policy unfolded throughout the 1988 U.S. presidential elections.

The complaints filed by American citizens at U.S. domestic courts clearly indicate increasing popular dissatisfaction with U.S. administration policies in Central America.[438] The popular dissent had tremedous impact on the incoming administration of George Bush. The appointment of James Baker, President George Bush's former campaign manager, as the new Secretary of State reportedly made the Bush administration's foreign policy still more vulnerable to domestic criticism.[439] The popular dissent combined with the appointment of James Baker as Secretary of State made the Bush administration to openly recognized that President Reagan's policy in Nicaragua was a failure.[440] It then took just a few months to signal a new policy towards Nicaragua as well as the peace process in Central America.

As part of that new policy, the CIA started auditing the Contras' spending of secret aid.[441] The President showed great tolerance more than indifference to the Costa del Sol accords.[442] Secretary of State Baker announced a few days later the United States' plans to lift the embargo against Nicaragua and "ease other curbs in return for democracy."[443] In March 1989, the White House also announced a cut on stipends to the Contras' civilian leaders by more than half and the elimination of payments for all the Contras' political operations.[444] Likewise, the administration publicly indicated that it had not ruled out direct talks with the Sandinistas.[445] Most importantly, a bipartisan agreement was reached on March 23 and later approved by Congress to allocate $45 million in non-military aid to the contra rebels--about $4.5 million a month through February 1990 when Nicaragua had promised to hold free elections.[446]

At the same time that President Bush and Secretary of State Baker termed Reagan's policy a failure, they also conceded that the March 1989 bipartisan proposal responded to the five Central America Presidents' Costa del Sol agreement and the Esquipulas II accords of 1987. The bipartisan agreement was followed by a favorable United States vote at the UN Security Council to support the creation of the first UN peace-keeping force in Central America and the U.S's promise to finance about one-third of the cost under customary peace-keeping rules.[447] Viewed in light of Nicaraguan President Daniel Ortega's declaration to suspend the cease-fire his government worked out with the Contras in Sapoá on March 1988,[448] U.S.

vote in favor of a UN peace-keeping force in Central America is an even more significant indicator of change.

The later developments in American policy towards the Contras and Central America in general suggested the emergence of more consensus on the part of the U.S. to abide by the principles guiding the Esquipulas negotiations. However, the United States' continued distrust of Sandinistas' alleged willingness to comply with the agreement and distaste for a Marxist-Leninist regime in Central America--or a "second Cuba"--may indicate that U.S. policy makers adapted but not yet truly learned anything new with regard to Central America. The goal of the United States in Central America remained static while the means to get rid of the Sandinistas were just adjusted to conform to the Esquipulas process. Underlying the United States' adjustment of means was the expectation that representative, plural, and free elections in Nicaragua would indeed happen and that they would be able to accomplish what the Contras have not achieved after a decade of armed struggle.

Decision Making and Bargaining Styles
Esquipulas II

Participants	Legal Knowledge	Political Goals	D.M./Bargaining	Change
Time range: 1988-early 1989				
Central American Presidents	More Consensual within coalitions as to basic negotiation norms but not yet consensual on the implementation of the accords	Interconnected but not expanding	Pragmatic Issues linked fragmentally	**Adaptation**
United States	Dissenting from all other participants shared meanings and thus not consensual	Specific/Static Less rigid attitude on means	Less skeptical than as of 1986 Some issues linked fragmentally and some tactically	**Adaptation**
Time range: early 1989-Dec. 1989				
Central American Presidents	More Consensual	Interconnected and expanding with implementation of Esquipulas II Agreement	More analytic Some issues linked substantively some fragmentally	**Learning**
United States	Not Consensual	Specific/Static Change of means	More pragmatic Issues linked fragmentally	**Adaptation**

Diagram 5

CHAPTER VIII

GUIDELINE FOR THE FUTURE:

REDUCING PROCEDURAL UNCERTAINTY IN CENTRAL AMERICA

A. The Lesson In Brief

I have summarized above the various attempts international organizations have made during the past decade to settle disputes in Central America. This exercise was done to address the question of what role, if any, international law and organizations have played in facilitating or obstructing conflict resolution in the region.

A substantial part of the discussion has been devoted to reveal the impact of Nicaragua's applications and ICJ orders and judgments on the way actors made decisions and behaved during the course of the negotiations. As pointed out, the ICJ was the only international organization who significantly participated in Central America during the Contadora years. ICJ's procedures were initiated by Nicaragua as soon as Contadora proved unable to clarify the main norms on which the several issues of its agenda were to be addressed. Contadora could not limit the uncertainties surrounding those norms and barred the participation of international organizations in the preparation and implementation of the Group's proposed agreements. The Contadora Group was active both at the United Nations and the OAS, but only to keep key actors exclusively negotiating within the Group's realm. Being successful in its initial stage to achieve some incremental growth,[449] Contadora's attempt to manage interdependence was either too ambitious or premature.[450]

Contadora attempted full autonomy with respect to international organizations without having previously achieved the necessary degrees of consensus by actors on basic knowledge. Contadora lost its chance to cope with uncertainty when its members attempted *de facto* exclusivity over Central America issues. The decline of Contadora's negotiations was finally assured by the Group's neglect to seek and achieve consensual normative expectations among Central American actors both in the 1985 and 1986 Contadora rounds.

The ICJ, an organ of the United Nations, disrupted the preeminence of Contadora on Central American issues. The Court's chief task was to reduce the ambiguity of the principles underlying most of the hard issues at stake. In contrast to Contadora, the Court, far from refusing the challenge, gave more precise content to the principle of nonintervention. The Court refused to accept those normative expectations advancing the inapplicability of the principle in the following cases: intervention in response to the threat or use of force, intervention as a matter of collective security defense, intervention to protect human rights, counterintervention without clear existence of an armed attack, and intervention to secure the right of peoples to self-government. From this perspective, the Court basically rejected the normative expectations on which the U.S. bloc had grounded their decision-making and bargaining styles.

A series of changes in the attitude of the actors arouse when the Court determined which expectations were to prevail in the judicial debate. By holding that no collective self-defense nor counterintervention was permissible in the absence of an armed attack, the Court pushed participants to reexamine those arguments in favor of forcible bargaining techniques. As such, participants more actively sought to achieve their traditional goals by putting the emphasis on negotiating means. This is what happened in mid-1986 when U.S. allies in the region decided to reactivate and improve the negotiation process instead of supporting the Contras, despite the fact that their goal was the same: to achieve representative and plural democracy in Nicaragua.

Consensual legal knowledge, acquired by the parties through the involvement of the World Court in the conflict, was a break through that marked the transition from the lifeless negotiations of Contadora to a new and more significant negotiating arena: the Esquipulas II process. The decisions of the Court and the continuing judicial procedures against Honduras served to constrain the parties to clarify traditional political goals and adopt less tactical and non-forcible bargaining styles. With renovated normative expectations--as authoritatively determined by the Court--, the strong leadership of the 1987 Nobel Peace Prize Winner Oscar Arias, and a fresher attitude, the five Central American Presidents undertook new and similar bargaining styles to change the configuration of alliances within the region. Along with the increasing similarity in bargaining styles among the Central American governments, the United States, who did not fully share the new knowledge, had to adapt and assume a less aggressive policy towards the region. In the final analysis, bargaining became less dissimilar even in the intercoalitional context.

However, this process of change, though providing the basis for agreement in Esquipulas II in August 1987, did not assure that the implementation of the accords would work with equal easiness. While most political goals remained specific and static during the Esquipulas II and Alajuela meetings, the Costa del Sol and Tela commitments had to expand the issues to include those concerned with implementation of the basic Esquipulas commitments. The expansion took the form of further agreements by the parties on the rules and procedures required for compliance with previous commitments. Since then, the Esquipulas II negotiations experienced some incremental growth and more important, the five Presidents started to understand how to manage their newly acquired interdependence.

B. International Organizations and the Implementation of the Esquipulas II Accords

The trend of the five Presidents towards more similar decision-making styles increased roles for international organizations in the implementation phase of the Esquipulas II accords. The August 1987 Esquipulas II commitments, for instance, stipulated that the UN and the OAS became active participants on verification and follow-up matters, especially in the areas of free elections in Nicaragua and resettlement of refugees. The Joint Declaration of Costa del Sol made express reference to a special invitation "to delegates of the Secretaries General of the United Nations and the Organization of American States" to co-operate on matters of verification and to a request for "technical assistance from specialized organizations of the United Nations." The Costa del Sol agreement includes the first specific mention of verification of security matters under the auspices of the Secretary General of the United Nations. Moreover, the Tela agreement envisioned the direct and active participation of international organizations in general. In order to facilitate the voluntary demobilization of insurrectional groups, for instance, the five Presidents agreed in Tela to create an International Commission of Support and Verification (CIAV). The Secretary Generals of the United Nations and the Organization of American States were called upon to join the Commission.

The relevance of this new role assigned to IGOs by Esquipulas II should not be assessed only by looking at the letter of the agreements. The importance of that role greatly depended on the IGOs capability to provide new consensual knowledge for the actors to improve on previous performance. Such new knowledge in turn depended on the kind of uncertainties that new political goals generated.

The five Presidents understood the flaw underlying the complexity of the Contadora Agenda and the responsibility incumbent on them to redefine Contadora's issue-areas.

Their effort helped identify the matters on which the parties still disagreed, but, more importantly, those efforts helped the Presidents to reexamine their political goals.

It was at the Costa del Sol meeting that the five Presidents confronted their dissatisfaction with previously held political goals. In the process, they decided to pool efforts to avoid the turbulence into which Esquipulas had fallen since the Alajuela meeting one year earlier. What had earlier appeared as a simple trade-off (Contras disbandment v. free elections in Nicaragua) in fact amounted to a readjustment of purposes under more consensual criteria for conflict resolution. But the Costa del Sol agreements themselves generated additional, equally important uncertainties that were related mostly with the management of the new interdependence. Issue-linkage again acquired complexity but seemed more manageable than during the Contadora years. Instead of looking for political will in support of an agenda of aggregated demands, participants now had to focus, as they did, on measures to comply with and implement the accords. The implementation process after the August 1987 Esquipulas II Accords certainly deserves to be addressed in detail.

The Alajuela meeting, the first presidential meeting after the Esquipulas accords were signed, indicated to the Presidents their need to discover more effective implementation mechanisms. On that occasion, the CIV not surprisingly found that the parties only partially complied with most of their commitments. The five governments consulted intensively to implement and monitor some of the provisions of the agreement only to find out that they were submerged into an ocean of uncertainties. It was clear, for example, that Nicaragua had to democratize; the problem, however, was to find the appropriate means to observe and verify that such elections were really honest and participative. Obviously, no free and representative elections were possible in Nicaragua unless the Contras were substantially demobilized. A demobilization of the Contras seemed extremely difficult, especially in light of the U.S.'s intention to keep the Contras as a military pressure on the Sandinistas to abdicate from government. To cope with this kind of uncertainty, someone had, as much as the ICJ had earlier, to provide new knowledge for participants to share and accept.

Right after the 1988 Alajuela meeting the peace process entered into a period of uncertainty and stagnation that lasted almost one year. However, the February 1989 Costa del Sol and, later on the same year, the Tela agreements, endowed upon the peace process a new impulse and vigor. Much of the details related to the implementation mechanisms agreed at Costa del Sol and Tela came from consultations between the Central American Presidents, their foreign ministers, and UN Secretary General Javier Pérez de Cuéllar. The five Presidents asked for some form of UN operation to verify compliance with the accords, in the following terms:

> That as a matter of urgency (the Secretary General) create, coordinate and assure the effective function of an impartial mechanism of on-site verification, control, and supervision of the provisions for a cessation of aid to insurrectional groups and irregular forces that operate in the region and the nonuse of territory to help them.[451]

The UN Secretary General took advantage of the request to explain to the five Presidents the necessary steps for establishing a UN peacekeeping force in Central America. A letter from Mr. Pérez de Cuéllar to the Central American foreign ministers of January 5, 1989 and, to a lesser degree, a report by the OAS Secretary General Joao Baena Soares contained important information that allowed the five Presidents to set forth the basic mechanisms to demobilize the Contras. These mechanisms, in turn, constituted the basis for a precise agreement to mandate the first UN peacekeeping operation in the Western Hemisphere.[452]

Though the Central American governments had not specifically asked for a peacekeeping operation, Mr. Pérez de Cuéllar suggested and explained to the five Presidents, in peculiarly professorial style, "what the United Nations calls peacekeeping operations," including a detailed account of the principles and practice as well as an overview of the activities that the United Nations could undertake, once approved. In his letter, Pérez de Cuéllar also requested that the Presidents state in "greater precision" what were their actual needs. He informed the Presidents about his conversations with the governments of Canada, Spain, and the Federal Republic of Germany on the nature and extent of the collaboration they had offered. He also pointed out the additional complexity and delicacy of "trying to put together or reconcile proposals [those of Canada, Spain, and Germany] that were inherently distinct and somewhat contradictory among themselves."

The Secretary General requested further precision on the kind of role to be played by the Executive Commission, that is the verification mechanism the Central American ministers of foreign affairs envisaged, as well as by the Secretary General of the OAS. As to the OAS, Pérez de Cuéllar emphatically warned that the OAS Secretary General and staff must not "interfere in the line of authority exercised by the Security Council." To the request of a number of regional governments that the operations be set out without going through the Security Council, Mr. Pérez de Cuéllar responded that such an approach was not possible. In the same professorial style, the Secretary General explained that though there was "no rigid methodology or formula to be automatically applied," all such operations since 1962 have been authorized by the Council in order to legitimize the force involved in the operations. In brief, Pérez de Cuéllar's letter attempted both to inform the Central American Presidents on and persuade them to take UN peacekeeping forces into account.

Beyond this, Pérez de Cuéllar's letter advised the Presidents that their political will had to be shared by all actors in the conflict, even those who were not party to the Guatemala accord of August, 1987. "In sum," he concluded,

> "given the circumstances, it appears best to limit myself for now to sending you the note on precedents which I enclose, in the hope that this, along with the observations contained in this letter, will help in finalizing the criteria and coming to a clear agreement on the mandate--or mandates--which should be given to the mechanism to be established."[453]

One month later, the five Presidents adopted the *Costa del Sol Declaration* and agreed to draw up within 90 days a joint plan to demobilize, repatriate, and resettle the Nicaraguan Resistance in Nicaragua or third countries. They also asked the Secretary General to proceed with arrangements to set up a group to verify the security provisions of Esquipulas II.[454] On March 31, the Ministers of Foreign Affairs of the five Central American countries, following the guidelines contained in Pérez de Cuéllar's letter of January 1988, requested the setting up of ONUCA, the UN peacekeeping operation to verify the security provisions of the Esquipulas Accords. Nonetheless, the Secretary General was unable to act on this request because it contained a reservation by Honduras related to its pending case with Nicaragua at the ICJ.[455]

Despite the delay in the creation of ONUCA, in April and May 1989 preliminary missions were sent to Nicaragua to verify preparations for free elections. After reviewing the reports produced by these missions, the Secretary General agreed in July 3 to monitor the process. He then signed with the Government of Nicaragua an agreement to create and implement the more comprehensive mission, thereafter known as ONUVEN.[456] The Secretary General was also successful in persuading the Security Council to adopt resolution 637/1989 which expressed support for the Guatemala Agreement and the Joint Declarations as well as for the Secretary General's good offices in support of the Central

American agreements.[457] On August 7, the Tela documents were adopted with the specific purpose of fleshing out the necessary details for the creation by the UN and the OAS Secretaries General of an *International Support and Verification Commission* (CIAV).[458] On the same day, Honduras and Nicaragua agreed to suspend their case at the World Court with the expressed understanding that Nicaragua would withdraw its application once conditions regarding prevention of the use of the Honduran territory by irregular forces had been met.[459] This latter agreement allowed the UN Secretary General to send a reconnaissance mission to the region to prepare a formal proposal to the Security Council for the establishment of ONUCA. This initiative gave form to the Central American governments' request to the UN and the OAS to conduct on-site verification of: a) the cessation of aid to irregular forces and insurrectionist movements and b) the non-use of the territory of one State for attacks on other States. The proposal of the UN Secretary General was preceded by his Report to the Security Council of October 11, 1989.[460] Both the proposal and the report described the mandate of ONUCA in full detail and persuaded the Security Council that it was both necessary and viable.

In general, Mr. Pérez de Cuéllar's initiative before the Security Council accomplished three important goals: a) it resolved remaining uncertainty about details of the mandate and the role of the United Nations; b) it resolved remaining uncertainty about the nature and scope of the verification efforts by giving preeminence to universal verification (UN) over the regional (OAS); and c) it achieved a consensual criteria on means for the implementation of the Esquipulas II accords, especially after the United States found both the report and the proposal of the Secretary General persuasive enough as to support them.

Indeed, the UN Secretary General made ONUCA's mandate more precise on purposes, rules, and procedures, and allocated authority both within ONUCA and for the operation itself. The Secretary General also detailed the organization of ONUCA, the personnel required by it to carry out its tasks, the equipment and the military elements, as well as the costs and proposals concerning the necessary budgetary appropriations for General Assembly approval.[461] The Secretary General also clearly determined the kind of co-operation the OAS was expected to provide. Mr. Pérez de Cuéllar reported in this regard:

> The five Central American Governments have expressed to me their desire that the co-operation of the Secretary General of the Organization of American States (OAS) be enlisted for the purposes of the verification mission. With a view to establishing the details of such co-operation, I would initiate contacts with the Secretary General of OAS, should the Security Council decide to establish ONUCA. The co-operation could take the form of the attachment to ONUCA headquarters, of a civilian liaison officer from the OAS Secretariat.[462]

The attachment of a civilian officer of the OAS to ONUCA simply confirmed the UN's predominance in the operation. However, since ONUCA is mainly a United Nations operation, the precision of a major role within it for the OAS would have been inopportune, particularly if examined in light of the traditional opposition between universal and regional mechanisms. Indeed, while the 1987 Protocol of Cartagena, amending the OAS Charter, diminished the jurisdictional conflict between the OAS and the UN Security Council in the settlement of regional disputes, it is doubtful that the OAS is ready to assume larger responsibilities for carrying out peacekeeping operations in the near future. That is to be the case at least while no consensus is achieved at the OAS on the main purposes and methods for conserving and maintaining peace in the Western Hemisphere. The collapse of the "collective security" formula that the US and the Latin American countries utilized until the 1970's to relieve the pervasive tension between other guiding principles --nonintervention v. union and confederation, self-determination and reliance v. dependency--has increased disagreement among coalitions and promoted empty rhetoric within the organization.[463]

The UN Secretary General also insisted in its reports to the Security Council that the political will of the Central American countries was not strong enough to comply with the provisions of Esquipulas II, but that "regional and extra-regional" governments should stop supplying aid to irregular forces, either openly or covertly. In this respect, the initiative of the Secretary General seems to have been very successful. The UN Security Council went farther than simply supporting the Central American Peace negotiations and the Secretary General's implementation efforts. On November 7, 1989, the United States was reported to have voted, after weeks of hesitation, with other Security Council members, to create the first UN peacekeeping force in the Western Hemisphere.[464]

In addition to the persuasive skills of the Secretary General, there seems to exist an additional--though complementary--explanation to the United States' support of ONUCA. Peacekeeping operations have usually played a "face-saving" role that is designed to help disputing states step out of a difficulty.[465] Alan James has explained in this regard that:

> If...one party is in the ascendant, it must be willing to stay its hand so that the other can disengage itself in a manner that can be given the appearance of not being forced upon it....The UN's role in this procedure will be to facilitate the disputants' disengagement and withdrawal by despatching a body of nonfighting troops or an observer group to the point of confrontation."[466]

The decaying US-sponsored Contras proved to be both a failed policy and an inefficient military force. The US vote favoring the creation of ONUCA clearly sets forth the administration's new approach against previous dissatisfaction and disappointment.

C. Perspective: Central America And The Future of Peacekeeping Operations

The peace process in Central America is well developed at the time of this writing and its implementation still unfolding. The three operations in Central America effectively implemented their respective mandates. CIAV invited the government of Nicaragua and the Nicaraguan resistance to meet at the United Nations on November 6 and 7, 1989. Negotiations actually took place at the OAS after the breakup of the nineteen-month cease-fire between the two contending parties in Nicaragua.[467] ONUVEN actively observed the elections in Nicaragua. ONUCA, which included about 625 military observers, was deployed incrementally.[468]

In fact, an advance party of UN troops was sent on December 3 to Central America in response to the aggravation of the internal conflict in El Salvador.[469] This deployment of 80 military and civilian observers to the region, even before the General Assembly passed the $41-million budget for the mission, indicates that the actual deployment of ONUCA was taken seriously and that the peacekeeping plans were much more than "words and paper." Pérez de Cuéllar's orchestration of ONUCA can even be seen as a step towards further institutionalization of peacekeeping within the United Nations.

All of this does not necessarily mean more consensual knowledge among the five Permanent Members of the UN Security Council and the international community in general as to the adequacy of peacekeeping for crisis management. But with peacekeeping now becoming less episodic,[470] the Central American operation would seem to involve more decision-making routines of the sort which the Secretary General has so far handled. Further institutionalization of peacekeeping mechanisms, of the kind involved in the Central American case, would surely pave the way for a greater legitimacy of UN peacekeeping practices. If so, the UN in general will also gain greater legitimacy and authority. Thus, we may say that there is an increasing trend towards the institutionalization of peacekeeping operations as a customary practice. When knowledge is consensual and attitudes similar in peacekeeping operations, the Secretary General is able to look persuasively into where, when ando how such operations are to be decided and implemented.

D. Conclusion

It took a decade for the Central American countries to shift from adaptation and stagnation to learning. The clue for this change has lain upon a simple formula: consensual knowledge is the main ingredient for any attempt to manage interdependence. Free elections and peaceful transition of power in Nicaragua in early 1990 confirms the validity of our assumptions. But the road to reconciliation in Nicaragua and the rest of the region is long and winding. In Central America, several other issues are nested with today's more salient ones. Central Americans will have to learn enough about the sources of knowledge and the kind of substantive and procedural questions that are required to tackle other equally difficult problems, such as the Guatemalan and Salvadoran conflicts, and matters related with regional refugees and economic recovery. The agenda is complex and so is the task of decisionmakers on the Isthmus, who must continue to deal with their responsibilities by first identifying the norms, rules, and procedures that will enable them to cope with remaining or further uncertainty.

PART III

THE INFLUENCE OF INTERNATIONAL LEGAL DYNAMICS ON DECISION-MAKING AND VICE VERSA: A DOUBLE APPRAISAL

CHAPTER IX

AN OBSERVATIONAL STANDPOINT: THE FACTUAL VARIABLES APPLIED

A. The Framework Summarized

I have attempted so far to describe the international conflict-resolution process from the perspective of a framework that I call International Legal Dynamics (ILD). My ultimate objective has been to lay down the basis for a methodology that may allow us to appraise the influence of international law on decision making. This same methodology, however, also enable us to observe how the decision-making process affects international law. What follows is my attempt to arrange, in probable sequence of occurrence, the "factual variables" and the "appraising indicators" that reciprocally influence between law and decision making within a conflict-resolution process. I define as "factual variables," the alternative conduct, procedures, and outcomes that may result from the parties' struggle to eradicate uncertainty and to assure that their expectations prevail in a dispute. In the Central American peace negotiations of the 1980's, the variables unfolded in the sequence outlined below (Figure 2) and, with more or less foreseeable variation, a similar sequence may be arranged for other cases as well. Whatever the arrangement of variables that the analyst utilizes, he/she must apply those variables in strict observance of the facts of the situation under examination.

As "appraising indicators," I refer to the individual elements of the mythical and operational systems--briefly discussed above--and their roles in affecting the outcome of international disputes. Appraising indicators may also be expected to unfold in a particular sequence the identification of which may help international scholars to assess the influence of international law on decision making and *vice versa*.

B. Sequence Of Factual Variables

The conceptual basis of the following variables are intended to apply to international conflict-resolution efforts in general. For explanatory purposes however, they have been ordered here specifically in accordance with the observable facts of the case study on Central America 1979-1989. In other instances, similar variables may be arranged in more or less identical sequence, depending on the particular facts of the cases. This qualification applies to the appraising indicators as well.

B.1. Actors and Target Audiences

A conflict may involve two or more parties who may act individually or within coalitions. In international settings, target audiences may also constitute active participants. International disputes also affect individuals, governmental and non-governmental organizations, and states, even though they may not be direct parties to the controversy. Even the attitudes and responses of the international community to the normative and political expectations of the parties directly involved may affect the disputing parties' motivations, political goals, and bargaining styles. To be sure, a conflict may be influenced by the geopolitical, economic, and sociological conditions surrounding the actors. Thus, the questions concerning who are the parties and who are the target audiences assume great relevance for our understanding of the development of a dispute and of the various efforts aimed at its resolution.

The Central American countries were obviously direct actors in the regional conflict-resolution efforts of the 1980's. The United States and the Contadora Group (Mexico, Venezuela, Colombia, and Panama) played significant roles as well. Other less visible participants, like Cuba and the Soviet Union, certainly influenced and supported most of Sandinistas' claims and expectations.[471] The Support Group (Peru, Brazil, Argentina, and Uruguay) joined the mediation process in the mid-1980's and gave important moral and political support to the Contadora Group. Various international organizations including many of a non-governmental character, like Amnesty International, served as means for informing target audiences. The responses of these international and other domestic audiences constituted both restraint and reference for direct and indirect actors. For analytical convenience, we can arrange these many actors as coalitions and target audiences. From 1979 to late-1986, a) Costa Rica, El Salvador, and Honduras, along with the United States occupied the front line of the U.S. bloc; b) Nicaragua and its Soviet bloc supporters were clearly situated on the opposite side; c) the Contadora Four and its Support Group acted as mediators; and d) a number of non-governmental organizations, international organizations, individuals, and states comprised the main target audiences and as such constantly monitored and responded to the ups and downs of the process.

From late 1986 through 1989--right after the judgment of the International Court of Justice on the Nicaragua case and the submission of Nicaragua's applications against Costa Rica and Honduras--, regional alliances changed. From then on, new groupings could be identified: a) the U.S. bloc lost cohesion and became somewhat isolated while the five Central American countries adopted more compatible bar-

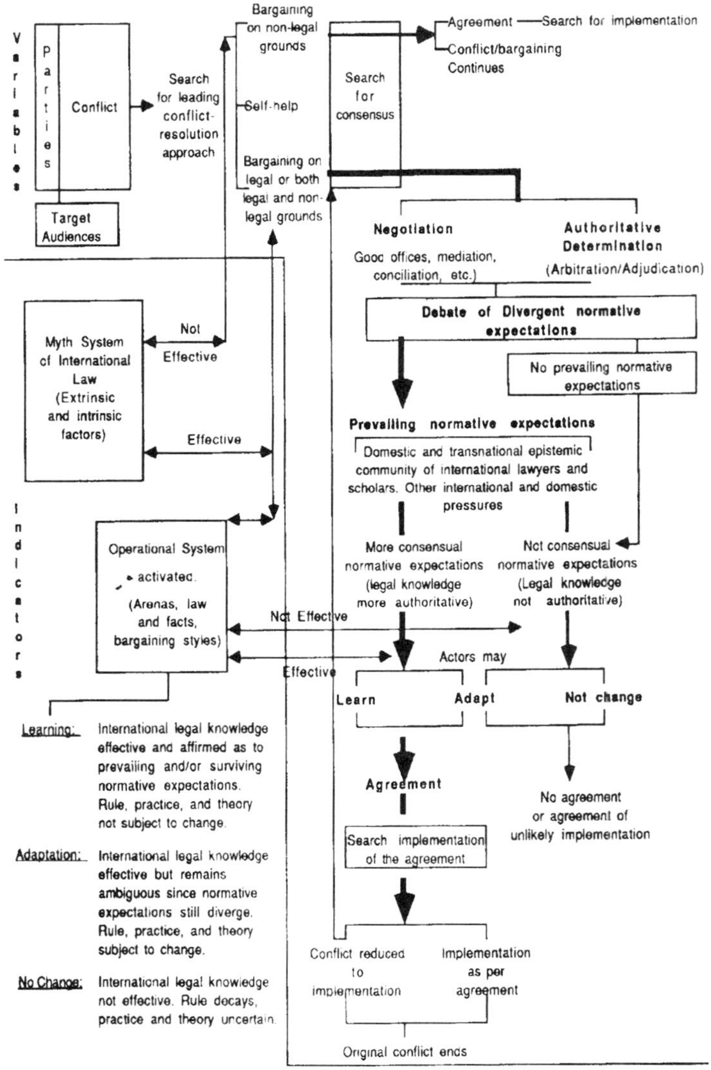

Figure 2.
International Legal Dynamics. Variables and Indicators

gaining styles around the August 1987 Esquipulas II Accords and actually united on a few common resolution criteria; b) the Contadora Group was gradually excluded from the process; and c) target audiences became more involved through the increasing role that the parties then assigned to international organizations in the implementation of the Esquipulas II Accords.

B.2. Conflict, Uncertainty And Contending Conflict Resolution Approaches

When a conflict arises it is always difficult to isolate and identify the real causes. This difficulty is an important source of uncertainty. Often equally difficult is the determination of the basic means for resolving the dispute because participants' divergent demands and expectations usually diverge enormously and even the several alternate procedures and strategies each actor contemplates rarely coincide with those of his or her opponent. The climate such differences and lack of common ground generates is often one of apprehensiveness if not actually turbulence. When actors start struggling against uncertainty, they tend to take the steps they think are more adequate to their interests and ideologies. That is to say, actors attempt to impose their own particular conflict-resolution approach. While some actors seek negotiated outcomes, others prefer to act unilaterally. Unilateral action, however, involves high risks and costs and is difficult to justify; consequently, collective bargaining is most frequently adopted approach for resolving conflicts. This approach, however, is potentially effective only when all parties realize that they need common criteria around which to link issues and build consensus.

As we know, the United States never rejected the possibility of an unilateral solution to the Central American problem. The U.S. bloc countries envisioned a more collective approach, but did not exclude forcible measures against

Nicaragua.[472] In contrast, Mexico, Venezuela, and Nicaragua advocated a negotiated alternative.

Tension over efforts to determine a conflict-resolution approach increased throughout 1982. The so-called "Central American Democratic Community" (CDC) advanced and pursued through the "Declaration of San Jose" the U.S. bloc's expectations by adopting and attempting to implement the *Declaración de San José*, a declaration that justified collective foreign involvement in Nicaragua.[473] Mexico and Venezuela, however, feared that the CDC's approach would lead to a U.S. invasion of Nicaragua, that is to say, a repetition of action like that the U.S. took against the Dominican Republic in the 1960's.[474] The tension between these two rival approaches, unilateral action on the part of the U.S. bloc and negotiated settlement on the part of Mexico, Venezuela, and Panama, was apparently resolved in January 1983 by the formation of the Contadora Group.

Contadora was indeed the result of a successful diplomatic and rhetorical move by Mexico, Venezuela, Colombia, Panama, that gained sufficient support from target audiences and set forth the basis for adopting negotiations as the leading conflict-resolution approach in Central America. As such, the Contadora negotiations could have proceeded on such non-legal grounds as we discussed below. However, they did not; as we shall discuss further in the following section, the Contadora Group framed the bargaining process within the core principles of the Inter-American legal system.

B.3. Bargaining

B.3.1. On Non-Legal Grounds:

Bargaining may be grounded exclusively on non-legal considerations. The threat or use of force is clearly one method to pressure an opponent to yield to the aggressor's bargaining demands. The threat or use of force as means of persuasion within a bargaining process, however, differs from the threat or use of force as a means for resolving a conflict. While the former unfolds as part of a larger and simultaneous conflict-resolution process, the latter seeks to end the conflict for once and for all. Thus, bargaining on non-legal grounds may not necessarily preclude the use of forcible measures to manipulate dialogue. Bargaining on non-legal grounds may also represent a search for consensus on the basis of reasonableness, common sense, values, ideologies and/or the relative power of the parties, as well as many other non-legal criteria for resolving conflict. It may possibly lead to agreement or the termination of the conflict by coercion, but it may also allow the controversy to continue. Though actors may advance some legal justifications, when a conflict is being resolved largely on non- legal grounds, none of these legal claims seem credible or viable.

B.3.2. On Legal Or Both Legal And Non-Legal Grounds:

Bargaining may also be based on legal or a mixture of legal and non-legal grounds. Bargaining on legal grounds means that actors use legal rules, language, and reasoning to formulate and transmit their expectations and demands; that actors intend to search through legal norms to find common conflict-resolution criteria; and that actors will eventually translate the major issues of debate into more or less sophisticated technical legal arguments. Though parties to international disputes have certainly been known to manipulate international law in decidedly non-legal ways, such parties often enough choose to bargain on legal grounds because international law permits less of a range of manipulative calculation than other types of bargaining. In other words, as a frame of reference, legal knowledge constrains manipulative argumentation. In legally grounded bargaining, for instance, the "requirement of justification" of demands limits relevance to legal questions and legal experts. It also strengthens the need to link the "interplay of personal, bureaucratic, and political factors" that characterizes actual decision-making process with "the idealized picture of rational choice on the basis of objectively coherent criteria."[475] Bargaining on legal grounds attracts decision makers when the myth system of international legal norms effectively enough guides and restrains the search for common-conflict resolution criteria.

From another perspective, we may say that actors choose to bargain on legal grounds when they judge that the myth system of international legal norms can effectively guide and restrain the search for common-conflict resolution criteria.

From the preceding discussion of "bargaining on legal grounds," it becomes apparent that international law and bargaining are compatible concepts and do not, as has often been claimed, exclude each other. "Legal conflicts, it is said, are 'conflicts of value', while bargaining invokes 'conflicts of interest'."[476] This claim arises from the notion that where rules are binding, no bargaining is feasible. And indeed, if a legal rule is commanding enough to decide the issues in conflict, then there is no margin for further bargaining. To assert, however, that international legal norms are always binding is too ambitious, for binding character implies some ability to compel and be enforced that international law does not entirely possess. International law does exert normative restraint, but that character of international law by no means excludes bargaining from the operation of that law.

From its inception in early 1983, the Contadora process was handled as bargaining on a combination of legal and non-legal grounds. The Group used legal principles and norms--in particular those concerning nonintervention, self-determination, and human rights--together with several other moral and rhetorical questions like the need for South-South dialogue and co-operation, the South-North debate for a just distribution of labor, and the bicentennial of the birth of Simon Bolivar--to achieve internal cohesion and bring the parties to the negotiation table. The hard issues came seven months later at the Cancún meeting of July 17, 1983. The huge agenda of political, security, social, and economic matters was presumptively grounded on the "clear compromise of absolute respect for the principles of self-determination and nonintervention."[477] There is no doubt that those principles were chosen by the parties, at least at a rhetorical level, to serve as the common conflict-resolution criteria to guide the negotiations. Actors, however, perceived these principles as deriving different normative expectations.

B.4. Ambiguity And Indeterminacy

The remainder of this study focuses exclusively on bargaining that is conducted on both legal and non-legal grounds. This is the type of bargaining that prevailed in Central America under the aegis of the Contadora Group, and our intention is to assess the effectiveness of international law in that conflict resolution process.

The Central American bargaining/searching process could have been resolved earlier had the principles at stake in fact provided definite, fixed, and unequivocal criteria of permissible and prohibited conduct. That criteria might then have served as a common conflict-resolution formula on which the parties could build consensus and agreement. However, Contadora's legal guidelines, as most legal norms, were far from constituting a self-defining body of knowledge. The general problem has been aptly described by Professor Abram Chayes:

> International law, in its normative sense, must be seen as indeterminate with respect to much of the array of concrete choices open in a particular situation. Often the rules have no authoritative formulation in words. Even when they do, the terms are open to a broad range of interpretation and emphasis. They do not dictate conduct so much as orient deliberation, order priorities, guide within broad limits. Moreover, institutional structures that are the

> product of law can be as important as rules, and more so in organizing and channelling decision.[478]

Indeed, the ambiguity of legal norms commonly and seriously obstructs efforts to reach consensus on legal grounds. Although the search for common conflict-resolution criteria based on legal norms usually involves less uncertainty than searches for resolution criteria based upon vague notions like "common sense" or "reasonableness," actors only rarely reach consensus at the initial stages of the bargaining process on the meaning and effects of a particular legal standard, and, it stands to reason, the more general the normative standard, the greater its indeterminacy. Nevertheless, international law cannot fulfill any significant role, even as an instrument for orienting deliberation, unless actors reach substantive consensus on the meaning and effects of the legal norm from which common conflict-resolution criteria might derive.

The principles of self-determination and nonintervention, as they entered into the Central American debate, illustrate this point. While the Sandinistas argued that the U.S. bloc's intervention in Nicaragua's internal affairs suppressed the Nicaraguan people's right to self-government and other fundamental human rights, the U.S. bloc argued that all such intervention was permissible.[479] The U.S. bloc regarded the Sandinistas' refusal to respect the Nicaraguan peoples' right to determine its own form of government as the real cause of the internal armed struggle in Nicaragua and the border tensions in the region. The U.S. bloc went on to argue that this refusal on the part of the Nicaraguan government amounted to a significant threat to the peace of the Americas. The U.S. bloc considered its "pro-democracy cause" justified in light of the Rio Treaty and legitimate enough to authorize unilateral U.S. economic and military pressure on the Sandinistas. The CDC countries reinforced this latter expectation with their conviction that the only reason behind the OAS reluctance to adopt collective measures of self-defense against Nicaragua was the unfortunate fact that the Contadora Group and Nicaragua constituted a majority within that regional organization.[480] The Reagan administration, encouraged by these expectations of its regional allies, emphasized national security and individual and collective self-defense as the core normative guidelines for its policy.

The interplay of nonintervention with self-determination, individual and collective self-defense, and the international protection of human rights, provoked very divergent expectations and demands in the Central American crisis. Conflicting expectations first arose out of the actors' manipulative uses of indeterminate legal norms and principles. The uncertainty that followed the Contadora process further distanced actors' normative expectations and decision-making styles. If the OAS had at any previous time taken measures to prevent actors from deriving dissimilar expectations from the principle of nonintervention,[481] the factual and normative intricacies of this case-study would serve to illustrate that such diplomatic and intellectual efforts did not event try to eradicate normative ambiguity.

B.5. Normative Expectations

B.5.1. Similar:

When parties conduct bargaining on legal grounds with similar normative expectations, their probabilities of agreement increase.[482] When the parties' political goals are influenced by increasing normative consensus (general acceptance of a common conflict-resolution criteria), these goals are likely to expand and interconnect throughout the bargaining process.[483] According to Ernst Haas, the decision-making styles of parties that share a similar or who have built an increasingly consensual knowledge base and interconnected political goals, tend to be more "analytic," and such parties tend to link relevant issues "more substantively" together. The decision-making styles of parties whose political goals remain specific and/or static, however, are generally more pragmatic, and insofar as such parties do link issues together, those links are generally fragmented. Haas's typology and terminology provides us the means for understanding the way knowledge interacts with interest.[484] Indeed, technical legal knowledge, when more consensual, both orients deliberation and exerts restraining influence on the actors' goals and decision-making styles. This type of normative expectations is further analyzed below in Section B.7.

B.5.2. Divergent

It may also happen that through bargaining, the parties are unable to reconcile rival normative expectations so that, as a result, normative divergence prevails. They advance legal arguments based on the same legal rules but do not reach the consensus necessary for substantive decision making. When normative expectations remain divergent, uncertainty prevails and may thwart the entire bargaining process, unless participants initiate a different effort to search for consensus.

Divergent expectations may lead the negotiations to stall and the parties to shift the bargaining criteria from legal to non-legal. But if negotiations stall only after the parties have decided to bargain on legal grounds, these same parties can still operate other international legal procedures to cope with divergence. The legal mechanisms for coping with normative uncertainty include further negotiation under extant legally specified procedures or calling on a third party to authoritatively settle their legal technical discrepancies. The former alternative includes methods like good offices, mediation, and conciliation under particular conventions, treaties and organizational frameworks. The latter comprises international arbitration and adjudication. These post-deadlock conflict-resolution mechanisms make the normative approach unparalleled and longer-reaching than other kinds of bargaining. Where non-legal bargaining would end in stalemate--since participants share no substantial criteria on which to resolve the conflict--, bargaining on legal grounds offers participants additional ways out.

As pointed out in the previous section, the legal expectations of the coalitions of actors in the Central American crisis were not consensual. The Contadora process failed to provide a common basis of understanding and consensus for the competing parties in part because the Group was unable to identify diverging normative expectations. Instead, issues and demands were tactically and artificially accumulated into a complex agenda of political, security, economic, and social matters that could not produce a clear and unequivocal basis for conflict resolution. The parties remained attached to their originally divergent normative expectations, and their decision-making styles became increasingly dissimilar. Thus, rival positions hardened and the controversy deepened. In this sense, Contadora's several stalemates were just early expressions of its final and inevitable deadlock.

In the midst of Contadora's uncertainty and in view of an imminent increase of U.S. military pressure, the Sandinistas sought international adjudication. They viewed the International Court of Justice as the best alternative to failing negotiations.[485] Though the Sandinistas contended that judicial proceedings would isolate their bilateral dispute with the United States from specifically Central American matters,[486] it later became apparent that this contention was an excuse to conceal the fact that the Sandinistas were using the Court to pressure the U.S. bloc to negotiate more in accordance with Nicaragua's normative expectations.[487] Nicaragua's move proved most effective for its purposes. Not only did the Court clarify and authoritatively determine the normative expectations that were to prevail and survive in Central America, but the Court's decision and proceedings also compelled the parties to revitalize negotiations on more similar normative grounds. This outcome was the product of an intensive exchange of claims through a meaningful debate of normative expectations.

B.6. Debate of Normative Expectations

When parties that hold divergent normative expectations continue to bargain on legal grounds, they run the risk of extending their differences into every issue in the dispute. Lacking common legal grounds on which to solve their problems, participants often manipulate legal argument according to their specific purposes. By such means, legal issues gain focus, but the results are usually disappointing. As parties--and third parties--in such cases disregard the relation between a common legal criteria and meaningful debate, they generate more and more confusion. The law at some point may be declared ineffective and the matter deemed resolvable only through diplomatic give-and-take strategies or self-help. But where the parties decide to cope with normative ambiguity either through negotiated means or authoritative determination, the possibility to debate divergent normative expectations increases. What formerly was bargaining on legal grounds becomes--or may become--a technical legal debate through which certain normative expectations either prevail (are upheld) or survive (are not contended or denied). The mediator's ability to persuade participants, the lawyerly skills of direct actors, the respectability of the judge or the arbitrator--these are some of the factors that would determine which of the rival normative expectations will survive and/or prevail.

An extensive literature has endeavored to describe in detail the legal technical issues that were submitted by the parties for decision by the International Court of Justice in the *Nicaragua case*.[488] It would thus be unnecessarily repetitious to duplicate that discussion here. Briefly, though, the major accomplishment of the Court's decision on the merits of the *Nicaragua case* was to rule against individual forcible intervention in the affairs of another state, as a means to safeguard self-government and representative democracy. By "forcible intervention" the Court included all methods of coercion affecting the state's free choice of "political, economic, social and cultural system, and the formulation of foreign policy."[489] Among the methods of coercion the Court cited the use of force, either in the direct form of military intervention, or in the indirect form of support for subversive or terrorist activities. To be sure, the Court authoritatively answered important questions regarding the interconnection between the wide interpretation of the concepts of self-determination and nonintervention. The Court considered that the United States' grounds for intervening in the affairs of a foreign state for reasons connected with domestic policies, ideology, and foreign policy, were merely "statements of international policy," and not an assertion of rules of existing international law.[490] The Court therefore, held that unilateral forcible intervention was impermissible even to protect the right of peoples to democracy or to pursue the international advancement of human rights. As to human rights, the Court emphasized that their protection should only be secured through the monitoring arrangements "as are provided for in the conventions themselves." The same tenet applied to collective self-defense.

Irrespective of the rightfulness of the Court's determinations, the fact is that when it came to resolving technical legal uncertainty, judicial proceedings proved to be far more effective than previous negotiating attempts. Even though the United States did not alleged arguments concerning "ideological intervention", the Court went on by its own initiative to examine all the legal questions that it thought were "relevant to the settlement of the dispute even if these rules have not been invoked by a party."[491] But again, for judicial authoritative determination to have any effect on decision making something more is required. As observers, who may want to know what we gain from a very clear and unequivocal decision, if the parties are not willing to comply with it or there are no feasible means to secure its enforcement. Indeed, not a significant step has been accomplished to resolve the dispute if the newly determined knowledge of the decision is not eventually shared by all or most disputants. Thus, two questions arise: How does authoritatively determined legal knowledge seep into the minds and attitudes of decision makers? And, how did the Court's decision and procedures influence the subsequent reconduction of the Central American peace negotiations?

B.7. Consensual Legal Knowledge

The idea of *consensual knowledge* is most helpful in answering the previous questions. Haas defines consensual knowledge as

> the sum both of technical information and theories about it that command sufficient agreement among interested actors and target audiences at a given time to serve as a guide to public policy."[492]

New knowledge from a Court decision becomes consensual if it passes the "test of truth" imposed on it by the usual users of such knowledge. As pointed out by Haas, "the ultimate test of truth is the collective decision by the users of knowledge as to which claim (by the contending parties) is more successful in solving a problem agreed by all as requiring solution."[493]

The concept of "epistemic communities" is also useful for understanding the effect of authoritatively determined legal knowledge on relevant actors in general and in the case of Central America 1979-1989, because this concept highlights and explains the users of *knowledge* to which Haas refers in the previous quotation. Epistemic communities are constituted by

> professionals who are united by a belief in the truth of their model and by a commitment to translate this truth into public policy, in the conviction that human welfare will be enhanced as a result.[494]

Professor Schachter has proposed that though it is dispersed throughout the world and engaged in diverse occupations, the professional community of international lawyers constitutes a kind of *invisible college* dedicated to a common intellectual enterprise.[495] This *invisible college* of international lawyers--to which the judges of the International Court of Justice belong--is certainly an epistemic community and is the most likely of such communities to apply the test of truth to particular legal or normative expectations.

In fact, the Court, which is comprised of those professionals who are appointed as judges, acts as a transnational body within the community of international lawyers. To frame its judgments, the Court generally uses the leading problem-solving techniques utilized by the larger community of international lawyers. This linguistic and technical interconnection between the Court and the larger community of lawyers enables the Court to lead and unify that larger community; it makes it very likely that the normative expectations that prevail at the Court will become consensual within the epistemic community of international lawyers. To strengthen the possibility that Court judgments will become consensual in the larger community, Court judges generally work out a high degree of consensus among themselves on most decisions they render. And, as evidence that Court decisions do become consensual, we may note that within the international legal profession, Court decisions are commonly cited as incontestable authority.[496]

The process, however, by which the legal knowledge that most international lawyers accept as truth seeps into decision making is a still more complex phenomena. One part of the process involves the authority and legitimacy that political elites, and not just international lawyers, bestow on the International Court of Justice as a transnational producer of international legal knowledge. Under certain circumstances, for instance, epistemic communities influence political actors to translate their technical "truth" into policy. Oscar Schachter has demonstrated that the invisible college of international lawyers extends into the sphere of government to create "penetration pacifique" of ideas from the nongovernmental into the official channels; Schachter concludes that most governments facing difficult choices "are likely to be influenced by a professional opinion" as expressed by the international legal community through either their national or international associations. Theorists of international relations have supported a similar position, but they relate the success of an epistemic community to two conditions: 1) the claim to truth it advances must be more persuasive to the dominant political decision makers than some other claim, and 2) it must make a successful alliance with the dominant political coalition.[497]

Not even these two conditions, however, may suffice to assure the success of an epistemic community because actors show a series of habitual social practices that tend to offset the influence of epistemic communities and the knowledge they espouse. International actors are human beings, and as such, they are significantly motivated by habit. No epistemic community can inject its *truth* into decision making unless they are able to break through habit. As Haas explains,

> we can claim only that epistemic communities, as triggers for learning, are likely to be heeded when political decision makers find it congruent with their career interests to do so; and this is more likely to happen during a crisis, when knowledge promises better solutions to old problems.[498]

Indeed, one should not forget that actors construct their normative expectations to justify their actions. In times of crisis, especially in light of disappointment, the most pervasive legal expectations tend to be replaced only when they no longer can be justify or serve to justify particular actions. International legal epistemic communities may play a decisive role in helping actors adjust or replace losing expectations because they can help actors "reflect...on their poor performance" and on their future chances of succeeding or failing in the controversy. The adoption by international lawyers of the expectations that prevail in a judicial debate enforces on decision makers the perception that old expectations should be adjusted to conform to prevailing ones. Thus, though habit is certainly a limit to the effectiveness of an epistemic community, failure and disappointment with previous results make actors more attentive to those who claim to possess the most relevant expertise. In other words, actors may act according to their habitual practices, but they also learn or adapt when their habits make them fail. In this sense, at least when the debate is conducted on the basis of legal technicalities and in the light of previous disappointment, the epistemic community of international lawyers may have a role in translating the prevailing and surviving normative expectations into consensual or authoritative legal knowledge.[499]

No matter how important the credibility and authority of the Court and the role of epistemic communities as providers of "consensual legal knowledge," there is always the possibility that consensual knowledge will not spring out of the debate. This sort of "fragmented" knowledge may well be desirable to some decision makers, particularly to those "who tend to entertain static and specific goals."[500] But if fragmented knowledge becomes recurrent, then the legal norm will more likely decay and be replaced by a different normative standard.

Our case-study on Central America shows that the Court decision passed the test of truth of international lawyers and became consensual knowledge among all actors except the United States.[501] While it shows that the epistemic community of international lawyers was one major factor facilitating the realization of more consensual meanings, our case study does not reveal that this community was the only engine in the transformation of prevailing and surviving expectations into consensual and authoritative knowledge. A few international lawyers opposed the Court's decision alleging either procedural concerns, like lack of jurisdiction, or considerations of fact and evidence.[502] An even smaller number of lawyers who opposed the Court's decision criticized it on substantive legal grounds.[503] For the most part, however, the community of international lawyers, U.S. members included, welcomed the several clarifications of conventional and customary international law that the Court conveyed through its decision of the Nicaragua case.[504]

At a number of conferences, workshops, and universities in the United States, domestic constituencies echoed international lawyers' remarks that overall the U.S. violated international law as determined by the 1986 I.C.J. judgment.[505] Important factions in the U.S. Congress acknowledged such reaction.[506] As a result, the division between the executive and the legislative branches of the American government widened. Fear that the executive would violate U.S. domestic law arose from the certainty that the President was violating international law. Such concern materialized during the Iran-Contra scandal, where it became clear that high functionaries of the Executive branch had violated the Boland Amendment, a law designed to ban aid to the Contras.[507] That domestic constituencies and international lawyers were now supporting the decision of the Court may have dissuaded presidential legal advisors from criticizing the judgment on substantive grounds. The U.S. government, however, decided not to abide by the judgment and made its decision on jurisdictional grounds; the U.S. argued that the Court lacked authority to take cognizance of the Nicaraguan application. Indeed, at the U.N. Security Council, the United States justified its veto by blaming Nicaragua for using the Court for strategic political purposes. Thus, the United States never really accepted the Court's authoritative determination of prevailing expectations; at best, leading U.S. government officials only felt constrained to adapt to the indisputable effects of that determination on the expectations of domestic constituencies, congressmen, and the political goals and bargaining styles of the main actors in the Central American region.

Costa Rica, Honduras, and El Salvador (the Tegucigalpa Bloc of U.S. allies), unlike the U.S., may not have had strong domestic epistemic communities of international lawyers, but their politicians and domestic constituencies evinced greater concern about the lawfulness of their respective foreign policies. Honduras and Costa Rica are very interesting examples in this regard. The Nicaraguan applications against these two countries activated a double process. First, the governments of both countries hired international lawyers to lead national group of legal advisers, and both public opinion and the government became highly sensitive to the comments of these local international legal experts. Second, the decision of the Court in the Nicaragua case provided the basis for legal argument and litigation strategy. For instance, legal advisers both in Honduras and Costa Rica frequently entertained the following questions: What did the Court say about Contadora as a special mechanism within the Inter-American system in the Nicaragua case? What are the differences in jurisdiction and admissibility between the new cases Nicaragua brought against Costa Rica and Honduras and the original Nicaragua case? What norms apply in these new cases that were not referred to by the Court in the Nicaragua case?[508] All this is to demonstrate that, the various holdings of the Court, whether beneficial or not for Costa Rica or Honduras, were not officially contested by the legal advisers of these countries. Instead, the Court's findings were closely examined in order "not to make the same mistakes" as had the United States's legal team in the earlier case. Both the opinions of local and international counsels and the prevailing and surviving expectations from the Court's decision of the Nicaragua case informed, guided, and restrained the Tegucigalpa bloc's foreign policy. For Costa Rican and Honduran political leaders, losing a case in Court would have brought great embarrassment; it would have meant the end of their political futures. For this reason in particular, the Honduran government persistently and notoriously asked Nicaragua to withdraw its case from the Court's list.

The acceptance by the epistemic community of international lawyers of the Court's decision thus certainly helped to translate the Court's prevailing expectations into more consensual knowledge and public policy in Central America. The Court too played an important role in this regard. The Court is endowed with significant legitimacy and authority by governments in general. This becomes more evident and meaningful when the decisions of the Court are discussed within the "medium" of the United Nations. There, a process is activated, one that Haas calls learning by "transideological communication"[509] and defines as "organizational learning," that takes place when "shared meanings among politically and culturally diverse actors emerge often enough"[510] to become apparent as such. Certainly, a decision from the International Court of Justice is normally written in a language that provokes lawyers and decision makers in transideological and transcultural settings to share meanings. The judgments of the International Court of Justice themselves, extensive as they are, are the product of the transcultural and transideological interaction of judges coming from different regions in the world. The Court's decisions are intended to be understood and shared by the members of the world community rather than by "Westerners" or "Easterners" only. The learning that a Court's decision activates within an international organization tends to seep directly into the minds and attitudes of decision makers independently of the action of epistemic communities. Transideological communication of legal matters clearly provides for a major involvement of international lawyers in helping decision makers to translate technical details into public policy.

On the basis of my assessment in this section of the role of epistemic communities and of the Court during the Central American crisis of the 80's, we may make the following observations. First, the decisions of the Court in the Nicaragua case achieved general acceptance from the international epistemic community of international lawyers and their domestic branches both in the U.S. and the Central American countries. Second, discussion of the Court's judgments in the Nicaragua case at the United Nations and other international forums paved the way for changes in the actors' decision-making styles. Third, factors such as the Nicaraguan applications against Costa Rica and Honduras and domestic events in the United States enhanced the role of international lawyers in the decision-making process of some of the Central American countries. Finally, the Court's clarification of normative expectations and the acceptance of those expectations by the epistemic community of international lawyers carved the normative expectations of domestic branches of that epistemic community and of other important sections of local governments and constituencies. Thus, while the U.S. government adapted to the Court's prevailing expectations, the Central American Presidents shared them and applied them more substantively in the way learners do.

B.8. Adaptation, Learning, and No Change

Political interests may not need to be informed by knowledge, but "it is hard to imagine any political issue in modern international relations that is not informed to some extent by experts' claims that command some respect, mixed with a fair amount of ridicule and contempt."[511] To be sure, by the time most actors begin to debate normative expectations, they have already significantly linked legal knowledge and interest. That is to say, most, if not all, actors have by then begun to assess and define facts and interests according to their legal expectations. By then most have also started defending their own normative expectations so as to attach credibility to their arguments. Actors who argue on legal grounds are, as we have discussed above, constrained by the normative expectations that eventually prevail in or survive the debate. Due to the pressure of normative constraint and because actors generally prefer to argue on legal grounds, we may with some accuracy predict when most of the relevant actors, target audiences, and epistemic communities are likely to accept and "internalize" the expectations that prevail or survive a determination process. This combination of factors--normative restraint and preference for legal argumentation--may help us, in other words, to predict in many cases which expectations are likely to become consensual knowledge.

At the stage of the conflict-resolution process at which the debate of normative expectations gives way to consensual legal knowledge, the bargaining context begins to change in many ways. Political goals begin to interconnect and expand in line with prevailing and surviving expectations. Actors begin to link substantively or at least fragmentally issues that they could only link tactically before. They begin to redefine the problem to the extent that they actually begin to share normative expectations and a common framework of meanings. Thus, issues and concerns begin to "nest" into "problem-sets" and, hence, become less decomposable, a phenomenon that is particularly important in resolving "complex crises." As a result, the "package-deal" acquires cohesion and composability so that actors can calculate more substantively and the overall sense of uncertainty diminishes.

The above does not always occur, and may not all necessarily occurs, but, as legal knowledge achieves more consensual status, actors usually do change their decision-making styles. The term *adaptation* refers to one set of these non-substantive effects,[512] that is to say, the tactical or pragmatic, or even skeptical, changes in the decision-making style of the so-called *persistent dissenters*, those actors or coalitions of actors who are not prepared to share the common knowledge that arises out of the debate of normative expectations but who instead remain stubbornly attached to their original specific-static position. The example I have used throughout the present discussion of the Central American peace process to illustrate adaptation is the case of the United States. Despite its static and specific goals, the U.S. adapted its foreign policy to Nicaragua after the five Central American Presidents signed the Esquipulas II Accords and U.S. domestic pressure became significant in the internal political arena.

The term *learning* indicates changes that are more *analytic*, than those of *adaptation*. Actors who learn actually take up and use the common conflict-resolution criterion provided by more consensual legal expectations and re-build expectations around it. Learning is rarely visible in international relations, but approximations to learning are far less uncommon. The Central American Presidents came close to *learning* when the Esquipulas II Accords were signed and its implementation was underway in the late 1980's.

In the absence of consensual knowledge, *adaptation* or else *no change* at all is the likely result and the chances of reaching agreement are very limited. Moreover, in the unlikely case that some kind of agreement is attained without consensual legal knowledge, no meaningful implementation of the agreement can realistically be expected.

B.9. The Agreement And Its Implementation

Consensual knowledge and the movement toward it certainly facilitate agreement. But is there any guarantee that an agreement reached through the formation of consensual knowledge will be implemented? The logic of the ILD framework leaves open two possibilities. First, implementation may be affected through the provisions of the agreement. Second, actors may be constrained to seek further knowledge to cope with the uncertainty surrounding implementation. As a consequence of any attempt for implementation, the original conflict either terminates or continues. If it continues, the issues concerning implementation of the agreement will of course remain subject to controversy.

After the signing of the Esquipulas II Accords, the Central American countries committed themselves to two major tasks: first, to cease all military pressure and all methods of coercion against Nicaragua and, second, to monitor and verify compliance with the rest of the promises under the agreement.

The first task--to stop military pressure against the Sandinistas--was successfully accomplished when the Reagan Administration and, later and more conclusively, the Bush Administration adapted to the changes taking place among alliances in Central America and within domestic circles of the various states. The second task--monitoring and verifying compliance and compliance itself--has not by the time of this writing yet been fully achieved. However, the Alajuela meeting of February 1988 made the five Central American Presidents realize that further knowledge and consensus were required to verify and comply with the accords.[513] That knowledge was not readily available, but conditions were most suitable for new expectations to become consensual. Enormous dissatisfaction had arisen from both the Investigation and Verification Commission (CIV), the implementation and verification commission that was created by the Esquipulas II Accords and the Executive Commission that replaced the CIV after the Alajuela meeting of January 1988, when the peace process stalemated for a full year.[514] Once again, the Court required the parties to double their efforts to cope with uncertainty. For example, the 1988 decision of the Court on the jurisdictional phase of the Nicaragua/Honduras case deemed it unnecessary for the parties expressly to enact a declaration to terminate a negotiating procedure.[515] The Court considered that a long period of inaction and stagnation, as occurred in Contadora, may constitute enough evidence of termination. Thus, the five Presidents felt pressed to call for another summit in early 1989 with the purpose of agreeing on procedures to verify and implement the Esquipulas Accords in order not to let the peace process terminate.[516] Nicaragua, on the other hand, kept on utilizing judicial proceedings for strategic negotiation purposes. During the upsurge of armed conflicts with Honduras and the U.S. troop deployments to the Honduras border in mid-1988, Nicaragua threatened to resume its case at the Court.[517] The Nicaraguan initiative prompted further interest in a 1989 Summit, despite Honduras' reservation against participating in further negotiations while judicial proceedings were still going on in the Court.[518]

The UN Secretary General Javier Pérez de Cuéllar furnished the parties information they needed to implement the most immediate objectives of Esquipulas II. His letter of January 5, 1989 proposed and explained to the five Presidents the kind of consensus and details required to send a UN peacekeeping operation to Central America. The five Presidents took advantage of the Secretary General's advice and, as we now know, invited international organizations to observe and assist in three major efforts: disbandment of the contras, elections in Nicaragua, and general cessation of hostilities. The undeniable efficiency of Mr. Pérez de Cuéllar not only endowed the five Presidents with new knowledge but also helped them to gain more consensual responses from the Bush Administration. The United States both approved the constitution of ONUCA, Spanish acronym to the United Nations Operation in Central America, and promised to finance one third of its costs. It is now for the international community and the Central American countries to find the legal expertise and knowledge to guarantee that every single one of the Esquipulas II commitments is fulfilled within the next few years.

B.10. The Outcome and The Framework

Despite the dramatic changes we have recently seen in Eastern Europe, modern international relations does not allow for much optimism. To believe that international law may bring about world peace and order is even more optimistic. This realization does not mean that we must remain wholly skeptical of the effectiveness of international law in resolving conflicts. The variables of our framework, summarized herein, are not designed to demonstrate that international law will always or definitely solve conflicts or that it is the only or even the most important element for doing so. Our variables are intended only to order complicated events for analytic purposes and to highlight the kind of role that international law has played therein. The reason I leave outcomes open is to avoid placing taxonomy in a governing position. Indeed, it is the "open search for the facts and a sensitivity to their changing effects that are the necessary conditions for understanding the development of law".[519]

CHAPTER X

APPRAISING INDICATORS: ITS SEQUENTIAL APPLICATION TO PEACE NEGOTIATIONS IN CENTRAL AMERICA DURING THE 1980'S

The indicators of effectiveness utilized in our framework are a set of independent variables that are intended to measure effectiveness of international law in conflict resolution. Thus, our interest is to ascertain the reliability of these variables in making such measurements. Extrinsic and intrinsic features of legal norms will be used to inquire into the greater or lesser effectiveness of the myth system of international law. Arenas, law-and-facts, bargaining styles, and changes in actors' attitudes are expected to inform us about the effectiveness of the operational system.

A. Myth System: Extrinsic and Intrinsic Characteristics

Actors searching for a common conflict-resolution criterion ideally review all available information that would allow them to link ideology, interests, factual constructs, and perceptions with some ideal objective and "authoritative" behavior. As we have seen, such information includes, on the one hand, non-legal standards of "appropriate" conduct and public policy and, on the other, international legal principles, norms, rules, and procedures. The myth system of international law--which we now understand as a body of normative knowledge that is neither self-defining nor self-applicable--may under certain circumstances appeal to decision makers and compel them to frame their expectations and demands in legal terms, but there is certainly no guarantee that disputing parties will choose international law as the main frame of reference from which to draw their demands and expectations. Our extrinsic and intrinsic indicators are expected to show us why actors decide or decide not to resort to international law when resolving a conflict. As discussed above, we categorize as "extrinsic" those indicators that inform us about the sociopolitical and economic conditions of decision makers that may promote them to utilize legal rules. "Intrinsic" indicators inform us about the features of the legal rules *per se* that attract or compel actors to utilize the law while building expectations and demands.

In the early stages of the Central American crisis, the United States and its allies in the Central American Democratic Community (CDC) viewed the Rio Pact as a useful device to "justify" building up severe controls and pressures upon the Sandinistas. The U.S. and the CDC expected the Sandinistas to comply with its previous promises to the Organization of American States to maintain representative and democratic institutions and free and pluralist elections. The CDC's potential invocation of the Rio Pact was premised on its projection of probable events both within Nicaragua and in the region. To the CDC countries, internal instability, civil war, and a Marxist-Leninist regime in Nicaragua threatened regional stability, including increasing border tensions, armed conflicts between neighbors, and overall disruption of the peace of the Americas. Rather than the threat Nicaragua may have represented, the Contadora Group concerned itself with the principles of nonintervention, self-determination, and the prohibition against the use or threat of force in international relations. The Group later managed to impose these principles in mid-1983, when the Contadora mediation took precedence over other conflict-resolution approaches.

This summary of the division between the normative expectations and approaches of the CDC and the Contadora Group demonstrates that the Central American conflict from its very origin was pitched on legal grounds. Thus, the myth system seems to have attracted the actors' attention to provide them an important frame of reference for conflict resolution. At least on a mythical level then, we can say that international law was effective from the beginning of the decade of Central American peace negotiations. In other words, a conflict that could have been reduced to its non-legal issues and handled exclusively on non-legal terms was significantly penetrated with legal concepts and constructions, no matter how ambiguous and indeterminate they might have been.

Some "extrinsic" factors influenced the prevailing conflict-resolution approach to unfold on legal grounds. First, Latin American countries have a traditionally strong inclination to achieve unity on idealized legal concepts, and, second, these countries generally feel that resorting to legal argument may be useful to defend national interests and achieve self-reliance in the face of hegemonic influences.[520] Guided by these values, Latin leaders have traditionally invoked legal instruments and institutions, often only rhetorically by usually as a sign of their collective achievement over the "selfish" opposition of industrialized countries.[521] The best evidence of this trend can be found in the diplomatic postures of the Latin American states in several diplomatic instances since the 1960's. The Latin American active participation at the General Assembly of the United Nations, the UN Conference on Trade and Development (UNCTAD), the "Group of 77," and the Non-Aligned Movement are only a few examples of such Latin American diplomatic efforts. In all of these fora, the Latin American countries have greatly relied on the principles of sovereign equality, political and economic independence, and nonintervention. Thus, it seems clear that Latin Americans would develop and utilize legal means and norms in their relations with the industrialized powers. Latin America's active participation in drafting and developing the 1974 UN Charter of Economic Rights and Duties of States and its adoption of more regional arrangements like the

Andean Pact also express Latin leaders' strong commitment to set forth their demands in legal fashion. All of the above are extrinsic causes that explain the mythical and rhetorical use of international law in the Central American crisis.

Extrinsic indicators seem to apply in Central America more easily and responsively than intrinsic ones. This is so because it is normally very difficult to isolate empirical evidence of the impact that intrinsic features of the law have on the motivations of decision makers. *Symbolic validation*, however, emerges from the present study as an evident intrinsic feature to promote the use of legal precepts in the Central American crisis.[522]

Symbolic validation is most apparent in the example of the principle of nonintervention. As pointed out elsewhere, the principle of nonintervention was at the core of legal expectations in the region. Nevertheless, the Latin American concept of nonintervention not only lacked substantive determinacy but historically has also been very incoherently applied.[523] From this, it would seem unlikely that nointervention would guide or restrain the political impulses of actors and coalitions in Central America. Indeed, the U.S. bloc construed Article 18 of the OAS Charter--the most comprehensive ever formulation of the principle--as admitting some exceptions.[524] That is to say, the "Central American Democratic Community" (CDC), mainly comprised of U.S. allies, interpreted Article 18 as permitting some methods of coercion and even forcible intervention against the Sandinistas in Nicaragua. The CDC considered the principle, as embodied in Article 18, to fully apply to the Nicaraguan question because of the "anti-democratic" and "aggressive" stance of the Sandinista government. Contadora and Nicaragua, however, viewed nonintervention strictly by the letter of Article 18. Despite the contradiction between these two interpretations, the Contadora Group surprisingly managed to introduce and sustain the principle throughout the mediation process without any sign of reluctance or opposition from the CDC countries.

Indeed, neither the indeterminacy nor the incoherence of the principle created an obstacle to the salient invocation of nonintervention in Central American bargainings.

The explanation for this paradox is that through *symbolic validation*--that is, repeated rhetorical and symbolic affirmations--of the principle, at a number of conferences and fora since before the adoption of the Bogota Charter in 1848, the principle of nonintervention has achieved paramount historical and moral validation in Latin America and in the developing world in general.[525] Despite its indeterminacy and incoherent application in the region, the principle of nonintervention has been idealized in Latin America as a norm according to which several other normative provisions and doctrines are usually constructed. Among the most notable doctrines that have been formulated around the principle are the Calvo and the Drago doctrines.[526] The Latin American application of the Estrada doctrine to the U.S. invasion of Panama on December 1989 is perhaps the most recent event evincing strong symbolic validation of the principle of nonintervention, one worth examining in some detail.[527]

The Estrada doctrine is intended to eliminate the need for States to make express statements in order to recognize foreign governments, express recognition being viewed under the doctrine as a critical interference in the internal affairs of other sovereigns. It thereby limits the power of the government of one state to recognize the government of another to the right to send or withdraw diplomatic representatives or accept or refuse the other nation's diplomats. The Estrada doctrine is clearly a useful way to accommodate the vague notion of nonintervention to avoid the often embarrassing situations involved with making express recognitions. It is doubtful, however, that express recognition in fact violates the political independence and sovereign rights of other states.[528] Recognition or non-recognition has tremendous importance for a new government both internally and internationally, especially when coming into power by non-elected means, but no significant practical difference exists between express non-recognition and the withdrawal of diplomatic relations. The Estrada doctrine simply makes tacit what otherwise would be express. Still, the connection between the Estrada doctrine and nonintervention--weak as it is--has been widely accepted in Latin America as a pillar in modern Latin American diplomatic practices.

This example serves to illustrate how deeply embedded is the symbolic notion of nonintervention in the region's diplomatic rituals, even though the principle itself does not provide for certain and unequivocal normative expectations. The example also illustrates that the habitual and rhetorical uses of certain principles like nonintervention and self-determination in Latin America is a factor that has influenced Latin decision makers repeatedly to apply those principles irrespectively of their indeterminacy. The introduction of major abstract legal principles in Contadora necessarily reponded to this trend.

B. Operational System

B.1. Arenas

When parties to a dispute frame their positions in legal terms, that is to say, when they incorporate the myth system into the bargaining process, these actors indicate a willingness to operationalize the law. Use of the myth system, however, does not necessarily entail use of the operational system. Actors may make "mythical" uses of the law without seriously considering the law as an important tool for solving problems. When, however, important participants persist in framing their arguments in legal terms, other actors are compelled to operationalize the law.[529] The question then is how to effectively operationalize legal norms. The factual variables mapped above indicate us that actors may enter either into more legally grounded negotiations or into third-party authoritative determination. The choice between these two methods or arenas determines the procedures that the parties will pursue in their efforts to operationalize the law.

An arena, as we understand it here, is the procedural setting within which participants exchange their conflicting expectations as they search for a common conflict-resolution criterion, the place, in short, where legal knowledge will be processed. The point at which actors identify their major arenas marks a threshold for both the actors who seek to frame arguments in legal terms and for the analyst who is trying to understand the process. Though in reality it might not prove so, actors logically select the arena that seems to be the most appropriate to promote and translate their expectations into authoritative knowledge. Thus, if actors choose the wrong arena, if they are unable within that procedural setting to translate their conflicting expectations into consensual knowledge, then the law appears to have been ineffectively operated and the operational system proves ineffective.

Arenas can be identified and classified according to the methods that are used within them to process legal knowledge. Negotiation seeks to achieve more consensual knowledge through the exchange of demands and expectations in bilateral or multilateral diplomatic contexts. Good offices, mediation, and conciliation are the most regularly used negotiating arenas. Authoritative determination involves a third-party who is endowed with the authority to resolve the tension between one or more rival normative expectations. Arbitration and judicial adjudication are both forms of authoritative determination arenas.

Since 1983, the Contadora process was clearly the first mediation arena that was chosen by all main participants in the Central American crisis. As a negotiating process, Contadora failed to achieve shared normative meanings through which issues could be linked and political goals interconnected and within which decision-making and bargaining strategies could be framed. The major evidence of the failure of Contadora is Nicaragua's decision in April 1984 to submit the main legal issues to a second arena, the International Court of Justice, for authoritative determination. The Court, unlike Contadora, was able to clarify legal meanings, determine the "appropiate" normative expectations, and establish the legal framework for the parties' future behavior. Right after the Court rendered its judgment on the merits of the Nicaragua Case and Nicaragua submitted its applications against Costa Rica and Honduras, most actors adjusted their political goals and bargaining styles in accordance with the normative expectations that prevailed in court. These changes in attitude and approach provided the "political will" needed to reach agreement in the third arena, the Esquipulas negotiations which took place from late 1986 to August 1987. The Court's determination of prevailing normative expectations led to more compatible bargaining and decision-making styles in the Esquipulas meetings. Further knowledge, as acquired by the Central American Presidents during 1988-1989, on the subsequent implementation of the Esquipulas II Accords marks the emergence of international organizations as the fourth arena in the peace process. The United Nations and, to a lesser degree, the Organization of American States served as knowledge-producers that assisted the parties in putting forward the basis for the implementation of the Esquipulas Accords. ONUCA, CIAV, and ONUVEN are part of the aftermath of the activation of this latter "supervisory" and mediating arena. The ultimate conclusion is yet to be seen. Still, distinguishing between the various arenas the parties operate from one point to the next in a particular conflict helps us explain and verify the effectiveness of the legal dynamics within such complex crises as that of Central America during the past decade.

The effectiveness of a particular arena in attaining consensual legal grounds impinges on the effectiveness of others and on the ultimate effectiveness of international law in the process of conflict resolution. That a conflict is peacefully and successfully resolved does not necessarily mean that an effective operational legal system was the decisive element. There are a number of different variables that intervene in conflict resolution, many of which are non-legal. What matters, as pointed out elsewhere in this discussion, is the extent to which legal knowledge affects decision-making and political goals as to promote changes in the motivations and bargaining styles of actors. Much of the effectiveness of the law depends on the actors' ability to operationalize procedural means. In so doing, an actors' diplomatic strategies and resources for implementation play significant roles, as do the actors' abilities to interconnect normative expectations with factual evidence.

B.2. Law And Facts

Authoritative determination, as opposed to negotiation, is normally considered to be strictly legal. Indeed, while good offices, mediation, and conciliation involve discussions of social, economic and political questions, both the arbitrator and the judiciary are mainly concerned with legal issues. And whereas in a negotiating environment bargaining strategies tend to involve complex issue-linkages and tradeoffs, in an environment of authoritative determination consistency between law and facts are of primary importance. That is to say that in a court of law, operators of international legal norms are responsible to provide the evidence that supports their legal arguments and demands, and the final outcome of the judicial debate depends highly on their interconnection of legal arguments and factual evidence. Indeed, the expectations that prevail or survive are normally those which the court considers to be well supported by law and evidence.[530]

In Central America, the non-appearance of the United States in the merits phase of the *Nicaragua Case* presented the Court with a very difficult task. It had to decide a dispute without the benefit of the legal arguments and evidence from one of the parties. The credibility of the decision might therefore have been severely damaged. However, the Court managed to render a decision that was later accepted by most international lawyers as one balanced in both law and facts.[531]

The success of the Court in rendering a widely accepted decision was due partly to its statutory duty to decide the dispute even in the absence of one of the parties[532] and to the so-called "discretionary elements in the art of judging."[533] Both components may have assuaged criticism of the substantive findings of the Court, because, first, the Court had to comply with its own statute and regulations and, second, it was expected by the international community to apply its best assessment of the case despite the "disappearance" of the U.S. They international community would have severely criticized the Court if the judgment had unpersuasively construed law and facts.[534]

Yet, the effectiveness of legal knowledge on decision making does not depend solely upon the ability of the adjudicator to produce credible judgments. The parties as the direct operators of the law also share great responsibility in this regard. They are expected to validate their normative expectations in light of the relevant facts of the conflict. As mentioned, the normative expectations that are most logically correlated to legal arguments and evidence tend to prevail in third-party authoritative-determination processes. In the Nicaragua case, normative expectations of the Sandinistas had better chances to prevail in Court, because the Sandinistas provided far more evidence and normative evaluations of the relevant facts than the United States. Measured from this perspective, the United States' failure to appear in the merits phase of the case was no achievement. The major effect of the proceedings at the Court was to narrow the bargaining process down to legal issues. By refusing to participate, the U.S. denied itself the opportunity to counter Nicaraguan law-and-facts constructions and to advance its own. The absence of the U.S. in the proceedings neither prevented its defeat in court, nor supported the U.S. bloc's normative expectations in the legal dynamics of the process.

Prevailing expectations that are strongly supported with facts and evidence are likewise most capable of passing the *test of truth* within the "transnational epistemic community of international lawyers"; they also have the potential of being translated into consensual and authoritative knowledge; and ultimately, they are the most likely to inform foreign policy. Even though, as discussed in Part II, the Court did infer and consider the arguments the United States might have advanced in its defense, the lack of a decisive participation by the United States in the Nicaragua case allowed the expectations of the Sandinistas to survive the *test of truth* of the Court and the main *legal transnational epistemic community*.[535]

B.3. Bargaining Styles

Negotiating arenas do not clearly respond to the "law-and-fact" mode of validation. This is particularly true in negotiations where issues have not been framed within legal norms and principles.[536] We are concerned here, however, only with negotiating contexts in which the actors utilize both the myth and the operational systems of international law,[537] and turn our attention to negotiations in which the major issues do in fact translate into legal questions.[538] Again, negotiations that are legally framed are those conducted on legal or both legal and non-legal grounds, that is to say, where the parties expect the law to provide them--wholly or partially--with an idealized objective standard on which to bargain. Within such normative negotiating contexts, the effectiveness of the law is best ascertained by observing the various moves the actors make to fabricate consensus out of a number of divergent normative expectations.[539] Those moves define the bargaining styles of the parties, which in turn reflect the extent to which legal knowledge has seeped into the minds and attitudes of actors.

Therefore, we may only know how influential legal knowledge has been in policy making if we trace the most prominent bargaining styles the actors use during the negotiation process.

By "bargaining styles," I refer to the ways actors link and trade off issues, make decisions, and endeavor to achieve their political goals while negotiating. Bargaining styles can be more or less compatible. They are compatible or similar when the knowledge base that informs them is consensual. Bargaining styles are less compatible or incompatible when each group of actors maintains different and competing sets of normative expectations and the negotiating knowledge base is therefore not consensual.

During the Contadora process, the bargaining styles of the actors within coalitions--say within the U.S. bloc--were more compatible, but the styles of actors across coalitions--say the U.S. bloc and the Contadora Group--were less. As pointed out before, the Contadora process did not achieve a basis of authoritative knowledge for most participants on the main principles that would guide the negotiations. While in Contadora, each coalition of actors rather tended to link issues according to its own unique set of normative expectations. By contrast, during the subsequent Esquipulas II negotiations, both intra-coalitional and inter-coalitional bargaining styles become more compatible. The Tegucigalpa bloc--Costa Rica, Honduras, and El Salvador--only started to link issues harmoniously with the Sandinistas during the Esquipulas talks, almost one year after the termination of the Contadora process. Likewise, during the Esquipulas II talks, the five Central American Presidents began to bargain more compatibly; they found points of agreement around the legal knowledge produced at the International Court of Justice as pertained both to the Nicaragua case and to the jurisdiction phase of the Honduras/Nicaragua case. In Esquipulas, the five Presidents seemed to have acted upon the more common expectations set forth by the Court that, however laudable the objective, any act of coercion against a foreign nation is unacceptable. Thus, the five Presidents conveyed a new set of shared meanings in their common pledge to end U.S. military aid to the Contras and through the Presidents' agreement to disband all revolutionary groups in the region. This change in rationale and goals directed Nicaragua and the Tegucigalpa bloc countries to agree on other equally important issues like national reconciliation and democratic elections. True, legal knowledge and constraint were not the only causes for more compatible bargaining within Esquipulas. The nine-year contra war and the economic difficulties that the Sandinistas were undergoing at the time of the Esquipulas II meeting may have "persuaded" Daniel Ortega to call for free, representative, and democratic elections in Nicaragua.[540] Likewise, the leadership of President Arias could have influenced and changed the attitude of the Tegucigalpa bloc with respect to the contras.[541] In fairness, however, we must accept that no elections would have been possible in Nicaragua without the a consensual legal base that supported the strong commitment of Costa Rica, Honduras, El Salvador, and Guatemala to join efforts to stop U.S. contra aid and disband the guerrilla forces in Honduras and El Salvador. Changes in the political goals and bargaining styles of the Tegucigalpa bloc countries with respect to the contras would have had difficult consequences had those countries remained within the same set of normative expectations that they displayed during the Contadora years. The five Presidents' acceptance of the legal knowledge produced by the Court in the Nicaragua case facilitated their decision on the undesirability of the contras. Even President Arias's approach to the contras, which likewise sought their disbandment, would not have received the same support it gained from the other Presidents, had the Court not ruled that intervention by coercion in the domestic affairs of a foreign state was impermissible.[542]

We have so far examined bargaining styles in the light of actors' knowledge and political goals, the interplay of which determines how actors and coalitions link issues and make decisions.[543] According to the Haas's model, there are *four* ways that knowledge seeps into the minds and attitudes of actors to provoke changes in their bargaining styles. First, when the *legal knowledge base* "does not" become consensual or authoritative between coalitions and the "political goals" of the parties remain *specific-static*, we should not expect any change from any of the parties (*no change*). At most, one party may *adapt* to some of the other party's expectations. The competing positions tend to harden and disrupt or stall the negotiations. The United States' bargaining style during the Contadora process illustrates this outcome. As we have seen, legal knowledge was not consensual in the overall Contadora context, and the U.S. maintained the specific and static goal of getting rid of the Sandinistas. The U.S. attitude did not change throughout the Contadora years and the negotiations failed. Second, when the contending coalitions *do not reach a consensual base of legal knowledge* but their political goals are *interconnected* or flexible but *not specific or static*, we may expect one actor or coalition to *adapt* to some of the opponent's expectations. The Contadora group's accumulation of issues between the years 1983 and 1986 exemplarized this second alternative. All in an effort to keep actors at the negotiation table, the group frequently adjusted or adapted its goals and objectives to the diverging demands and expectations of the parties without providing an authoritative normative base. Third, when the legal knowledge base becomes *consensual* but political goals remain *specific or static*, it is more likely that actors will *adapt* to the majority expectations. The bargaining attitude of the U.S. during the Esquipulas negotiations falls within this third category. Though the United States' goal continued to be the same specific and static objective of overthrowing the Sandinista regime, the increase of consensual knowledge among the Central American countries and target audiences forced the Reagan and the Bush administrations to adapt to the Peace Plan of the Esquipulas II agreement.

Finally, when legal knowledge is *more consensual* and political goals are *flexible or interconnected*, actors tend to *learn* by *internalizing* the knowledge and reflecting it through a common set of political goals and analytic modes. For the Central American countries, the Esquipulas meetings resembled this fourth mode of bargaining. Legal knowledge became more consensual to the five Central American Presidents, as provided by the Court, and political goals were completely reformulated in accordance with the shared normative expectations of the parties.

When examined in light of the mroe evident goals of the actors, the causal relationship between knowledge and bargaining styles enables us to monitor changes in decision-making. Thus, bargaining styles indicate whether or not knowledge is becoming increasingly consensual, enabling the parties to link issues together in more compatible or similar ways. Bargaining styles also indicate the levels of authoritativeness and the impact and change that consensual knowledge has produced on the participants. As I just mentioned, because of the influence of consensual knowledge on the bargaining process, actors may adapt, learn, or simply not change at all. Ernst Haas establishes the connection between bargaining styles and changes in decision-making as follows:

> Adapting and declining organizations both tend to be subjected to situations in which all bargaining, among all possible groups of opponents, pits different ways of linking issues and different decision-making styles against one another; dissimilarity prevails across the board. This is not the case under learning. Intragovernmental encounters feature dissimilarity, intracoalitional negotiations are similar, and intercoalitional bargaining is based on almost similar modes and principles.[544]

Our case study shows that the normative expectations that prevailed at the Court actually seeped into the bargaining styles of those actors who had persistently refused to accept them within the Contadora process. The Central American countries belonging to the U.S. bloc accepted the expectations prevailing in Court as valid legal knowledge and, thus, adjusted their bargaining styles more in consonance with Nicaragua. The political goals of the Tegucigalpa Bloc became more receptive to the idea that other governments could affect Nicaragua's domestic affairs only through the consent and full acceptance of the Sandinistas. The previous U.S. bloc's more specific goal of throwing the Sandinista regime from power was gradually replaced by other goals, such as the disbandment of guerrilla groups, national reconciliation, democratic elections, and repatriation and relocation of refugees. Thus, the ICJ-produced knowledge became consensual among the five Presidents, which is to say that these Presidents either learned or nearly learned such knowledge by internalizing and reflecting it in their bargaining styles. The U.S., on the other hand, did not fully share the prevailing expectations from the Court and maintained the same specific and static goal of getting rid of the leftist government in Nicaragua. Therefore, the United States continued to link issues tactically and merely adapted its bargaining to the emerging circumstances. Consequently, the U.S. Department of State justified continued military support of the contras to pressure the Sandinistas into complying with its promises in Esquipulas II.[545] Though the Presidents of the United States did not share in the consensus held by the five Central American Presidents, the multiple effects originating from the consolidation of the Court's decision among the Central American allies and within the U.S. domestic sphere of government and constituencies forced the U.S. towards adaptation.

B.4. Change of Attitude Among the Actors

Changes in decision-making styles are themselves indicators of the effectiveness of international law in influencing relevant political elites. At the same time, changing trends in decision-making styles reflect the present and future status of the law. A double appraisal is therefore available. As just discussed, changes in decision-making styles can be categorized as *adaptation, learning,* and *no change*. When knowledge remains *fragmented* because none of the parties share the same normative expectations, we may find actors either *adapting or not changing*. *Adaptation,* however, is more likely to occur when knowledge is becoming more consensual, that is when most of the participants are beginning to share the same legal expectations. In such circumstances, the dissenting actor or coalition will be constrained to adjust its policy to the preferred expectations of most participants. However, when none of the divergent expectations prevail, chances are that no change will take place. In cases when an actor is constrained to adapt by more consensual knowledge, the law proves to be effective but some degree of normative ambiguity remains. Since the adapter still dissents from the expectations that prevail, normative expectations remain divergent. *Adaptation*, therefore, indicates that the legal norm is subject to change or replacement, unless relevant actors derive similar expectations from it in the future. In cases of *no change*, the law is not effective and the legal norm tends to decay. *No change* in actors' bargaining styles indicates that the norm is too ambiguous to provoke similar expectations and authoritative knowledge and, thus, to promote either one of the parties to adjust. Should a pattern of *no change* recur with respect to a particular norm, the norm will likely be replaced by other legal standards that are able to produce more compatible expectations. *Learning* indicates that the law has produced or has been determined to produce more compatible or similar expectations and that it has effectively prompted parties to internalize and affirm it.

It is hard to imagine the ultimate impact of legal knowledge in the larger context of U.S./Latin American relations. The most recent evidence of dissenting normative expectations between the U.S. and several Latin American nations is the invasion of Panama in December 1989. The deployment of U.S. troops to Panama and the subsequent overthrow of Manuel Noriega's regime evince that the United States still believes that a "just cause" legitimizes U.S. forcible intervention in the internal affairs of a foreign state, particularly in Latin America. The Latin Americans, by contrast, condemned the invasion and regard it as a flagrant violation of the principle of nonintervention, even though the whole hemisphere disliked both Mr. Noriega and his regime.[546] Operation "just cause," as President Bush named it, is also the most recent expression of the pervasive uncertainty that still accompanies the basic principles of international law in the Western Hemisphere. As we have seen, such uncertainty has and will continue to produce divisive effects over past, present, and future U.S. and Latin American relations.

CONCLUDING REMARKS

Decision making during situations of conflict affects international law, either affirming or changing it. Likewise, international law affects decision-making by constraining actors to learn or to adapt.

With these two perspectives in mind, it is possible to attempt a comprehensive appraisal of the dynamics of international law in conflict resolution. In doing so, it is not enough to find out that the law has been affected by the global social and political process. It is equally important to know *why* has that effect occurred and whether the law itself has directly or indirectly influenced policy making. We cannot ascertain this, simply by looking at international law from the traditional perspective that maintains that it is an objective, binding, and *almost* enforceable set of rules.

The interrelation between international law and decision making is the product of complex and dynamic interconnections between normative and political expectations. Political actors may frame their political goals and bargaining styles within the normative realm of available international legal knowledge. Because of this, actors may end up changing political goals and bargaining styles by exchanging legal demands and expectations. Adaptation, learning, and no change are the concepts we have used to categorize these results. Changes in decision-making, whatsoever, would reflect the present and suggest the future effectiveness of legal principles and norms in affecting the motivations and the behavior of political actors.

In our case-study, we observed that international law and institutions impacted on the Central American peace process. Thus, in response to the problem raised in Part I and from which this discussion originally departed, we may assert that international law--when duly operated by decision makers--continues to play an important role in helping to solve situations of crisis. The more consensual the legal knowledge among actors and coalitions, the more likely that their bargaining will become compatible, that political goals will be harmonize, and that decision-making will change to represent this consensus.

During the 1980s, legal knowledge in Central America was initially fragmented. Actors derived different expectations from the interplay between the principle of nointervention and other related principles. By 1987, that same knowledge had become more consensual between the five regional Presidents. The International Court of Justice and the United Nations played substantial roles in forging consensual knowledge in the region. The epistemic community of international lawyers helped to translate prevailing and surviving normative expectations into consensual conflict-resolution criteria. The five Presidents, under the leadership of President Oscar Arias, *internalized* the new knowledge and fueled it into the Esquipulas II process. Further proceedings at the International Court of Justice and increasing involvement of international organizations in the peace process set the stage for the effective implementation of the Esquipulas II Accords.

We cannot, however, extend the same conclusion to the larger context of U.S.-Latin American relations. U.S. and Latin leaders still do not seem to derive the same normative expectations from main principles and it is not clear whether such principles will serve as common basis for resolving future conflicts in the Americas. Though the most recent political developments in the five Central American countries suggest that the meaning and scope of those principles have been clarified and affirmed, the United States' December 1989 invasion of Panama indicates quite the contrary. The unanimous reaction in Latin America condemning the U.S. military intervention in Panama and the grounds on which the Bush Administration attempted to justify such action emphasizes the fragmentated normative expectations of U.S. and Latin leaders.

A meaningful investigation of the mechanisms through which knowledge fragmentation can be overcome certainly exceeds the scope of this discussion. However, these explanatory efforts have been intended to trace the path for future scholarly and political investigation.

An examination of the impact of international law on decision-making should allow the international legal analyst to recommend adjustments to improve legal effectiveness. Such recommendations might include changing or recreating old legal norms according to the observable outcomes of a number of attempts to resolve conflicts. Likewise, new norms may be drafted to prevent normative ambiguity from bringing further unresolvable uncertainty to the conflict. To fulfill either of these objectives well, one would have to look at the historical trends of international practice with a clear framework in mind to identify the most appropriate language and content of the prospective norm. With admirable courage and distinctive knowledge, this is indeed the task that the United Nations has pursued through the codification efforts of the International Law Commission. But the creation and recreation of the law should not only and strictly look for the achievement of absolutely certain and clear-code rules. The development of international law should also look at unwritten or emerging normative criteria on which to approach the different political, economic, social, and cultural issues where new potential for conflict exists. Many areas of international law still require additional normative standards--no matter how ambiguous they might be--so that it would be possible to reduce most international conflicts to legal issues and narrow them in legal terms. International lawyers and scholars therefore need to assume the duty not only to present international actors with propositions de *lex lata*, but also with considerations that in a particular context may even look as *desiderata de lege ferenda*.[547]

At the same time that we need to develop and strengthen modern international law-making, we must also clearly remember that we need more certain, coherent, consistent and validated legal norms. Normative determinacy and legitimacy are in general, however, intimately connected with another more urgent task, the reinforcement and proliferation of expeditous and accessible procedures for debating and translating normative expectations into more consensual forms of legal knowledge. Again, this is not the appropriate place to embark upon a long discussion about the adjustments that present international institutions and procedures for conflict-resolution require. We must acknowledge, however, that significant efforts have since long been undertaken in this direction by the various governmental and non-governmental international organizations, and epistemic communities of international legal and non-legal scholars.[548] Neither is this the place to advance or advocate new institutional arrangements such as the constitution of regional international courts, regional parliaments, regional arbitration mechanisms, or both universal and regional conciliatory panels.[549] But an important qualification may certainly be advanced here. No further effort should be made to create more legal institutions for settling conflicts until we first clarify the main purpose and means that are to be assigned to it. The determination of consensual conflict-resolution criteria should be the leading purpose, rather than artificial agreements barely displaying a likelihood of being implemented. The means to achieve consensual knowledge should at least allow for a free exchange of expectations, provide the mechanisms for determining the expectations that prevail and survive, and supply the methods for translating prevailing expectations into consensual knowledge among the parties to a controversy. Thus, future conflict-resolution institutions must replace rhetoric with knowledge, tactics with substance, and improvisation with more analytical attitudes.

Further development of procedures for conflict-resolution requires more than the "political will" to institutionalize; it must also involve effective methods to identify and interpret cooperative efforts and to orient them towards more meaninful realizations.

NOTES

PART I

CHAPTER I

METHODOLOGICAL QUESTIONS

[1] *Military and Paramilitary Activities in and against Nicaragua* (Nicar. v. U. S.), hereinafter the Nicaragua case, 1986 I.C.J. 146. The International Court of Justice hereinafter the "Court" or the "ICJ."

[2] *Id.* at 147.

[3] *Id.* at 148.

[4] U.S. Dep't of St., *The Situation in Central America*, Bureau of Public Affairs, Public Information Series, November 1988, Washington, D.C., at 3.

[5] This is the bottom-line of what is called the U.S. Hegemonic Strategic Vision in Central America. See M.J. Blachman, W.M. Leogrande, and K. Sharpe, *Confronting Revolution: Security Through Diplomacy In Central America, at 329, (1986).*

[6] *Id.* at 17.

[7] *Statement on the U.S. Withdrawal from the Proceedings Initiated by Nicaragua in the International Court of Justice*, note of October 7, 1985, Department of State, Washington, D.C., reproduced in 24 I.L.M. 246 (1985).

[8] For example, Richard Falk cites "the U.S. government's blatant reliance on extensive covert operations to overthrow the Sandinista government together with its brazen repudiation of the authority of the International Court of Justice in the Nicaraguan conflict" to help explain the decline of normative restraint in international relations. R. Falk, *Revitalizing International Law, at 97 (1989).*

[9] See A.S.I.L, *U.S. Relations with Central American Nations: Legal and Political Aspects*, at 144-169 ASIL Proc. 78th Ann.

Meeting, Am. Soc'y Int'l L. (1984); J. Rowles, *Secret Wars, Self-defense and the Charter: A Reply to Professor Moore*, 82 AJIL 568; Farer, T., *Id. at 155-212*; *Sidestepping International Law*, Int'l Herald Tribune, Apr. 12, 1984, at 6, col.1. For a perspective in favor of the United States, see J.N. Moore, T*he Secret War in Central America and the Future of World Order,* 80 AJIL 43 (1986); *U.S. Can't Observe Laws Violated by Its Foes, Kirkpatrick Tells Jurists*, Int'l Herald Tribune, Apr. 14-15, 1984, at 6, col.7.

10 See Kennedy, *Theses about International Law Discourse*, 23 GYIL 353. Also Richard Falk who, by drawing from Thomas Khun's work, advocates a "paradigmatic" change in our vision and attitude toward the world's future and international law as well, see Falk, *supra* note 8.

11 These conceptual gaps may have resulted from the paucity of greater theoretical works in the field of international law. As McDonald and Johnston explain, "[p]artly because of the immensity of the field, an increasing number of international lawyers today are virtually driven to specialization...the literature of international law as a science of international law seems seriously deficient in major theoretical works." McDonald and Johnston, *International Legal Theory: New Frontiers of the Discipline*, in "The Structure and Process of International Law (1986), at 1. For an illustration of these gaps in a comparative analysis of modern theories of international law, See R. Falk, *New Approaches to the Study of International Law*, in "New Approaches to International Relations" (Kaplan, ed., 1968), at 357.

12 The labels used herein are not intended to represent rigid or even standard classifications but are helpful for illustrative purposes. Specific reference is made for neopositivism to T. Nardin, *Law, Morality And The Relations of States*, Princeton, (1983); and for policy-science or instrumentalism to M. McDougal, et al., *infra* note 28. I believe that my labeling McDougal as a "policy-scientist" should not create controversy at all, since he himself has called his framework a "policy-science oriented jurisprudence" and his opponents often categorize such method as "instrumentalist." However, to label Nardin as a "neopositivist" requires some explanation. According to my understanding of Nardin's concept of international law as a "common body of authoritative norms," as I describe further in Section B.2., Nardin views international law as

an international order that expands its horizons not necessarily only when the nation-states agree to accept certain defined limitations upon their behavior. The traditional "positivist," view, in contrast, generally holds that international law constitutes a series of rules restricting the actions of independent states and forming exceptions to state sovereignty only when the "consent" or the "will" of those states is present and clearly demonstrated for every single rule. Nardin, however, maintains that "[a]lthough entities other than states increasingly have certain rights and duties under international law, this law is still one that is created and applied by states." See T. Nardin, *Law, Morality, and the Relations of States,* (1983), at 47. Moreover, his definition of international law suggests that the positivist conception is still present in his argument. Nardin defines international law as "a body of common rules, rooted in the customary practice of the society of states, on the basis of which independent political communities pursuing diverse and often incompatible ends are related to one another, and which itself defines the terms of their coexistence...," Id., at 308. Thus, while traditional positivism understands international law as a set of objective standards of legal validation that can derive only from the will of sovereign states as manifested in their relevant conduct, Nardin draws this body of rules from the customary practice of nation-states. The Neopositivist school of international law is analyzed in A. D'Amato, *The Neo-Positivist Conception of International Law,* 59 A.J.I.L. 321 (1965). Variations of traditional positivism may be seen in L. Oppenheim, *International Law: A Treatise*, (1912); H. Kelsen, *Theorie de Droit International Public*, extrait du Recueil des Cours (1953); following Kelsen's conception, see J.L. Kunz, *The Changing Law of Nations*, (1968), at 80; other versions of positivism may be found in G. Schwarzenberger, *International Law* (1949) and J.L. Brierly, *The Law of Nations* (1967). For a comprehensive, and easy-to-understand description of modern currents of thought in today's international law, see M. Shaw, *International Law* (1986), at 39-49.

[13] On the influence that classical approaches have exerted on moderns see, A. Cassese, *International Law in a Divided World, 1986.*

[14] See our discussion *infra* Section C.1.

[15] See generally Koskenniemi, *From Apology to Utopia*,(1989).

[16] L. Henkin, *How Nations Behave*, (1979).

[17] R. Falk *The Future of the International World Order*, (1969). See also I. Detter De Lupis *The Concept of International Law*, (1987) and A. D'Amato, *International Law: Process and Prospect*, (1987).

[18] As will be seen below, my understanding of theory linkage has profited from the works of Ernst B. Haas and J. David Singer. See *infra* notes 59 and 60.

[19] For definitions of these terms see *infra* note 47.

[20] One commentator has aptly described the limitations imposed on authors by a particular "level of analysis," he indicates that "[e]ach group is trapped, as it were, in its own conceptual jail, like all prisoners, its members rarely get a glimpse at the life of those incarcerated elsewhere...[T]here are equally compelling reasons to remain confined within the boundaries of either field...Each field contains more of its own distinctive problems that can be studied in a lifetime of research, and there is plenty to do without also worrying about the problems that lie in the area of overlap between fields." Rosenau, *Linkage Politics*, (1969), at 8.

[21] I borrowed the term "external conceptual problems" from L. Laudan, *Progress and Its Problems: Towards a Theory of Scientific Growth*, at 50 (1977). According to Laudan, "[E]xternal conceptual problems are generated by a theory, T, when T is in conflict with another theory or doctrine which the proponents of T believe to be rationally well founded. It is the existence of this 'tension' which constitutes a conceptual problem," that is, when "a new theory in some scientific domain will make assumptions about the world which are incompatible with the assumptions of another scientific theory, a theory which we have good independent grounds for accepting," at 55. However, "noting of a logical inconsistency or a relation of non-reinforcement between two theories need not force scientists to abandon one or the other, or both.", at 56. My application of Laudan's insights at this lower level of abstraction, leads me to think that major criticism of international law is partly due to the great chasm between the leading theories in the discipline, both for the way they seem to contradict each other and for what each of them refuses to address. If and whenever possible, "progress" within international legal theory would be achieved when a new proposition helps to sur-

mount criticism, both by eliminating or sidestepping the incompatibilities and by fleshing out the gaps between the former leading theories.

[22] See T. Farer, *Law in a Decentralized Political System*, in **The Grand Strategy Of The United States In Latin America,** at 160-167 (1988).

[23] See M. McDougal, and W.M. Reisman, *International Law in Contemporary Perspective: The Public Order of the World Community*, (1981). See also, M. McDougal, and W.M. Reisman, *International Law in Policy-Oriented Perspective*, in **The Structure and Process of International Law,** 103 (Mcdonald & Johnston eds. 1986).

[24] *Id.* at 3.

[25] *Id.* at 91.

[26] McDougal and Reisman, *International Law in Policy-Oriented Perspective*, in **The Structure And Process of International Law,** at 105, (1986).

[27] Reisman, W.M., Nullity and Revision: *The Review and Enforcement of International Judgments and Awards*, at 4 (1971).

[28] McDougal and Reisman, *International Law in Policy-Oriented Perspective*, in **The Structure and Process of International Law,** 103 (Mcdonald & Johnston eds. 1986), at 118.

[29] *Id.* at 109.

[30] T. Farer, *supra* note 22, at 161.

[31] "Though the words 'human dignity' are asserted to be of relatively recent origin, the image of man as capable of respecting himself and others, and of participating constructively in a more abundant shaping and sharing of human dignity values, is a culmination of many converging trends in thought, both secular and religious, extending far back into antiquity and coming down through the centuries with expanding cultural and geographic reach." *Id.* at 123.

[32] Professor Oscar Schachter criticized and warned against excessive reliance on "fundamental goals" in sacrifice of determinacy. He also has pointed out that "[t]his is not to say that disciplined reliance on basic ends of the law is undesirable in applying rules and legal procedures. Such policies have a proper

place. They must be policies accepted by the international community (or the relevant group of states to which they apply). They must be applied in a way that is not destructive of a basic element of law --namely that an entity subject to the law cannot decide for itself in the last analysis whether and to what extent it is governed by a legal rule. It may of course disregard a rule and face its consequences, or it may seek to change the law for reasons of its policy. However, it cannot assert as a matter of law that its own political interest is a sufficient ground to deny the application of an accepted rule of law.". O. Schachter, Remarks, **Proc. 79th Ann. Meeting,** at 272, ASIL (1985). Schachter's criticism goes beyond the mere jurisprudential context when attacking "McDougal and others in the policy-oriented school to apply their theory in a highly selective manner to override the constraints of law in favor of the 'higher ends' sought by present U.S. policy." Id. at 273. See also, T. Farer, supra note 22, at 166: "McDougal's insistence on minimizing the guidance potential of verbal prescription facilitates myopically chauvinist decisions unresponsive to collective interests, and thus leads to obliteration of the line between legality and political expediency." Anthony D'Amato, one of the scholars who have purported to overcome McDougal's theoretical limits, has proposed to do so by asserting that, "legal prescriptions indicate to man that which he ought to refrain from doing. In this latter usage as a prohibition and not a power, legal rules communicate to the receiver the expectations of others (society other nations) who might retaliate if he disobeys the prescriptions." A. D'Amato, *The concept of Custom in International Law*, at 11 (1971).

[33] T. Farer, *supra* note 22, at 167.

[34] This is precisely what the New Haven school tries to do in M. McDougal, W.M. Reisman, and A. Willard, *The World Community*, 21 U. Cal. Davis L. Rev. 866 (1988).

[35] Some of the methods of interpretation, clarification, and recreation of legal knowledge used by the international community include procedures for peaceful settlement of disputes, resolutions and declarations of international organizations, and efforts directed to codify and develop legal institutions.

[36] For our explanation of this particular set of facts, see our discussion in Chapter VII.

37 Much has been written about the specific characteristics of legal reasoning as opposed to moral and philosophical reasoning. It has been said, for example, that "legal reasoning...is to...rhetoric what mathematics is to formal logic." Ch. Perelman, *Justice Law and Argument*, (1980) at vii. Moreover, "[i]t is the existence of an elaborated technique of the usage of presumptions and of the burden of proof which furnishes one of the characteristics of legal reasoning." *Id.* at 132-133. A recent and innovative discussion on the role of norms and legal reasoning in today's international relations may be found in F. Kratochwil, *Rule, Norms, and Decisions: On the conditions of practical and legal reasoning in international relations and domestic affairs*, (1989). For general reference on the most influential writings on this matter, see R. Alexy, *A Theory of Legal Argumentation*, (1989).

38 T. Nardin, *Law, Morality and the Relations of States*, (1983).

39 *Id.* at 5 and 14. In Nardin's own words: "[P]urposive and practical association can be distinguished both according to the authority of their rules and the kinds of end or good they make possible. Purposive association is a relationship among those who cooperate for the purpose of securing certain shared beliefs, values, and interests, who adopt certain practices as a means to that end, and who regard such practices as worthy of respect only to the extent that they are useful instruments of the common purpose. Practical association, in contrast, unites those engaged in the pursuit of different and sometimes incompatible ends through their recognition of the worth of those ways of life constituted by the authoritative practices that apply to them as moral agents or as members of a political community. The classic maxim 'Let justice be done though the heavens fall' is simply a hyperbolic way of expressing the outlook embodied in the conception of morality and law as essentially constraint-oriented (practical) rather than end-oriented (purposive)."

40 *Id.* at 18 and 219.

41 *Id.*, at 308-324.

42 *Id.*at 47.

43 *Id.* at 126.

44 *Id.* at 147. As we shall see in Chapter III, the answer to this question is an essential component for a framework that is intended

to appraise the effectiveness of international law in restraining and guiding decision making.

45 Though I have selected Nardin to represent the neopositivists, he is not, however, the only prominent scholar in present international legal theory who consider the law mainly as a body of rules and from whose writings we may obtain useful insights for our prospective linkage.

46 Overriding criticisms have been attempted by critical-structuralists and the so-called "deconstructivists." They make use of conceptual oppositions, such as rule versus process which, they argue, can neither be integrated nor prioritized one term over the other. Decontructivists regard this "problematique" as a false dilemma because the opposing positions, in the end, turn out to be the same. See M. Koskenniemi, *From Apology to Utopia*, Helsinki, 1989, at xx and xxi (1989), and D. Kennedy, *International Legal Structures*, (1987).

47 In the field of international relations the terms *levels of analysis* and *image* are both defined as "individuals, groups, states, and society or international system as separate points of focus....Such levels help scholars to be systematic in their approach to understanding international relations....In explaining a phenomenon such as war, for example, the theorist may identify possible causes as being some characteristic or characteristics of the international legal system, states and their societies, groups or individuals....In accounting for or explaining such a phenomenon, one may look both within a unit such as a state (subsystemic level or second image) as well as how the unit relates to its external environment (systemic level or third image), which are different levels of analysis." See P. Viotti and M. Kauppi, *International Relations Theory*, (1987) at 596, parentheses added. The term *variables* is used in international relations as "[a] characteristic of an object or class of objects that may take on different values....The variable may be quantitative (such as height) or qualitative (such as marital status)....In international relations research, for example, the class of objects may be states and the variable military power....Researchers wish to 'operationalize' a variable, which means finding a way to measure the variable....Military power may be operationalized, for example, by using such indicators as number of nuclear weapons, amount of the gross national product devoted

to military expenditures, or number of persons under arms....*A dependent variable* is simply what one is trying to explain, such as the frequency and intensity of war since 1800....*Independent variables* are factors that may help to explain or predict the dependent variable." *Id.* at 607.

48 Disciplinary embeddedness refers to the area of scientific knowledge upon which a theory is constructed either by drawing metaphors or patterns of behavior from that discipline to explain particular international phenomena, or by using such knowledge as the basic foundation of a major argument.

49 The concept of "linkage" has been developed and defined in the field of international relations as "any recurrent sequence of behavior that originates in one system and is reacted to in another." See J. Rosenau, ed., *Linkage Politics: Essays on the Convergence of National and International Systems*, (1969). The basic purpose of the advocates of "linkage theory" is to study the full complexity of relations between national and international systems. They seek to study the interconnections between world forces and domestic factors in the development of international events. Our concept of "bridging" differs in appearance from the original "linkage theory" in the sense that we are not trying to create a new theory that would link levels of analysis. Instead, we are linking theories that are based upon one or more images. In the final analysis, however, our bridging effort entails "linkage theory," because the resulting framework attempts to study international phenomena from the perspective of various analytical images.

50 For views and illustrations on bridging alternatives, see generally E. B. Haas, *Beyond the Nation-State*, (1968).

51 This is the case of theories T and T' that build arguments on identical levels of analysis, variables, and degrees of embeddedness just to demonstrate different aspects of the same general conclusion.

52 For example, when a theory T that explains a particular conflict by focusing on the influence of domestic factors to explain systemic forces, arrives at similar or compatible explanations as T', which happens to focus more on systemic forces. The basic approach of "linkage theory" tends to resemble these types of cases. See Rosenau, *supra*, note 49.

[53] See examples of the third alternative, in E. B. Haas, *supra* note 50.

[54] Internal conceptual problems arise when a theory is self-contradictory or shows conceptual ambiguity or circularity within itself. External conceptual problems denote logical inconsistencies between the theories. See L. Laudan, *Progress And Its Problems: Towards a Theory of Scientific Growth*, Chapter II.

[55] K. Waltz, *Man, State and War*, at 226 (1954).

[56] T. Nardin, *supra*, note 38, at 322.

[57] *Id.* at 322-323. In a recent article, Robert Putnam, Professor of Government at Harvard University, elaborates a theory on the ratification of treaties that departs from the identification of these two different levels of analysis. The reader may find in Putnam's article a comprehensive explanation of what he calls a two-level game. R. Putnam, *Diplomacy and Domestic Politics: the logic of two level games*, 42 I.O. 427 (1988).

[58] See E.B. Haas and J.D. Singer, *infra* notes 59 and 60.

[59] J.D. Singer, *The Level-of-Analysis Problem in International Relations*, in J. Rosenau, International Politics And Foreign Policy, at 29 (1969). Singer provides the following illustration of the problem: "One might, for example, postulate that when the international system is characterized by political conflict between two of its most powerful actors, there is a strong tendency for the system to bipolarize. This is a systemic-oriented proposition. A sub-systemic proposition, dealing with the same general empirical referents, would state that when a powerful actor finds itself in political conflict with another of approximate parity, it will tend to exert pressure on its weaker neighbors to join its coalition. Each proposition, assuming it is true, is theoretically useful by itself, but each is verified by a different intellectual operation. Moreover --and this is the crucial thing for theoretical development--one could not add these two kinds of statements together to achieve a cumulative growth of empirical generalizations." *Id.* at 28-29.

[60] E.B. Haas, *Beyond The Nation-State*, at 55 (1964).

[61] *Id.* at 107.

[62] *Id.* at 108.

[63] T. Nardin, *supra* note 38, at 306-307.

64 *Id.* at 308-309.

65 W. Reisman, and A. Willard, *International Incidents: The Law that Counts in World Politics*, at 4 (1988).

66 K. Waltz, *Man, the State, and War*, at 231 (1954).

67 "[I]nternational society appears to be an association of states...where international society is understood in cosmopolitan terms, of individuals linked across national boundaries by shared beliefs....But it would be a mistake to regard all international relations as defined and governed by the pursuit of shared purposes. I want to argue that there is another mode of relationship [practical] that is more fundamental because it exists among those pursuing divergent as well as shared purposes." T. Nardin, *supra* note 38, at 5.

68 *Id.* at ix.

69 W. Reisman and A. Willard, *supra* note 65, at 263-264.

70 T. Nardin, *supra* note 38, at 176-177. For Nardin, international lawyers seem to constitute an invisible college, a form of "epistemic community." An epistemic community is a network of specialists who share common styles of reasoning and similar views about cause and effect relationships in a particular area of expertise, 16.

71 *Id.* at 179.

72 For a critique of the New Haven school's concept of "human dignity," see O. Schachter, *The Legality of Pro-Democratic Intervention*, 78 AJIL 645 (1984).

73 The risk of coming and going between images rather than bridging them has been clearly shown by Martii Koskenniemi, who warns about falling in "descending and ascending patterns of justification." Koskenniemi explains that the two patterns are "both exhaustive and mutually exclusive" since the former is premised on the assumption that normative code overrides individual State behavior, will or interest, while the latter assumes that State behavior, will or interest determine of the law. He excludes any middle position because it would constantly shift between the opposing positions and ultimately ends up being either descendant or ascendant. See M., Koskenniemi, *From Apology to Utopia*, at 42 (1989). To overcome this "false dilemma," he suggests that the international lawyer should desist in pursuing "utopic" objectivism

(descending argument) while at the same time reject being too "apologetic" (ascending argument). *Id.* at 40-41. Though Koskenniemi aptly spots the two working levels of analysis and warns against shifting between them, his "ascendant-descendant" description tends to create the illusion of "opposition" or "conflict" between what in reality may be different parts of a single whole.

[74] According to Ernst Haas's seminal definition "consensual knowledge" consists of "a body of beliefs about cause-effect and end-means relationships among variables (activities, aspirations, values, demands) that is widely accepted by the relevant actors, irrespective of the absolute final "truth" of these beliefs. See R. Rothstein, *Consensual Knowledge and International Collaboration: some lessons from the commodity negotiations*, 38 I.O. 736 (1984).

[75] L. Henkin, *How Nations Behave*, at 50-56 (1979).

[76] See T. Nardin, *supra* note 38.

CHAPTER II

THEORETICAL SKETCH

[77] E.B. Haas, *Why We Still Need the United Nations*, at 1 (1986). Haas uses this argument with respect to international organizations.

[78] In connection with international organizations, Ernst B. Haas writes: "But should we blame a leopard for having spots? The superpowers are often blamed for ignoring the United Nations and for causing disputes which are ultimately dealt with by hortatory and ineffectual U.N. resolutions. Respect for the U.N. is said to be low because words, repeated *ad nauseam,* take the place of action. States of all kinds are accused of ignoring the machinery for the peaceful settlement of disputes and preferring to confront each other outside international forums. All of these charges are correct--but beside the point." *Id.*, at 1.

[79] I use the term "self-activating" to borrow Professor A. Chayes's argument that international law does not project itself into the deliberations (of decision makers) on its own motion. Professor Chayes adds, "someone must call the lawyers." A. Chayes, *The*

Cuban Missile Crisis, in **International Law: a Contemporary Perspective** (Falk, ėt al., eds. 1985] at 343.

80 "That reality is socially constructed is not meant as an empty figure of speech; rather, it emphasizes the fact that those experiences to which actors attach the stigma 'real' occur in socially allocated situations and are perceived and interpreted in terms of socially derived and validated as well as differentiated meanings." See B. Holzner, et al., *Knowledge Application: The Knowledge System in Society*, at 85, (1979).

81 R. Falk, *Revitalizing International Law*, at 97 (1989).

82 See United Nations Association of the U.S.A., *Issues Before the 42nd General Assembly of the United Nations*, at 11 (1987-88).

83 See Scheman, R., *The Inter-American Dilemma*, 1988, 184.

84 *Military And Paramilitary Activities in and Against Nicaragua* (Nicar. v. U.S.A.), 1986 I.C.J. Reports 14, at 126 and ff. Hereinafter referred to as the *Nicaragua Case*.

85 Soon after the diplomatic disappointment leading to the termination of the Contadora process in mid-1986, the Court rendered its judgment on the *Nicaragua Case,* and Nicaragua submitted its applications against Costa Rica and Honduras. Negotiations resumed after a short impasse arriving at the signing of the Esquipulas II Accords by the Presidents of the five Central American countries in August 1987. For a detailed recollection of facts and my accompanying analysis, see Part II and Part III of this study.

86 *Border and Transborder Armed Actions, (Nicar. v. Hond.) and Border and Transborder Armed Actions*, (Nicar. v. Costa Rica), reprinted in 25 I.L.M. 1290 and 1293 (1986).

87 W. Reisman & A. Willard, *International Incidents*, at 37 (1988).

88 For classic studies on the role and attributions of the U.N. Secretary General and international bureaucracies in general, see S. Schwebel, *The Secretary-General of the United Nations*, (1952); T. Weiss, *International Bureaucracies*, (1975); T. Franck, *Nation Against Nation: What Happened to the UN Dream and What the U.S. Can Do About It*, (1985); R. Jordan, *"Truly" International Bureaucracies: Real or Imagined?*, in Finkelstein, L., *Politics in the United Nations*, at 424 (1988).

[89] See R. Falk, *supra* note 8.

[90] See for example I. Detter De Lupis, *The Concept of International Law*, (1987).

[91] De Lupis' more extreme assertion is her denial of the existence of a customary international law.

[92] "Norms comprise symbols of normative conceptions about reality. A translation of these conceptions is operationalized by the user." B. Holzner et al., *Knowledge Application: The Knowledge System In Society*, at 95 (1979).

[93] The terms "operator," "international participants," "decision-makers," and even "states" are used here to refer to international legal subjects that enjoy sufficient access and standing to activate a legal process. Thus, for example, states are the only operators and participants with access and standing at the International Court of Justice, though individuals may also become operators before an international human rights court. For more detailed discussion on the various international subjects in contemporary international law, see I. De Lupis, supra note 90; McDougal and Reisman, *International Law in Contemporary Perspective*, in **The Structure And Process Of International Law,** at 107 (1986).

[94] See F. Boyle, *World Politics and International Law*, (1985); W. Coplin, *The Functions of International Law*, (1966); G. Niemayer, *Law Without Force*, (1941).

[95] The term "norm" or "rule" is used here and elsewhere in this work to refer to all pre-established, written or unwritten, recognized or less recognized normative commands. The distinction between general principles, *jus cogens*, norms, rules and procedures is irrelevant to this discussion, except where expressly indicated. All these terms are used indiscriminately to suggest the various components of international legal regulation.

[96] For a recent discussion on the role of practical and legal reasoning in international relations and domestic affairs, see F. Kratochwil, *Rule, Norms, and Decisions, (1989).* See also B. Holzner et al., *supra* note 80, at 102-3; see also in general R. Alexy, *A Theory of Legal Argumentation, (1989).*

[97] For discussions about the indeterminacy of legal arguments see generally M. Koskenniemi, *supra* note 15; Kennedy, supra note 10; H. Lauterpacht, *The Function of Law in the International*

Community, at 426 (1933). But see T. Franck, *Legitimacy in the International System,* 82 A.J.I.L. 705 (1988); and T. Nardin, *supra* note 38.

98 I relate the notions of prevailing and surviving expectations with Holzner and Marx's "authoritative" and "consensual" reality tests, seeking to assess the reality and reliability of knowledge or belief in terms of criteria of consensual validation. "Authoritative" and "consensual" validity tests are powerful constraints on knowledge and knowledge use. See Holzner and Marx, *supra* note 80, at 103-106.

99 See T. Nardin, *supra* note 38. See also O. Schachter, *Rule and Purpose in International Society,* (Book Review), 85 Columbia L. Rev. 895 (1985).

100 See M. MacDougal et. al., *supra* notes 23 and 28.

101 Reisman defines an "international incident" as "an overt conflict between two or more actors in the international system," which must be perceived as such by other key actors and resolved in some nonjudicial fashion. "Its resolution must provide some indication of what elites in a variety of effective processes consider to be acceptable behavior." In this manner, rather than examining what is written in books about law, the scholar or advisor locates the functional elites whose behavior determined the outcome and makes inferences about international law accordingly. Reisman and Willard, *supra* note 87, at 15.

102 F. Boyle, supra note 94, at 66. See also O. Schachter, *Remarks,* Proc. 79th Ann. Meeting A.S.I.L. (1985).

103 For an interesting debate on this subject, see G. Dorsey, *The McDougal-Lasswell Proposal to Build a World Public Order,* and McDougal's response, *The Dorsey Comment,* both articles in *Agora: McDougal-Lasswell Redux, 82* AJIL 41 (1988); see also O. Schachter et al., *Remarks,* Proc. 79th Annual Meeting A.S.I.L, (1985). For McDougal's and Reisman's comprehensive view on this matter, see generally M. McDougal, W. Michael Reisman, and R. Willard, *The World Community,* 21 U. Cal. Davis L. Rev. 807 (1988).

104 Technological changes bringing environmental deterioration produce massive social and economic dislocations. The way McDougal and disciples seek to appraise these "crises" is by

conveniently arranging them in terms of values. M. McDougal, W. Michael Reisman, R. Willard, *The World Community*, 21 U.Cal. Davis L. Rev. 866 (1988).

105 "The critical point is whether policy choices and decisions take into account the other participants. It is not necessary for each participant to think of all the other participants; but it is pertinent for those who make important decisions to do so." *Id*., at 851.

106 G. Tunkin, *Theory of International Law*, at 300 (1974).

107 See M. Koskenniemi, *supra* note 15, at 152.

108 *Id*., at 152. Building such criteria is one of our main concerns in this study.

109 12 J.L. Brierly, *The Basis of Obligation in International Law And Other Papers,* at 201 (1977).

110 J. Austin, *The Province of Jurisprudence Determined*, at 14 (1955).

111 A. D'Amato, *International Law*, at 1 (1987).

112 R. Fisher, *Bringing Law to Bear on Governments*, 74 Harv. L. Rev. 1130 (1961).

113 L. Henkin, *How Nations Behave*, as cited in D'Amato, supra note 114, at 2.

114 J.L. Brierly, *supra* note 109, at 202. Arguing that a necessary precaution of the state is not to defy the disapprobation of the majority.

115 These energies curbed the militarist excesses of royalty in thirteenth-century England and produced the Magna Carta. "International law, if it is to be effective in the war and peace area, will develop more in response to pressure from citizens for a lawful policy than as a shift in official stance by the leading governments of the world." R. Falk, *Revitalizing International Law*, 100 (1989).

116 Hart, *The Concept of Law*, at 80; H. Kelsen, *Pure Theory of the Law*, at 211.

117 A. D'Amato, *supra* note 111.

118 *Id*. at 14.

119 *Id*. at 24.

120 *Id*. at 119.

[121] For a discussion about the illegality of the U.S. invasion of Grenada, see F. Boyle, *supra* note 94, at 272.

[122] Hart H.L, *The Concept of Law*, cited by T. Nardin, supra note 38, at 131.

[123] T. Nardin, *supra* note 38, at 131.

CHAPTER III

THE FRAMEWORK: INDICATORS OF EFFECTIVENESS IN INTERNATIONAL LAW

[124] W.M. Reisman and A. Willard, *supra* note 87, at 12. Though I borrowed the terms "Myth" and "Operational" systems from Reisman and Willard, the way in which I use the terms in this discussion does not need to resemble Reisman's and Willard's particular treatment.

[125] B. Haas, E.B., *Why Collaborate*, 31 World Politics 357 (1980).

[126] *Id.* at 368.

[127] Expectations may prevail either because they are shared by participants through negotiation and interaction or because they are authoritatively determined by impartial third party action.

[128] For a selective review of Theories of Practical Discourse, see R. Alexy, *A Theory of Legal Argumentation,* (1989).

[129] 32 This is not only due to the system's assigning of a marginal role to lawyers in international affairs but also to the limited self-confined role of legal advisors. Reisman has rightly warned that "international lawyers make themselves irrelevant by failing to identify what international law in this context is and by failing to report it to those to whom they are responsible." W. M. Reisman et. al, *International Incidents*, at 6 (1988).

[130] E.B. Haas, *Why We Still Need The United Nations*, at 10 (1986).

[131] T. Jackson, *Quasi-state, Dual Regimes, and Neoclassical Theory: International Jurisprudence and the Third World*, 41 Int'l Org 537 (1987). See also A. Cassese, *International Law in a Divided World*, at 119 and 145 (1986).

[132] M. Bedjaoui, *A Third World View of International Organization*, cited by R. Jackson, supra note 134, at 537.

[133] Haas E.B., *supra* note 125, at 10.

[134] M. McDougal & W.M. Reisman, *International Law in Policy-Oriented Perspective*, at 112, in **the Structure and Process of International Law** (Macdonald &Johnston eds. 1986).

[135] T. Franck, *Legitimacy in the International System*, 82 AJIL 705 (1988).

[136] *Id.* at 708.

[137] "Obviously, rules with a ready ascertainable meaning have a better chance than those that do not regulate the conduct of those to whom the rule is addressed or exert a compliance pull on their policy-making process. *Id.* at 713.

[138] *Id.* at 716.

[139] *Id.* at 719.

[140] *Id.* at 721.

[141] *Id.* at 725.

[142] *Declaration on the Inadmissibility of Intervention in the Domestic Affairs of States and the Protection of their Independence and Sovereignty*, Dec. 21, 1965, U.N.G.A. Res. 2131 (XX), 20 U.N. GAOR, Supp. (No. 14) 11, U.N. Doc. A/6014 (1966), reprinted in 5 I.L.M. 374 (1966), p. 2.

[143] See R. Sadurska, *Threats of Force*, 82 AJIL 241 (1989); R. Higgins, T*he Legal Limits to the Use of Force by Sovereign States: United Nations Practice,* 37 Brit. Y.B. Int'l L. 269, 276-77 (1961); D. Bowett, *Self Defence in International Law*, at 24 (1958).

[144] "The Court has found that a State is not bound to continue particular trade relations longer than it sees fit to do so, in the absence of a treaty commitment or other specific legal obligation....The cessation of economic aid, the giving of which is more of a unilateral and voluntary nature, could be regarded as such a violation only in exceptional circumstances....As to the opposition to the grant of loans from international institutions, the Court cannot regard this as sufficiently linked with the 1956 FCN Treaty to constitute an act directed to defeating its object and purpose."

Military and Paramilitary Activities in and Against Nicaragua, (Nicar. v. U.S.), 1986 ICJ Rep. at 128.

[145] T. Franck, *supra* note 135, at 726.

[146] *Id.* at 731.

[147] *Id.* at 733.

[148] Dworkin, R., *Law's Empire*, (1986) at 176.

[149] *Id.* 179. cited by Franck, *supra* note 138, at 741.

[150] T. Franck, *supra* note 135, at 741.

[151] R. Dworkin, *supra* note 148, at 184.

[152] *Id.* at 752.

[153] In direct reference to Article 53 of the UN Charter. *Id.* at 757.

[154] *Id.* at 757.

[155] *Id.* at 759.

[156] E.B. Haas, *Why We Still Need the United Nations*, at 68-69 (1986)

[157] Article 53 of the Vienna Convention on the Law of Treaties. Done at Vienna May 22, 1969. Opened for signature, May 23, 1969. U.N. Conference on the Law of Treaties, First and Second Sessions, Mar. 26-May 24, 1968 and April 9-May 22, 1969, U.N. Doc. 39/27, at 289 (1969), reprinted in 8 I.L.M. 679 (1969). For detailed discussions on the character of peremptory norms see Sinclair, *The Vienna Convention on the Law of Treaties*, at 203-226 (1984); Elias, *The Modern Law of Treaties*, at 192-194 (1974); Sztucki, *Jus Cogens and the Vienna Convention*, (1974); Gomez Robledo, *Le ius cogens international: sa genes*, sa nature, ses fonctions, 172 Rec. des Cours 13 (1981); L.A. Alexidze, *Legal Nature of Jus Cogens in Contemporary International Law*, 172 Rec. des Cours 219 (1981); G. Gaja, *Jus Cogens beyond the Vienna Convention*, 172 Rec. des Cours 317 (1981). Among the peremptory norms of

ius cogens, commentators usually include the following: prevention and repression of genocide, piracy, slave-trade, racial discrimination, terrorism or the taking of hostages.. According to Jimenez de Arechaga: "The substantive contents of jus cogens are likely to be constantly changing in accordance with the progress and development of international law and international morality. *Jus cogens* is not an immutable natural law but an evolving concept: the last phrase in the definition envisages the modification of *jus cogens* by the same process which led to its establishment". E. Jiménez de Aréchaga, *General Course*, 159 Rec. des Cours 9, 64-67 (1978-I).

[158] Article 33 of the UN Charter reads in part: "(1) The parties to any dispute, the continuance of which is likely to endanger the maintenance of international peace and security, shall, first of all, seek a solution by negotiation, enquiry, mediation, conciliation, arbitration, judicial settlement, resort to regional agencies or arrangements, or other peaceful means of their own choice...". Article 2(4) of the same Charter states that: "All Members shall refrain in their international relations from the threat or use of force against the territorial integrity or political independence of any state, or in any other manner inconsistent with the Purposes of the United Nations.".

[159] For example, in the Inter-American System, the *Pact of Bogota* establishes a detailed regulation of each of the methods set forth in the UN Charter and Article 24 of the Charter of the Organization of American States. See *American Treaty On Pacific Settlement (Pact of Bogota*, done at Bogota, April 30, 1948; entered into force May 6, 1949; 30 U.N.T.S. 55.

[160] In a recent article, Professor Oscar Schachter demostrates that a claim to self-defense is no longer a matter left solely to the particular calculations of states; rather "states usuin force do not escape community judgments even though they seek to avoid them," and "the right of self-defense, "inherent" though it may be, cannot be autonomuous." O. Schacther, *Self Defense and the Rule of Law*, 83 AJIL 277 (1989).

[161] *Id.* at 274.

[162] *Id.* at 274-75.

[163] M. Socarras, *The Argentine Invasion of the Falklands: International Norms of Signaling*, in **International Incidents,** 116 (W.M. Reisman and A. Willard eds. 1988).

[164] The December 1990 U.S.invasion of Panama, though capable of overthrowing the Noriega regime and capturing Noriega himself for trial in the United States, had devastating effects on Latin America's acceptance of U.S. normative expectations on matters of collective security, self-determination, and nonintervention. Diverging expectations as to the scope and content of these principles, which in turn, are the supporting pillars of the Inter-American system, tend to widen the gap between U.S. and Latin America and negatively affect hemispheric understanding and cooperation; all this, at a time when the United States wishes to find ways to integrate the region and secure the cooperation of Latin neighbors in controlling drug trafficking, money laundering, massive migrations and other matters of great domestic importance.

[165] **Military and Paramilitary Activities in and against Nicaragua,** (Nicar. v. U.S.) 1986 ICJ 149.

[166] A. George, *Presidential Decision Making in Foreign Policy*, at 26-27 (1980)

[167] E. Haas, *supra* note 128, at 390.

[168] *Id.* at 390.

[169] *Id.* at 390.

[170] See D. Rubino, *La Fattispecie E Gli Effetti Giuridici Preliminari*, at 3-10, (1939); for bibliographic references on the subject see A. Torrente, Manuale di diritto privato, (1985).

[171] V. Perez, *Derecho Privado*, at 152 (1988).

[172] We cannot exclude the possibility that actors may also try to distort the facts in the same way they try to manipulate legal knowledge. However, the margin of distortion of the facts is always limited to the number and capability of the neutral sources of information available to the other parties and target audiences. Manipulation of facts is also limited by the evidentiary requirements of a particular arena. We are tempted to assert, for example, that these evidentiary requirements are less demanding in negotiating arenas than in judicial proceedings. However, the increasingly abundant and accurate international coverage of modern media have clearly improved international actors' fact-finding capabilities generally to almost override such difference.

173 *Military and Paramilitary Activities in and against Nicaragua* (Nicar. v. U.S.) 1986 I.C.J. 39

174 S. Rosenne, *The Law and Practice of the International Court of Justice*, at 580 (1965).

175 Such an authority mainly derives from Article 36(c) of the Statute, which states that the Court has jurisdiction in all legal disputes concerning: "c) the existence of any fact which, if established, would constitute a breach of an international obligation." *Statute of the International Court of Justice*, done at San Francisco on June 26, 1945, I.C.J. Acts and Documents No. 4, at 60 (1978).

176 K. Highet, *Evidence, The Court, and the Nicaragua Case*, 81 AJIL 9 (1987).

177 Highet concludes that "(a)lthough the Court has broad flexibility and wide powers in matters relating to evidence, it has not yet used them to their full potential, any more than the Court itself has been used to its full potential. It did not fully use those power in (the Nicaragua Case)," *id.* at 9.

178 Highet cites remarks such as: "get the facts or the facts will get you" or "(i)f you get all the facts you can be right; if you don't get all the facts, you can't be right". *Id.* at 9.

179 D. Bowett, *Contemporary Developments in Legal Techniques in the Settlement of Disputes*, 180 Recueil Des Cours 177 (1983).

180 *Id.* at 177.

181 *Id.* at 191.

182 One of the most utilized arguments to attack the admissibility of an application before the ICJ is that grounded on the "non exhaustion of local remedies." See the *Interhandel Case* (Switz. v. U. S.) 1959 I.C.J. 6. In this case, the Court held that "Switzerland's claim during the pendency of litigation in the United States was premature and inadmissible due to Interhandel's failure to exhaust available remedies." In the Nicaragua Case (Jurisdiction), the Court had to entertain the United States' contention that Nicaragua's application was inadmissible because of the ongoing negotiation procedures within the context of the Contadora Process.

183 On the origin and the life cycle of ideas and the question of why some ideas prevail over others, see J. Goldstein, *The Impact*

of Ideas on Trade Policy, 43 Int'l Org 1 (1989); Ch. Kindleberger, The Rise of Free Trade in Western Europe, 35 Journal of Econ. Hist. 1 (1975).

184 The term "epistemic community" is used in the sociology of science. For example, Holzner and Marx consider that the faith in the scientific method which scientists apply, is, the shared technical and intellectual approaches by a group of specialists, as formative of such a community. See B. Holzner, and J. Marx, *supra* note 80, at 107-111. See also L. Fleck, *Genesis and Development of a Scientific Fact,* (1979) who defines a "thought collective" - as a sociological group with a common style of thought. Epistemic community is a very concrete version of Thomas Kuhn's definition of "paradigm" which he defines as "an entire constellation of beliefs, values, techniques and so on shared by the members of a given community...of practitioners. T. Kuhn,*The Structure of Scientific Revolutions*, at 175 (1970).

185 J. Habermas, *Legitimation Crisis*, at 108 (1976); see also *Knowledge and Human Interest,* appendix. Jurgen Habermas has developed what he calls a "Consensus Theory of Truth." According to Habermas, the truth of what is asserted is made to depend on the soundness of the assertion because of a well-founded consensus, "if and only if it is structurally possible to call into question, modify, and replace the prevailing language of justification in which experiences are interpreted." *Legitimation Crises*, at 108. In this sense, P. Alexy understands that "judgments of value and judgments of obligation are thereby basically put on an equal footing with empirical judgments in respect of their truth-value." R. Alexy, *A Theory of Legal Argumentation*, at 108 (1989).

186 See E.B. Haas, *Why Collaborate*, 32 World Politics 358 (1980). For the most recent formulation of Haas's model, see E.B., Haas, *When Knowledge is Power*, (1989). Haas's applications, however, are mainly connected with International Organizations theory, a framework in which it has proved to be very successful. I have thus had to personalize Professor Haas' theory a great deal here. It has been my understanding that since international disputes are usually conducted in the context of *ad hoc* or institutionalized arenas--very much resembling or taking place in organizational frameworks--Haas's has much to contribute to our building of an international legal dynamics framework.

187 E.B. Haas, *Why Collaborate*, 32 World Politics, at 379-85.

PART II
FROM ADAPTATION TO LEARNING: A DECADE OF PEACE NEGOTIATIONS IN CENTRAL AMERICA

188 *Legal knowledge*, as defined above, comprises the international legal norms and procedures that are embodied in conventional and customary international law and legal theory. It also includes the convergent and divergent expectations that international participants extract from that body of legal norms and use in their explicit or implicit legal arguments.

CHAPTER IV

THE CONTADORA YEARS: 1979-1986

189 See U.N. Doc. A/40/1128 and S/18143 (1986). See also 25 I.L.M. 1304 (1986).

190 R. Leiken and B. Rubin, *The Central American Crisis Reader,* at p. 20 (1987). Characterized by its relatively static societies, authoritarian military governments, and economic dependency on the United States (U.S.), the Central American countries are also known to have the most inequitable distribution of wealth in Latin America. Despite apparent economic growth during the heyday of the Central American Common Market (1950-1970), when the annual gross domestic product of all the member countries grew at an average rate of 5 percent, Central America's poorest class received only between 3 and 4 percent of the national income, whereas the top 20 percent of the population received 60 percent. Id., at 21-36. An almost identical proportion applies to land distribution. According to the 1952 Agricultural Census in Honduras, the top 4 percent of the farms spread over 57 percent of the territory while the bottom 65 percent of the farms occupied only 15 percent of the land. See M. Posas, *Politica Estatal y Estructura Agraria en Honduras (1950-1978),* 24 Estudios Sociales Centroamericanos 38 (1979). In El Salvador, during the same

period, the wealthiest 7.5 percent of the population owns 73 percent of the land. See PACCA, *The Alternative in Brief.*, at 6 (1987).

[191] The literature on Central America and the current crisis is extensive. Among the most recent works, see C. Eguizabal, *America Latina y la Crisis Centroamericana,* (1988); R. Fagen, *Forging Peace: The Challenge of Central America,* (1987); W. Hahn, ed., *Central America and The Reagan Doctrine,* (1987); N. Hamilton, *Crisis in Central America,* (1988); L. Hufford, *The United States in Central America,* (1987); S. Landau, *The Dangerous Doctrine,* (1988); R. Leiken, *The Central American Crisis Reader,* (1987); A. Lowenthal, *Partners in Conflict,* (1987); R. Pastor, *Condemned to Repetition,* (1987); P. Shearman eds., *The Superpower, Central America and the Middle East,* (1988). Earlier studies have been summarized and compared by J.D. Cochrane, *Crisis In Central America,* 39 Int'l Org. 755 (1985). Other books and articles not listed here are cited throughout this pages.

[192] M. Blachman, *Confronting Revolution,* at 16 (1986).

[193] *Id.* at 16.

[194] Comandante Bayardo Arce in May 1984, for example, considered that the future elections were bothersome to them and that the Sandinistas intended to remove the "facade of political pluralism" and establish "the party of the revolutionary, the single party". See J. Sorzano, *Contadora: A Process for Central American Peace.*, 85(2) Dep't St. Bull. 61, (1985). See also Daniel Ortega, *Nothing Will Hold Back Our Struggle for Liberation.*, (1979); Sergio Ramirez, *Socialism Cannot Be Instituted Overnight.*, (1980); Tomas Borge, *Social Classes and Political Power,* (1982).

[195] Pyongyang, KCNA in English, 0400 GMT, June 10, 1980, Foreign Broadcast Information Service, North Korea, cited by J.N. Moore, *The Secret War In Central America,* 80 AJIL 53 (1986).

[196] See in general *id.* at 43-69.

[197] See Anmesty International, *Human Rights in Nicaragua,* (1986); B. Niestschmann, *Statement to the OAS (October 1983),* in **The Central American Crisis Reader,** at 271, 312 R. Leiken and B. Rubin, eds. 1987), and B. Nietschmann, *Central America's Forgotten Wars,* Oakland Trib. Sept 29, 1987, at A-10.

[198] Later, when Colombia joined this group in a meeting in New York, on February 1982, the group became known as the "New York Five."

[199] See Inforpress Centroamericana, *Centroamerica,* at 22 (1982).

[200] *Id.* at 20. In the meantime, U.S. military aid to Central America increased from 4.2 million dollars in 1980 to 124.5 million in 1982.

[201] This static objective characterized Mexico's foreign policy toward Central America during the past decade despite its recurrent tactical efforts to show concern for other regional social and economic problems. Though Mexico advocated approaching the Central American crisis from "its social and economic roots," the fact is that it has not pursued "an active or generous aid program toward the area. S. Purcell, *Demystifying Contadora,* in **Contadora and the Diplomacy of Peace in Central America**, 164 (B. Bagley, ed. 1987) [hereinafter Contadora and Diplomacy]. To be sure, from 1979 to 1982 Mexico's aid to Central America included loans for up to $125 million and donations as high as $54 million. A discounted price in oil shipments and financial facilities under the August 1980 "San Jose Accords" were also granted by Mexico for *a* limited period of time. Mexico's efforts to create a Multilateral Economic Fund in 1981 in Nassau did not prosper and no other activities were pursued. On other frustrated Mexico's economic initiatives, M. Ojeda, *Las Relaciones de Mexico con los Paises de America Central,* (1985).

[202] B. Bagley, Contadora, in **Contadora and Diplomacy,** at 185.

[203] Colombia, Costa Rica, Honduras, El Salvador, Belize, Jamaica, Panama, the Dominican Republic, and the United States participated in this meeting. The text of the "Final Act of the Meeting of Foreign Ministers of Countries Interested in the Promotion of Democracy in Central America and the Caribbean (**Declaration of San Jose),**" see 82 Dep't of St. Bull. 69 (1982).

[204] See Bagley, *supra* note 202, at 185.

[205] *Id.* at 185.

206 See Inforpress, *supra* note 199, at 33. In 1981, the Security Council failed to adopt a draft resolution "under which it would

have appealed to all Member States to refrain from the direct, indirect, overt or covert use of force against any country of Central America and the Caribbean". See Draft Resolution, U.N. Doc. S/14941. Nicaragua brought new claims to the U.N. Security Council on July and August, 1982.

[207] Contadora Information Bulletin, (January 9, 1983). See also Inforpress, *Centroamerica 1983,* 20-21.

[208] M. Morris and V. Millan, *Controlling Latin American Conflicts: Ten Approaches,* at 166 (1983).

[209] See Inforpress, *Centroamerica 1983,* 21.

[210] The UN and the OAS organs before which Central American problems were addressed marked a clear trend toward sidestepping most of the issues by remitting them to Contadora. On the support granted to Contadora, see among other resolutions U.N. Doc. GA/38/10 (November 11, 1983); OAS AG/RES.675 (XIII-0/83); OAS AG/RES. 702 (XIV-/84); OAS AG/RES. 831 (XVI-0/86); OAS AG/RES. 770 (XV-0/85).

[211] See Inforpress, *supra* note 209.

[212] **Norms for the Implementation of the Commitments of the Document of Objectives,** Contadora Information Bulletin (January 8, 1984).

[213] All documents herein mentioned may be found in their English version in Morris Michael and Millan Victor, *Controlling Latin American Conflicts*. Ten Approaches, at. 164-217. (1983) See also R. Leiken, *The Central American Crisis Reader,* at 638-653 (1987).

[214] B. Bagley, *Contadora and Diplomacy,* at 190.

[215] S. Purcell, *Demystifying Contadora,* 64 Foreign Affairs, at 77 (1985). The United States interpreted that: "Its provisions (of the Act) for verification and enforcement were totally inadequate, and it deferred negotiations on foreign military and security advisers and arms and troop reductions until after signature of the treaty. On the other hand, the Act required the United States, upon signature, to cease military exercises and support for the Contras. Further military aid to El Salvador and Honduras had to be frozen, while Nicaragua was allowed to maintain its military advantage over these two countries. The provisions for democratization and

internal reconciliation were hortatory and unenforceable as drafted. They would have allowed the Sandinistas to claim that the Nicaraguan elections scheduled for November 1984 were in compliance with the Act despite charges by the democratic opposition, led by Arturo Cruz, that the electoral process was rigged," *id.* at 77.

This is the place to include a brief note on U.S. policy towards the region. Reagan's policy can be fairly described as developing from moderate acceptance to rigid reluctance towards the Contadora's negotiations. By April 1983, President Reagan declared that: "(t)he United States will support any agreement among Central American countries for the withdrawal--under verifiable and reciprocal conditions--of foreign military and security advisers and troops". See 85(2) Dep't St. Bull. 59-62 (1985). On October 1984, the U.S. was indicated that the Sandinistas "simply could not be trusted to comply with any diplomatic agreement" and that "long-term U.S. security interests in Central America would be threatened as long as the current Nicaraguan leadership remained in power". See R. Greenberger, *Reagan Administration Moves to Limit Treaty Ploy by Nicaraguan Marxists,* Wall St. J., September 26, 1984, at 36. In January 1985, the U.S. decided to suspend the Manzanillo talks with the Sandinistas (initiated in 1984) and rejected the jurisdiction of the ICJ on the Nicaraguan application. The political goal of the United States in Central America became each time more specific and inflexible. The aim was clearly to prevent another Cuba in the region, rather than seeking a negotiated agreement between the countries involved. Although on August 1, 1988, Secretary of State George Schultz, accompanied by Elliot Abrams and Morris Busby, met with the Foreign Ministers of Costa Rica, El Salvador, Honduras and Guatemala, to evince full support for the negotiated process proposed by the Arias Peace Plan, he later revealed that what he actually intended was a consensus on a document condemning the Sandinista regime. **La Nacion (Costa Rica) Aug. 3, 1988; Tiempo (Honduras) August 9,** 1988. U.S. inflexible goal was pursued through financial and military aid to the "Contras" under the Reagan Doctrine that where "Marxist Leninist regimes have allegedly come to power, in places such as Afghanistan, Nicaragua, and Angola, they are considered totalitarian and therefore incapable of evolving into democratic pluralistic systems... (i)n these states, U.S. interests are best served by supporting indigenous elements, so called freedom fighters, who seek the overthrow of existing regimes.". See **Institute of International Studies,** 9 Foreign Policy News Clips 1-35 (1987).

[216] B. Bagley, *Contadora and Diplomacy,* at 192. In light of the Tegucigalpa counterdraft, it might be unfair, however, to assert that these nations were merely acting as U.S. proxies in the negotiation process. As Bagley explains, "Honduras, for example, was especially concerned with the maintenance of U.S. bases and joint military maneuvers, for it feared that without a visible U.S. military presence it would be vulnerable to Nicaragua's larger armed force. El Salvador required continued U.S. arms shipments and advisors to conduct its ongoing war with the FMLN. For its part, Costa Rica was genuinely repelled by the Sandinistas' increasing authoritarianism and greatly feared the possibility of future cross-border subversion," *id.* at 193.

[217] See R. Russel, and J. Tokatlian, *Argentina y la Crisis Centroamericana,* FLACSO, Serie de Documentos e Informes de Investigacion No. 36, at 27-29 (1986). See also B. Bagley, *Contadora and Diplomacy,* at 208.

[218] The purpose of the meeting was "to make a detailed review of the regional situation." In the Caraballeda Message, the Contadora and the Support Group outlined what they considered the lasting foundations for peace in Central America. The document included, inter alia, the conclusion of negotiations on the Act, the cessation of outside support for irregular forces and insurrectional movements operating in the region, a freeze on the acquisition of armaments and a scheduled reduction thereof, and effective steps to achieve national reconciliation and full enjoyment of human rights and individual freedoms. See the **Caraballeda Message of 12 January 1986,** U.N. Doc. A/40/1075-S/17736, Annex.

[219] Guatemala's policy shift occurred after two meetings of the five Presidents of the Central American countries in Esquipulas on January and May 1986. The meetings were called upon by President Vinicio Cerezo to discuss Guatemala's proposal for the creation of a Central American Parliament. Guatemala's policy shift, from a passive de facto neutrality to active participation, is a direct consequence of Cerezo's assumption into power a few months before the Esquipulas meeting. See Inforpress, *Cronologia Basica del Proceso de Negociacion en Centroamerica,* 18 (1988).

[220] Point 9 of the Preamble of the 1986 Contadora Act defines "reasonable balance of forces" in the following terms: "it is highly desirable to set maximum limits for military development and consequently reduce and control armaments, troops under arms and military installations, in accordance with the requirements of stability and security in the area". See U.N. Doc. A/40/1136, reproduced in 25 I.L.M. 1302 (1986).

[221] The declaration included the following items: a) that no national territory be used to attack another country and no logistical or military support be given to irregular forces; b) that no country enter into military or political alliances which will, directly or indirectly, threaten the peace and security of the region; c) that no world power give military aid to irregular forces in the area. U.N. Doc. S/18143 of June 10, 1986, Annex.

[222] **"Contadora Act on Peace and Co-operation in Central America" U.N. Doc. A/40/1136-S/18184 Annex II (1986),** reproduced in 25 I.L.M. 1302 (1986). hereinafter **"The 1986 Contadora Act"**.

[223] See B. Bagley, *Contadora and Diplomacy,* at 201.

[224] The Group of 77 (G-77) is a coalition of less developed countries (LDCs) that currently includes more than 120 member states. It overlaps the Non-Aligned Movement (NAM). The G-77 is the instrument for orchestrating objectives, policies, and tactics among the LDCs in connection to the rules and structure of international economic relations. Since the G-77 taken together has more members than any group of industrialized nations, it seeks to employ U.N. General Assembly voting rules as instruments of real power. See L. Finkelstein, *Politics in the United Nations System*, 21 (1988).

[225] Rothstein explains, "The UNCTAD leadership and the Group of 77 rejected the traditional (and largely unsuccessful) case-by-case approach to commodity problems and instead sought 'global resource management in the interests of the development process' using means that were to encompass the totality of the commodity problem from production to consumption...(I)n short, they decided to shoot for revolution, not reform, to aim for a new regime with a different distribution of power, income, and wealth, not incremental adjustments to the old regime". R. Rothstein, *Consensual Knowledge and International Collaboration: Some*

Lessons From the Commodity Negotiations, 38 Int'l Org. 740 (1984).

[226] See R. Rothstein, *Regime Creation by a Coalition of the Weak*, 28 Int'l Studies Q. 307 (1984).

[227] Particularly drawing from the unilateral U.S. interventions in Guatemala (1954) and Dominican Republic (1965). See B. Bagley, *Contadora and Diplomacy*, at 185.

[228] See Presidents Herrera Campins' and López Portillo's "Letter to President Reagan of September 1982," in R. Leiken and B. Rubin, *The Central American Crisis Reader*, at 636 (1987).

[229] See The Caracas Declaration of September 1981, by which several Latin American nations, including Venezuela, denounced the Franco-Mexican declaration to the United Nations on the Salvadorean civil war. In the latter declaration both the Mexican and the French government recognized the FDR-FMLN as a "representative political force" and urged that foreign involvement be avoided by all parties. The Franco-Mexican Declaration and the Caracas Declaration are reproduced in R. Leiken and B. Rubin, *The Central American Crisis Reader*, 628-629 (1987).

[230] S. Purcell, *supra* note 215, at 167.

[231] *Panama And The Sandinistas: A Revolutionary Friendship Turns Sour*, Latin Am. Weekly Rep., Dec. 21, 1979, at 92.

[232] The bottom-line of Betancur's plans seemed to be the creation of the "appropriate" environment to negotiate amnesty for the domestic guerrillas in return for their peaceful incorporation into the political system. See S. Purcell, *supra* note 206, at 167.

[233] The "Panamericanist Movement," whose origins go back to 1822 and Bolivar's dreams for a united Latin America, is a Latin American historic and largely developed commitment to pursue order and cooperation in the Americas. Panamericanism has laid down the bases for the current "Inter-American System," a body of institutions, multilateral and bilateral conventions purporting to maintain peace and collaboration in the Western Hemisphere. See M. Monroy Cabra, *Derecho Internacional Público*, at 228 (1986).

[234] Rothstein, *supra* note 226, at 737.

[235] Finkelstein, *supra* note 224, at 21.

236 Indeed, Contadora's position in matters of collective security and nonintervention was seen by the Tegucigalpa Bloc and the U.S. as a firm commitment to Nicaragua's demands. This commonality between the Contadora Group and the Sandinistas made the U.S. and the Tegucigalpa Bloc in the final analysis to consider the Contadora Group more as Sandinistas' allies than as an impartial mediator.

237 In this connection, H. Raiffa writes, "[A]ny joint problem-solving effort that decomposes a problem into its component parts can run into difficulties, because the disputants may not agree on the structure, or on the prognostication of uncertainties, or on synergies and interactions within and between these component parts". *The Art And Science Of Negotiation*, at 220 (1982).

238 R. Scheman, *The Inter-American Dilemma*, at 184 (1988).

239 *Id.* at 184.

240 *Id.* at 184.

241 See Inter-American Committee on Human Rights, "Report on the situation of Human Rights in the Republic of Nicaragua", XVII Meeting of Foreign Affairs Ministers, June 1979, reproduced in R. Leiken and B. Rubin, *The Central American Crisis Reader*, at 195 (1987).

242 Article 18 reads: "No State or group of States has the right to intervene, directly or indirectly, for any reason whatever, in the internal or external affairs of any other State. The foregoing principle prohibits not only armed force but also any other form of interference or attempted threat against the personality of the State or against its political, economic, and cultural elements." Article 19 states that: "No State may use or encourage the use of coercive measures of an economic or political character in order to force the sovereign will of another State and obtain from it advantages of any kind". *Charter of the Organization of American States* (OAS). Done at Bogota, April 30, 1948. Entered into force for the United States, Dec. 13, 1951. 2 U.S.T. 2394, T.I.A.S. No. 2361, 119 U.N.T.S. 3. *Protocol of Amendment*. Done at Buenos Aires, Feb. 27 1967. Entered into force for the United States, Feb. 27, 1970, 21 U.S.T. 607, T.I.A.S. No 6847. *Protocol of Amendment*. Done at Cartagena de Indias, Dec. 5, 1985.

[243] On the indeterminacy of the Declaration on Intervention and the Friendly Relations Declaration which faithfully reflect the language of Articles 18 and 19 of the OAS Charter, see L. Damrosch, *Politics Across Borders: Nonintervention and Nonforcible Influence Over Domestic Affairs*, 83 AJIL 9 (1989).

[244] Professor Damrosch adds that "[t]he presence of some deviation would be less troublesome if other states could be shown to be protesting and imposing sanctions, but, again, the evidence is ambiguous: although verbal protests against interference are common enough, the protesters are often engaging in similar behavior themselves, and there is little indication of efforts to respond to violations with sanctions or demands for redress." *Id. at 3.*

[245] See *Inforpress Centroamericana*, Centroamerica 1982, at 21.

[246] The Spanish text of the CDC, *Id.* at 21-22. The Rio Treaty is the *Inter-American Treaty of Reciprocal Assistance*, done at Rio de Janeiro, Sept. 2, 1947. Entered into force for the United States, Dec. 3, 1948. 62 Stat. 1681, T.I.A.S., No 1838, 121 U.N.T.S. 77.

[247] Inter-American Conference for the Maintenance of Continental Peace and Security, Rio de Janeiro, 1947, (1953), OAS, *The Inter-American System*, at 265 (1983).

[248] "Collective intervention, on the other hand, is by definition intervention that has been authorized by some international body having widespread legitimacy." E. Luard, *Collective Intervention*, in Bull ed., **Intervention in World Politics,** 157 (1984).

[249] In section III(b) I try to demonstrate that both the U.N. and the OAS conferred *de facto* exclusivity to Contadora on all Central American issues.

[250] The U.S. and its Central American allies' mention of collective security both at the ICJ and at Contadora meetings supports the assertion that the notion of collective security was always used by the U.S. to justify its military pressure over the Sandinistas. The U.S. alleged in its counter-memorial during the jurisdictional phase of the *Nicaragua case* that "El Salvador, Honduras, and Costa Rica have each sought outside assistance, principally from the United States, in their self-defense against Nicaragua's aggression...[p]ursuant to their inherent right of individual and collective self-defense, and in accordance with the terms of the *Inter-American*

Treaty of Reciprocal Assistance, the United States has responded to these requests." International Court of Justice, *Counter-Memorial Submitted by the United States of America*, at 82 (Aug. 17 1984). See also Shultz, *Affidavit*, Annex 1, para. 7: "I hereby affirm that the United States...consider its policies and activities in Central America...[p]ursuant to the inherent right of collective self-defense, and in accord with its obligations under the Inter-American Treaty of Reciprocal Assistance, the United States has provided support for military activities against forces directed or supported by Nicaragua as a necessary and proportionate means of resisting and deterring Nicaraguan military and paramilitary acts against its neighbors...." Normative expectations like those of the U.S. bloc around the notion of collective security are more evident within some U.S. think tanks. The Heritage Foundation, for example, endorsed the view that "[g]iven Nicaragua's subversion of El Salvador, the United States is entitled to respond with whatever action is necessary and proportional in order to create and sustain an effective defense [based upon] Article 51 of the United Nations Charter and Article 3 of the Rio Treaty," *Thirty Myths About Nicaragua*, 54 The Heritage Lectures, March 8, 1986-March 9, 1986.

251 See R. Reagan, *World Peace and the Situation in Central America and the Caribbean*, 83 Dep't of St. Bull 81 (1983). Article 6 reads: "If the inviolability or the integrity of the territory or the sovereignty or political independence of any American State should be affected by an aggression which is not an armed attack or by an extra-continental or intra-continental conflict, or by any other fact or situation that might endanger the peace of America, the Organ of Consultation shall meet immediately in order to agree on the measures which must be taken in case of aggression to assist the victim of the aggression or, in any case, the measures which should be taken for the common defense and for the maintenance of the peace and security of the Continent". Article 7 reads: "In case of a conflict between two or more American States, without prejudice to the right of self-defense in conformity with Article 51 of the Charter of the United Nations, the High Contracting parties, meeting in consultation shall call upon the contending States to suspend hostilities and restore matters to the status quo ante bellum, and shall take in addition all other necessary measures to reestablish or maintain inter-American peace and security and give a solution

to the conflict by peaceful means. The rejection of the pacifying action will be considered to determine the aggressor and apply the measures which the consultative meeting may agree upon". In the past, Costa Rica and Honduras successfully invoked Article 7 of the Rio Treaty against Nicaragua. Article 7 was first applied during the conflict between Costa Rica and Nicaragua in 1948-49, and then again in 1955-56. It was again invoked in the Honduran-Nicaraguan border dispute over the validity of an arbitration award given by the King of Spain in 1906. See Garcia Amador, F., *Sistema Interamericano a Travês de Tratados, Convenciones y otros Documentos*, OAS 1981, 853-854.

252 See T. Enders, *Nicaragua: Threat to Peace in Central America*, 83 Dep't St. Bull 76 (1983).

253 See Dep't Statement, *Declaration on Democracy in Central America*, 82 Dep't. St. Bull. 69 (1982).

254 For a technical discussion supporting a broad concept of collective security on these same grounds vis a vis the notion of nonintervention, see F. García-Amador, *The Rio de Janeiro Treaty*: Genesis, Development, and Decline of a Regional System of Collective Security, 17 Inter-American Law Review 14 (1985). See also Dean, B.P., Self-Determination and US Supporting of Insurgents: A Policy Model, 27 Mil. Law R. 149 (1988).

255 The Conference emphatically condemned "[t]he activities of the international communist movement as constituting an intervention in American affairs [that had taken the form of] political aggression or aggression of non-military character." See Conferences, Supp II, cited in García-Amador, *The Rio de Janeiro Treaty*, 17 Inter-American L. Rev. 15 (1985).

256 See also *More* U.S. *Effort Yields Less Result; Haig Finds Quick Solutions in Central America Slip from Grip*, The Wash. Post, March 4, 1982, First Section, A1.

257 *Id.* at A1. See also U.S. Department of State, U.S. *Observations On the ICJ Judgment of Nov. 2*, 1984, reprinted in 24 ILM 249.

258 Dep't Statement, *supra* notes 252 and 253.

259 *Id.* at 71.

[260] Texts of these declarations in R. Leiken and B. Rubin, *supra* note 236, at 195.

[261] L. Damrosch, *supra* note 243, at 37.

[262] *United Nations Declaration of Principles of International Law Concerning Friendly Relations Among States In Accordance With the Charter of the United Nations,* Oct. 24, 1970, U.N.G.A. Res. 2625 (XXV), 25 U.N. GAOR, Supp. (No.28) 121, U.N. Doc A/8028 (1971), reprinted in 9 I.L.M. 1292 (1970), hereinafter referred to as the *Declaration of Principles.*

[263] See Rosenstock, *The Declaration of Principles of International Law Concerning Friendly Relations: A Survey*, 65 A.J.I.L. 713, 732 (1971); see also Reisman, *Coercion and Self-determination: Construing Charter Article* 2(4), 78 A.J.I.L. 642 (1984). Professor Reisman views the right of self-determination to include the "free choice of peoples about their government and political structure." He later concludes that there exists a right to use force in foreign countries to bring about 'ongoing self-determination'. A more moderate position can be found in Chowdhury, *The Status and Norms of Self-determination in Contemporary International Law,* in Snyder, F., and Surakiart, S., eds., **Third World Attitudes Toward International Law: An Introduction,** at 87 (1987). Chowdhury defends the wider interpretation of self-determination by arguing that "it is difficult to contend that an independent State can with impunity deny representative government to its people and yet claim that it has in good faith implemented the principle of self-determination." (p. 94). In doing so, he must acknowledge that the "denial of self-determination and human rights by a particular tate is bound to disturb the conditions of stability in an international order and thus impair peaceful and friendly relations among nations." (p. 99). In this regard, " a State not possessed of a representative government or a State guilty of violating with impunity human rights, cannot claim immunity by relying on the principle of nonintervention." (p. 98). In contrast with Reisman, Chowdhury seems to support only collective forms of intervention. For an application of self-determination to internal democracy, see the second paragraph of Principle VIII of the *Final Act of the Conference on Security and Cooperation in Europe*, done at Helsinki, Aug. 1, 1975. Reprinted in 14 I.L.M. 1292 (1975), also known as the **Helsinki Accords** of 1975. Principle VIII provides in part that

"[b]y virtue of the principle of equal rights and self-determination of peoples, all peoples always have the right, in full freedom, to determine, when and as they wish, *their internal* and external political status, without external interference, and to pursue as they wish their political, economic, social and cultural development."

264 See for example Argentina's arguments on self-determination and nonintervention in the Falklands question. Argentina maintained that the expressed desire of the Falklanders to remain linked to Britain "cannot be used to bypass Argentina's historical right to sovereignty over the islands and to disrupt Argentina's territorial integrity," M. Sánchez, *Self-determination and the Falkland Islands Dispute*, in F. Snyder and S. Surakiart, eds., **Third World Attitudes Toward International Law,** 104-105 (1987).

265 See E. Abrams, *Permanent Dictatorship in Nicaragua?*, U.S. Dept. of State, Bureau of Public Affairs, Pub. No. 802; see also *President Reagan's State of the Union Address of February 6*, 1985, reproduced in The Washington Post, Jan. 26, 1988, A10, col. 1. The Reagan doctrine resembled Professor Reisman's thesis that where a repressive government deprives the people of their free choice, a foreign state should be legally entitled to use force to bring about the desirable end of "ongoing self-determination." In the OAS Charter, however, we may also find some provisions which would justify normative expectations based upon the idea of self-determination as self-government. The clearest is the wording of Article 3(d) of the *Charter of the Organization of American States*, stating that "the solidarity of the American States and the high aims which are sought through it require the political organization of those States on the basis of the effective exercise of representative democracy."

266 See OAS AG/RES. 78 (II-0/72). See also Subsecretaría de Asuntos Juridicos, OEA, *Sistema Interamericano*, Vol. I, 93-106. Resolution 78 relates Article 3 of the OAS Charter with the provisions on self-determination of the Declaration of Principles.

267 See *Security Council Reaffirms Support for Contadora Efforts*, U.N. Chron., May 1985; U.N. Chron., August 1984.

268 Scheman *supra* note 238, at 184.

269 The term encompasses Costa Rica, El Salvador, and Honduras, the U.S. allies in Central America since mid-1984.

[270] See B. *Bagley Contadora and Diplomacy*, at 192; *U.S. Version of Contadora Draft Disputed*, Washington Post, Oct. 3, 1984, at A24. See also, N. Y. Times, Nov. 16, 1984; U.S. Dep't. of St., Office of Public Diplomacy for Latin America and the Caribbean (1985), Annex 3, at 1-3. See also, T. Farer, Contadora: *The Hidden Agenda*, 59 Foreign Policy 71 (1985).

[271] On the disadvantages of "passive consensus", see B. Buzan, Negotiating By Consensus, 75 AJIL 324 (1981).

[272] H. Raiffa aptly affirms: "Complex negotiations can often be resolved by compromises that exploit the role of time. Not everything must be decided here and now. Some actions can be deferred to a later time and be made contingent on information learned along the way." H. Raiffa, *The Art And Science of Negotiation*, at 220 (1982).

[273] See M. Morris and V. Millan, *Controlling Latin American Conflicts: Ten Approaches*, at 164. (1983)

[274] *Id.* at 172.

Contadora's verification capabilities proved to be very inefficient and inappropriate in various border incidents between Costa Rica and Nicaragua in 1984 and 1985.

[276] B. Bagley, *Contadora and Diplomacy*, at 185.

[277] The Rio Treaty is a fundamental part of the Inter-American System and the OAS encompasses the institutional apparatus of that same system.

[278] OAS AG/Res.675 (XIII-0/83), P*eace Efforts in Central America.*

[275] This role was assigned to the so-called Technical Group. 279 The OAS General Assembly alerted the parties in conflict that they had "available, for the peaceful settlement of disputes, the various procedures provided in the Charter of the Organization," and urged them to use these procedures as means for settling the disputes existing in the region. See OAS AG/Res. 680 (XIII-0/83), *Procedures for Peaceful Settlement of Disputes.*

[280] OAS AG/Res. 702 (XIV/84) *Peace Efforts in Central America.*

[281] See OAS CP/doc.1592/85 and OAS CP/Res.432(623/85).

[282] See *Incidents of Peñas Blancas*, October 1983 OEA/Ser.G CP/Acta 538/83; Conventillos, February 1984 OEA/Ser.G CP/Acta 553/84; and *Gulf of Fonseca*, May 1984 OEA/Ser.G CP/Acta 567/84 CP/INF 2161/84.

[283] See speeches by Nicaraguan delegates at OAS CP/doc.1592/85.

[284] D. Lincoff, *Annual Review of United Nations Affairs*, 103 (1982).

[285] *Id.* at 127, U.N. Doc. S/15651.

[286] *Id.* at 134, U.N. Doc. S/15746

[287] For example, the Security Council considered another Nicaraguan complaint on February 3, 1984. The U.S. once again vetoed a draft resoltion that called for an end to the "attacks against the sovereignty and independence of Nicaragua.", *id.* at 144. See also U.N. Doc. S/16449 (1984).

[288] See 7th *Summit of NOAL*, New Delhi, 1983, 15-20. This approach brought Nicaragua more favorable resolutions. For example,the General Assembly resolution 38/10 "condemned the acts of aggression against the States of the region and, in particular, the indiscriminate acts against Nicaragua." The same resolution also expressed its "firmest support for the Contadora Group, urging it to persevere in its efforts."

[289] See S. Purcell, *supra* note 215, at 88.

[290] M. Karns, *Ad hoc multilateral diplomacy: The United States*, the Contact Group, and Namibia, 41 Int'l Org. 122 (1987).

CHAPTER V

THE STRUGGLE AGAINST UNCERTAINTY

[291] This was the case despite the fact that Nicaragua had indicated that it was not asking the Court to bring the armed conflict to an end but to clarify Nicaragua's rights under conventional and customary international law. **Military and Paramilitary Activities in and against Nicaragua,** (Nicar. v. U.S.), Jurisdiction and Admissibility, 1984 ICJ 392, para. 100 (Judgment of Nov. 26, 1984). The case in its two phases, jurisdictional and merits will hereinafter be referred to as the *Nicaragua Case*.

292 **Military and Paramilitary Activities in and against Nicaragua (Nicar. v. U.S.),** Jurisdiction, ICJ Reports 1984, and Merits, Judgment, ICJ Reports 1986, 14.

[293] Nicaraguan Foreign Minister Miguel D'Escoto told reporters on June, 1986 that "you must not fall into the false illusion that the signing of the [Contadora] agreement is going to bring peace to the region...after all, the Central American governments are not at war....(T)here are tensions between the (Central American) governments, but only because of the war that the United States has unleashed against ...Nicaragua." See Reuters Ltd. June 6, 1986.

[294] Take for example the creation of the Tegucigalpa Bloc in September 1984 and the rejection by its members of the 1984 Contadora Act on verification and implementation grounds. See Wash. Post, Oct. 21, 1984, A12; Proprietary to the United Press International, September 27 and October 3, 1984 (NEXIS).

[295] This view acquired its maximum expression by June 1986, when Nicaragua clearly stated that the Contadora negotiations had failed and that "the time has come to start considering alternate solutions to Central America's political bloodshed." Reuters Ltd., June 6, 1986 (NEXIS).

[296] See Proprietary to the United Press International, October 3, 1984 (NEXIS); see also "Central Americans Meet On Contadora Changes; Nicaraguans Boycott Session in Honduras," Wash. Post, Oct. 20, 1984, A12.

[297] See N. Y. Times, April 9, 1986.

[298] **Military and Paramilitary Activities in and Against Nicaragua,** (Nicar.v.US), Provisional Measures, Order of May 10 1984, ICJ Reports 1984. Article 41(1) of the Court's statute reads: "The Court shall have the power to indicate, if it considers that circumstances so require, any provisional measures which ought to be taken to preserve the respective rights of either party.

[299] *Id.* at 18.

[300] *Id.* at 21.

[301] 1984 ICJ 187.

[302] *Id.* at 187.

[303] *Id.* at 187.

304 *Id.* at 189.

305 *Id.* at 190.

306 *Id.* at 196 (emphasis added).

307 Wash. Post, May 1, 1984, A16.

308 *Id.* at A16.

309 See B. Bagley, *supra* note 207, at 188.

310 *Report of the National Bipartisan Commission on Central America*, Jan. 1984, 120.

311 Article 63(2) provides that "[E]very state so notified has the right to intervene in the proceedings, but if it uses this right, the construction given by the judgment will be equally binding upon it." *Statute of the International Court of Justice*, Done at San Francisco, June 26, 1945, 59 Stat. 1055, T.S. No. 993, 3 Bevans 1153, 1976 Y.B.U.N. 1052.

312 **Military and Paramilitary Activities in and against Nicaragua,** (Nicar. v. U.S.), Declaration of Intervention of Aug. 15, 1984, 1984 ICJ 215.

313 *Id.* at 215

314 *Id.* at 215.

315 *Id.* at 216.

316 1984 ICJ Reports, para. 113.

317 *Id.* paras. 87 and 88.

318 U.S. Department of State, *U.S. Observations On the ICJ Judgment of November 2, 1984*, reproduced in 24 ILM 249.

319 ICJ Reports 1984, para. 108.

320 **Letter from the U.S. Secretary of State to the Secretary-General of the U. N. of October 7,** 1985, reproduced in 24 ILM 1742.

321 *U.S. Rules Out New Nicaragua Talks*, N. Y. Times, Dec. 3, 1984.

322 **Military and Paramilitary Activities in and against Nicaragua (Nicar. v. U.S.),** Merits, 1986 ICJ 14 (Judgment of June 27).

323 *Id.* at 146.

[324] *Id.* at para. 292.

[325] Issues 7, 10, and 11. *Id.* at 149.

[326] Issues 12 and 13. *Id.* at 149.

[327] The Court upheld the Vandenberg reservation but concluded that the normative content of the treaty rules on which Nicaraguan demands were grounded were also part of customary international law. In examining the merits of the case, the Court revisited the U.S. argument that "the provisions of the United Nations Charter relevant here subsume and supervene related principles of customary and general international law." The Court also entertained the U.S. position that "the multilateral treaty reservation bars adjudication of claims based on those treaties, [and thus] it bars all of Nicaragua's claims." The Court concluded, however, that "customary international law continues to exist and to apply, separately from international treaty law, even where the two categories of law have an identical content." *Id.* at paras. 42-56 and 173-174

[328] *Id.* paras. 26-31.

[329] The Court observed that it did "not believe that the concept of armed attack includes not only acts by armed bands where such acts occur on a significant scale but also assistance to rebels in the form of the provision of weapons or logistical or other support. Such assistance may be regarded as a threat or use of force, or amount to intervention in the internal or external affairs of other States...Nevertheless, such activities may well constitute a breach of the principle of the nonuse of force and an intervention in the internal affairs of a State, that is, a form of conduct which is certainly wrongful, but is of lesser gravity than an armed attack." *Id.* at para. 195.

[330] *Id.* at para. 195

[331] *Id.* at para. 198.

[332] *Id.* at para. 201.

[333] *Id.* at para. 205.

[334] *Id.* at para. 207.

[335] *Id.* at paras. 210-211.

[336] R. Falk, *The World Court Achievement*, 81 AJIL 110 (1987).

[337] *supra* note 322, at para. 223.

338 *Id.* at para. 212.

339 *Id.* at para. 251.

340 *Id.* at paras. 257-259.

341 *Id.* at para. 261.

342 *Id.* at para. 262.

343 *Id.* at para. 263.

344 *Id.* at para. 266.

345 *Id.* at para. 268.

CHAPTER VI

THE WORLD COURT: EXCURSUS ON THE ANATOMY OF A TRANSNATIONAL AUTHORITATIVE DETERMINATION PROCESS

346 Only thirteen cases since 1945 may be said to have involved use of armed force. See O. Schachter, *Disputes Involving The Use of Force*, In L. Damrosch, **The International Court of Justice At A Crossroads,** at 223 (1987).

347 See H. Hubbard, *Separation of Powers Within the United Nations: A Revised Role For the International Court of Justice*, 38 Stanford L. R. 168 (1985). This article provides a list of previous force cases submitted before the ICJ, at 175-176, notes 69-88.

348 In the words of another commentator, "compulsory jurisdiction was fatally flawed from its inception, has never played a major role in resolving international disputes despite its many adherents, and has become an unfortunate talisman interfering with the development of more vital conflict resolution mechanisms." J. Kelly, *The International Court of Justice: Crisis and Reformation*, 12 Yale J. of Int'l L. 342 (1987).

349 See 1954-1955 ICJYB 187 (1955) and 1984-1985 ICJYB 66-101 (1985).

350 S. Schwebel, *Reflections on the Role of the International Court of Justice*, 61 Washington L. R. 1066 (1986).

351 The United States, France, and China (before 1949), formerly adhered.

[352] *Id.* at 1066.

[353] As Judge Schwebel explains, "even though under the United Nations Charter the Security Council is authorized to make recommendations or decide upon measures to be taken to give effect to a judgment of the Court, the Security Council does not appear to be seen as a reliable enforcer of the Court's judgments." *Id.* at 1067.

[354] For example, **Delimitation of the Maritime Boundary in the Gulf of Maine Area (Can. v. U.S.),** 1984 ICJ 246 (Judgment of Oct. 12), reprinted in 23 I.L.M. 1197 (1984).

[355] See 1984 I.C.J. 169 (I.C.J., May 10, 1984); also 1981 I.C.J. 3 and 1985 I.C.J. 3.

[356] A judgment given by a Chamber is considered as rendered by the Court. See Article 27 of the Statute of the International Court of Justice. Chambers of the Court offer what could prove to be an attractive half-way house between international arbitration and adjudication...in the real world chambers may sometimes afford states a likelier forum by permitting them a voice in the choice of judges...while at the same time providing the advantages over arbitration of an accepted body of rules of procedures and the facilities of the Court in the Hague. *Statute of the International Court of Justice, done at San Francisco*, June 26, 1945, 1976 Y.B.U.N. 1052. Four Chambers have been constituted to date.

[357] "One sees that the great majority of the judgments of the Court have been accepted by the states concerned, and carried out even where they did not like the judgment at all." S. Schwebel, *Judging the World*, Interview, 18 The Brief 15 (1989). For a comprehensive and persuasive analysis of the impact of ICJ's judgments and advisory opinions in the world today, see E. Jiménez de Aréchaga, *The Work and the Jurisprudence of the International Court of Justice*, 58 BYIL 1 (1987).

[358] See generally H. Lauterpacht, *The Development of International Law by the International Court*, (1958).

[359] See W. Evan, *Knowledge and Power in a Global Society* (1981).

[360] *Id.* at 13.

[361] Notably, **Military and Paramilitary Activities In and Against Nicaragua,** (Nicar. v. U.S.A.), 86 I.C.J. 14.

[362] H. Lauterpacht, *supra* note 358, at 21.

[363] E. Jiménez de Aréchaga, *supra* note 357, at 1.

[364] S. Schwebel, *supra* note 357, at 17.

[365] Partially through the notion of the national and the ad-hoc judges of Article 31 of the statute that guarantees at least that each party will have a judge of its nationality or appointment sitting in the case.

[366] Article 2 of the Court's statute establishes that the Court "is to be composed of a body of independent judges, elected regardless of their nationality from among persons of high moral character, who possess the qualifications required in their respective countries for appointment to the highest judicial offices, or are jurisconsults of recognized competence in international law." According to Article 3(1) the Court is to consist of "fifteen members, no two of whom may be nationals of the same state." Article 4 states that the members of the Court are to be elected by the UN General Assembly and by the Security Council from a list of persons "nominated by the National Groups in the Permanent Court of Arbitration." In the case of UN member-states that do not have such formally constituted National Groups, nominations are done by ad hoc National Groups specially appointed by UN member-states for that purpose. Article 6 adds further requirements to National Groups, who are "recommended to consult its highest court of justice, its legal faculties and schools of law, and its national academies and national sections of international academies devoted to the study of law." For a detailed explanation of the statutory and customary methods for the selection and election of judges to the ICJ, see E. McWhinney, *Law, Politics, and "Regionalism" in the Nomination and Election of World Court Judges*, 13 Syracuse J. of Int'l and C. L. 1 (1986).

[367] For arguments in the same direction, see M. Lachs, *A Few Thoughts on the Independence of Judges of the International Court of Justice*, 25 Columbia J. of Transnat'l L. 593 (1987); E. Gordon, *Observations on the Independence and Impartiality of the Members of the International Court of Justice*, 2 Connecticut J. of Int'l L. 397 (1987).

[368] See T. Franck, *Some Psychological Factors in International Third Party Decision-Making*, 19 Stan. L. Rev. 1217, 1220 (1967).

369 E. Brown Weiss, *Judicial Independence and Impartiality*, in Damrosch, L. *The International Court of Justice at a Crossroads,* (1987), at 123.

370 *Id.* at 134.

371 Some evidence of this effect may arguably be found in the current attitude of Third World states, Communist states and Japan toward the ICJ, in contrast to their old pervasive belief that the Court was simply a product of Western European culture and that its method was alien to the cultures of many non-European. See E. McWhinney, *Western And Nonwestern Legal Cultures and the International Court of Justice*, 65 Washington University Law Quarterly 873 (1987); see also, E. McWhinney, *The International Court of Justice and the Western Tradition of International Law* (1987). On the ICJ's appropriateness to adjudicate even those cases where the law is uncertain, such as those involving the use of force, see O. Schachter, *supra* note 351.

372 The Annual Meetings of the American Society of International Law and the American Bar Association are very consistent in this regard. See 13 International Law News 1-2 (1984). See also *Peace Organizations protest new U.S. policy toward World Court,* 116 New Jersey Law Journal 5 (1984).

373 *General Assembly demanded a halt of U.S. aid to the contras by overwhelming majority*, Reuters North European Service, Nov. 3 1986, Monday AM cycle.

374 See 23 UN Chronicle 83 (1986). See however the critique of the merits of the Court's 1986 judgment by the current Legal Adviser of the State Department, in A. Sofaer, *Adjudication in the International Court of Justice: progress through realism.* 44 The Record of the Association of the Bar of the City of New York 46, (1989).

375 1980 ICJ 67.

376 1962 ICJ 151.

377 **Interpretation of Peace Treaties with Bulgaria,** Hungary, and Rumania, 1950 ICJ 65 (Advisory Opinion).

378 See **Rights of Nationals of the United States of America in Morocco,** 1952 ICJ 176; **Right of Passage Over Indian Ter-**

ritory, 1960 ICJ 6; **International Status of South West Africa,** 1950 ICJ 128.

379 **Effect of Awards of Compensation made by the UN Administrative Tribunal,** 1954 ICJ 471; **Judgments of the Administrative Tribunal of the ILO upon Complaints made against UNESCO,** 1956 ICJ 77.

380 **Frontier Dispute,** 1986 ICJ 554 (Burkina Faso v. Mali), **Minquiers and Ecrehos,** 1953 ICJ 47 (France v. UK); **Arbitral Award made by the Kind of Spain on 23 December 1906,** 1960 ICJ 192 (Hond.v.Nicar); **Continental Shelf,** 1969 ICJ 50 (Tunisia v. Libyan Arab Jamahiriya); **Delimitation of the Maritime Boundary in the Gulf of Maine Area,** 1984 ICJ 246 (Canada v. US), etc.

381 Invariably all constitutive Charters of IOs make express reference to the ICJ as means for judicial settlement of disputes.

382 On the impact of ISPAs themselves, see Evan *supra* note 364.

383 1986 Reuters Ltd, July 3, 1986, Thursday, BC cycle.

384 Id.

385 See J. Goldklang, *House Approves Proposal Permitting ICJ to Advise Domestic Courts*, 77 AJIL 338 (1983); see also H. Mosler, Supra-national Judicial Decisions and National Courts, 4 Hastings International and Comparative Law R. 425 (1981). In the United States a series of complaints by private groups seeking injunctive and declaratory relief against the funding of the "Contras" in Nicaragua, have brought the ICJ's 1986 decision to the attention of U.S. courts. The most recent of those cases is *Committee of United States Citizens Living In Nicaragua v. Reagan*, 859 F.2d 929 (D.C.Cir.1988).

386 H. Dillard, *Law. Policy and the World Court: Attacking Some Misconceptions*, 17 Willamette Law Review 13 (1980).

387 1979 ICJ 7, reprinted in 19 ILM 139 (1980). Judge Dillard argued that time after time in the debates in the Security Council following the Court's decision against Iran, "the representatives of numerous nations, in calling on Iran to release the hostages, fortified their arguments by citing and stressing the World Court's order." These debates culminated in a unanimous resolution which, though killed by the Soviet veto and with no immediate effect, led

to world condemnation of Iranian action with significant long range consequences. H. Dillard, *supra* note 391, at 18.

388 *Id.* at 18.

389 See L. Gross, *Underutilization of the International Court of Justice*, 27 Harvard Int'l Law J. 571 (1986).

CHAPTER VII

COPING WITH UNCERTAINTY THROUGH CONSENSUAL KNOWLEDGE AND NORMATIVE RESTRAINT

390 Nicaragua: *Ortega Calls World Court Case in Region's Interest*, 1986 I.P.S., July 29, 1986; U.P.I. 1986, July 29, 1986.

391 Both Applications appear at 25 ILM 1293 (1986).

392 **American Treaty On Pacific Settlement,** done at Bogota, April 30, 1948. Entered into force, May 6, 1949, 30 U.N.T.S. 55.

393 In this perspective, see *Nicaragua Leader Visits Chicago, says he wants peace with U.S.*, N.Y. Times, Aug. 3, 1986, 7.

394 *Ortega at UN urges peace in low-key talk*, L.A. Times, July 30, 1986, Part 1, page 5, col. 1.

4395 *U.S. Vetoes Rebuke On Aid To Contras*, The N.Y. Times, August 1, 1986, A3. Col.1.

396 *Id.*

397 UN Docs S/18221, Letter, 11 July 1986 from Nicaragua to the UN Security Council, transmitting ICJ's judgment; *U.S. Senate Approves Aid to Nicaragua Contras,* 1986 Facts on File 595 B1 and 1986 Facts on File 804 D1; *Nicaragua Down U.S. Plane*, Charges CIA Contra Supply Operation, 1986 Facts On File 745 A1.

398 *UN Assembly demands Halt to U.S. Aid to Contras*, 1986 Reuters November 3, 1986, Monday, AM Cycle; see UN GA/Res/ 42/18 of 12 November 1987.

399 *Central America: Costa Rica May Sanction Contras*, I.P.S., July 29, 1986.

400 O. Arias, *El Camino de la Paz* (1989), 79.

[401] By August 17, 1986, President Arias had already focused most of his administration's attention to Nicaraguan issues. President Arias's speech to celebrate the one hundred days of his administration stressed Costa Rica's compliance with its duty not to allow the use of its territory by Nicaraguan insurrectional groups. An important part of that speech was also dedicated to comment on the inadmissibility of Nicaragua's application to the Court, which was unjustly questioning Costa Rica's international honor and dignity. Id., at 108-110. One month later, President Arias devoted a significant portion of his address to the UN General Assembly to defend Costa Rica's position at the World Court. Id. 115-123.

[402] 1986 Reuters, July 30, 1986, Wednesday, PM cycle.

[403] Monge officially proclaimed Costa Rican neutrality in the Central American conflicts. It was reported, however, that a secret airstrip functioned in Costa Rican northern territory with the specific purpose of supporting contras operations.

[404] **Agreement On Procedure For Establishing Firm and Lasting Peace In Central America,** 26 ILM 1164 (1987).

[405] *Honduran President Says He Wants Nicaraguan Rebels Out,* 1986 Reuters, November 6; Facts on File, October 31, 1986.

[406] *Central America Asks How Far U.S. will Go*, N.Y. Times, Nov. 2, 1986, 3.1. *Tense OAS Debate Expected On Regional Issues*, 1986 I.P.S., November 10; 1986 Reuters, November 10; 1986 Reuters North European Service, November 7.

[407] *OAS Opens Meeting Amid Anti-Nicaraguan Charges*, 1986 Reuters, Nov. 10, 1986.

[408] *Requiem For Contadora Group*, 1986 Reuters, Nov. 14; *Venezuelan Minister Gives Grim Outlook For Contador*a, 1986 Reuters Nov. 14; *Contadora Group Comes Under Fire At OAS Meeting*, 1986 Reuters North European Service, Nov. 14.

[409] 1987 Reuters North European Service, Jan. 23, 1987; The Xinhua General Overseas News Service, Jan 21, 1987; 1987 I.P.S., Jan. 20, 1987.

[410] 1987 Reuters North European Service, Feb. 14.

[411] Reproduced in 25 ILM 1168 (1987)

[412] *Joint Declaration of Esquipulas III of February 1988.*

413 *Final Report of the LASA Commission on Compliance with the Central America Peace Accord*, 4-7 (March 15, 1988).

414 *La Parálisis en Esquipulas II, Arias: La Paz es frágil en Centroamerica*, La Nación (Costa Rica) Aug. 7, 1988, at p. 3; *El Compromiso Aun No Cumplido*, El Heraldo (Honduras) Aug. 6, 1988, at 31; *El Acuerdo Esquipulas II un año después de su firma*, Tiempo (Honduras) Aug. 6, 1988; *Sin Pena Ni Gloria*, La Prensa (Nicaragua), Aug. 6, 1988; *El Plan de Paz, o el Mérito Puro y Simple de Sobrevivir*, La Hora (Guatemala), Aug 8, 1988; *Primer Aniversario de Esquipulas II*, Latino (El Salvador), Aug. 9, 1988.

415 *Id.* at 7.

416 **Case Concerning Border and Transborder Armed Actions,** (Nicar. v. Hond.), reproduced in 28 ILM 335 (1989). In its efforts to free itself from the legal and political burdens carried by Nicaragua's application, the Honduran government argued both lack of jurisdiction and inadmissibility of the claim. More significantly, Honduras alleged before the ICJ that the application was inadmissible. Honduras argued that since Nicaragua accepted the Contadora process as a "special procedure" under Article 2 of the Pact of Bogota, Nicaragua was precluded both by Article IV of the Pact and elementary considerations of good faith "from commencing any other procedure for pacific settlement until such time as the Contadora process has been concluded; and that time has not arrived." See id. at para 13. Many other issues were raised by the parties that deserve detailed examination. However, this is not the place to address them all adequately. It is Honduras's insistence in using the Pact of Bogota to question the admissibility of Nicaragua's claim that most concerns us in this discussion. Honduras' arguments on this issue paved the way for the Court's analysis of the interplay between the various means for the settlement of disputes the parties had available.

417 **Border and Transborder Actions,** Id. at 106.

418 See American Treaty On Pacific Settlement, 30 UNTS 55.

419 *Id.* at 106-107.

420 The contents of this letter are described and analyzed at pages 176 and 177 below.

421 **Joint Declaration of the Central American Presidents,** 1989 Envio 10 (Mar. 1989).

[422] *Id.* at 3. An unofficial translation of the Tela Agreement was furnished to the author by the Central America Resource Center, P.O. Box 2327, Austin, TX 78768.

[423] Spanish acronym for "United Nations Operation in Central America."

[424] See the list of references provided *supra* note 196.

[425] See U.S. Dep't. St., T*he Situation In Central America,* at 1 (1988).

[426] U.S. Dep't St., *Democracy in Latin America and the Caribbean: The Promise and the Challenge*, Special Rep., at 158, (March 1987).

[427] *Nicaraguan Obsession,* L. A. Times, Home Edition, 6. This situation was confirmed on November 3, when the UN General Assembly demanded a halt of U.S. aid to the contras by [an] overwhelming majority. See Reuters North European Service, Nov 3 1986, Monday AM cycle.

[428] 1987 I.P.S., Feb. 13, 1987.

[429] See *Central America: U.S. Claims Success Despite Reports of Failure*, 1988 I.P.S., Aug. 3, 1988; *Fracaso la Maniobra de Reagan contra Nicaragua,* Adelante, Aug. 11, 1988; *Honduras Sugiere Participación Directa de U.S.*, Tiempo, Aug. 9, 1988; E*stados Unidos Reconoce Revés En Guatemala*, La Nación, Aug. 3, 1988.

[430] *Central America: U.S. Claims Success Despite Reports of Failure*, 1988 I.P.S., Aug. 3 1988.

[431] See H.A. Ryan, *Arias Plan: Local Support Is Key*, 1987 The Christian Science Monitor 12 (Sept. 1, 1987).

[432] L, Etheredge, *Can Governments Learn: American Foreign Policy and Central American Revolutions*, at 196 (1985). Etheredge writes: "Only by strong emotional impact, in extremis and faced by nuclear deterrence, has a lesson...been accepted."

[433] *Id.* at 181.

[434] Etheredge comments that "Shultz's soporific style and personal decency aided the administration's public relations. As Shultz was interpreted as a moderating influence in Soviet-American relations, and this influence was greatly desired by potential critics of Central American policy, Shultz (and the ad-

ministration) has probably, for this reason as well, been the subject of fewer attacks." *Id.* at 208.

[435] *Reagan's Shadow CIA: How the White House Ran the Secret 'Contra' War*, 195 The New Republic 23 (Nov. 24, 1986). For a comprehensive picture of this division and the domestic factors impinging on it, see J. Omang, *The Contra Commitment*, 2 parts, Wash. Post, A1, Jan. 2, 1987.

[436] See *Nicaragua Case ICJ, U.S. Withdrawal*, 86 H381-15; *Reagan Policy Critique*, 87 H381-33.3; *Meeting with European Parliament*, 88 H382-14; *Democratic Transitions in Central America*, 88 H381-95; *Peace Accord Signed in 1987*, 88 H381-19. Congressional opposition to President Reagan's policy in Central America became more salient when the House Speaker Jim Wright himself took the lead in criticizing Washington's sending of 3200 U.S. combat troops to Honduras in March 1988. See *Troop Order Splits Congress*, The Tribune News Services, A1-2, March 18, 1988

[437] C. Giacomo,*Legal Experts Upset With U.S. Reaction to World Court Ruling*, 1986 Reuters, Jul. 3, 1986, BC cycle. See also *Peace Organizations Protest New U.S. Policy Toward World Court*, 116 New Jersey L. J. 5 (October 1986); *Jurists Condemn U.S. Over International Court Move, Reuters*, May 15, 1984; *Should the U.S. reconsider its Acceptance of World Court Jurisdiction?*, Proc. 79th Ann. Meet. A.S.I.L., at 93-109, (Apr. 1985); Ch. Brower, *Annual Meeting Focuses On Nicaraguan Case Before the World Court*, ABA Sect. Int'l L. and Prac., 13 Int'l Law News 1-2 (Fall 1984).

[438] See Crockett v. Reagan, 467 U.S. 1251; Meyer et al. v. U.S., 1987 U.S. Dist. Lexis 935; U.S. Congressman Robert K Dornan et al. v. U.S. Secretary of Defense, U.S. Secretary of State, Director, Central Intelligence Agency, Ronald W. Reagan, 676 F. Supp. 6., (The Court held that subjecting contra aid matters to Congressional approval was constitutional); Javier Sánchez et al. v. Ronald Reagan, 770 F2d 202; see also *Nicaragua: U.S. Pastor to Sue Reagan For Attempted Murder*, 1988 I.P.S., Aug. 3, 1988. The most salient and significant case arose from a suit filed by the Committee of United States Citizens v. Ronald Reagan, 859 F.2d 929; 1988 U.S. App. Lexis 14362. In this latter case the plaintiffs, unhappy with their government's failure to abide by the ICJ decision and

believing that continued funding of the Contras injured their own interest, filed suit in the United States District Court for the District of Columbia. Though the claim was dismissed by both the District Court and the Court of Appeals, the case gave American courts the opportunity to clarify the legal effects of the ICJ's judgment in the U.S. domestic legal system. The Court of Appeals rejected the "political question" as impeding enforcement of the ICJ judgments. Significantly, the Court of Appeals held that the questions submitted were justiciable, but at the same time dismissed the claims on the ground that private parties have no cause of action to enforce an ICJ decision. *Id.* at 932.

439 See Friedman, T.L., *Baker's World,* N. Y. Times, International Section, A7, September 21, 1989. Friedman writes: "With one sentence on Tuesday, Secretary of State James A. Baker 3d confirmed openly what everyone suspected: that he looks at this job and the world first and foremost through the prism of American politics....What kind of foreign policy will the United States ultimately have if you take Mr. Baker out of the campaign but cannot take the campaign out of Mr. Baker?"

440 See *Bush's Washington: Who is Who: Second Article of a Series,* N. Y. Times, Jan. 17, 1989: "Mr. Baker has told lawmakers on Capitol Hill that United States support for the anti-Communist rebels in Nicaragua--the contras--has been a failure." See also The Boston Globe, Jan. 7, 1989; *New Policy On Contras Told*, L.A. Times, March 25, 1989; *Nicaragua: U.S. Admits Military Pressure Failed To Bring Change*, I.P.S., March 27, 1989.

441 L.A. Times, Jan. 28, 1989.

442 U.P.I., Feb. 17, 1989.

443 L.A. Times, March 3, 1989.

444 N.Y. Times, March 29, 1989, 8.

445 Reuter Library Report, March 28, 1989, AM cycle.

446 1989 Examiner News Services, March 24, 1989, A1

547 U.S. *Supports UN Force for Latin America*, Boston Globe, Nov. 8, 1989, 1.

448 *Latin, U.S. Worlds Apart In Rating Talks*, Miami Herald, Oct. 31, 1989, 1.

CHAPTER VIII

GUIDELINE FOR THE FUTURE: REDUCING PROCEDURAL UNCERTAINTY IN CENTRAL AMERICA

449 The term *incremental growth* refers here to increasing agendas and goals within a particular arena. Incremental growth does not necessarily implies that actors change or that the relevant legal knowledge base is consensual. Though Contadora augmented the number of issues and achieved a comprehensive--almost overwhelming--agenda, knowledge for conflict-solving was never consensual and actors' bargaining styles remained dissimilar. As a result, after a series of stalemates, the process finally decayed. I have borrowed the notion *incremental growth* from Ernst B. Haas. He defines it as: "featur[ing] the successive augmentation of an organization's program as actors add new tasks to older ones without any change in the organization's decision-making dynamics or mode of choosing." The second model of organizational development elaborated by Haas is what he labels *turbulent non-growth*, which "involves major changes in organizational decision making: ends no longer cohere; internal consensus on both ends and means disintegrates." See E.B. Haas, *When Knowledge is Power,* at 4 (1989).

450 The term *managed interdependence* applies to actors who, having learned from their previous disappointments, achieve a consensual basis on which to handle the dispute and end up sharing similar bargaining styles. Again, I borrow the term *managed interdependence* from E.B. Haas, who defines it as: "the reexamination of purposes brought about by knowledge-mediated decision-making dynamics [normally associated with learning]." *Id.* at 4.

451 *Id.*

452 See document VF/CAM/ARIAS/11/CARC, Central American Resource Center.

453 *Id.* at 6-7.

454 UN Press Release, Note No. 4774, Sept. 6 1989, 2.

455 *Id.*

[456] See UN doc. A/44/375 of Jul. 7, 1989. ONUVEN officially opened its offices in Managua and started its activities on Aug. 25. The Secretary General appointed Elliot Richardson as his Personal Representative for the verification of the electoral process in Nicaragua. See Press Release SG/A/422/rev.1, Aug. 30, 1989. ONUVEN was mandated to develop direct and regular contacts with its main interlocutor, the *Consejo Supremo Electoral* (Supreme Electoral Council), as well as with the political parties. ONUVEN observers also had to monitor electoral activities and the access by political parties to media. To supplement the above responsibilities ONUVEN had to visit the regions and special zones of Nicaragua, and establish contacts in all the regions to ensure that its monitoring actually covered all parts of the country. ONUVEN had to report directly to the Secretary General who in turn reported to the General Assembly. The Mission was composed of twenty-three member international staff based in Managua. Additional United Nations personnel was expected to join the mission on Dec. 2, 1989 when the second phase of ONUVEN's activities were to start. See **UN Press Release,** Note No. 4777, Sept. 11, 1989.

[457] *Id.* at 3. The resolution of the Security Council, as drafted by the Secretary General, tacitly suggested that US policy become more supportive of the Central American accords. Indeed, the Security Council, unanimously (US vote included), appealed in point 4 "to all states, in particular to those which have links with the region and interests in it, to back the political will of the Central American countries to comply with the provisions of the Guatemala Agreement and of the Joint Declaration, particularly that regional and extra-regional Governments which either openly or covertly supply aid to irregular forces or insurrectionist movements in the area immediately halt such aid, with the exception of the humanitarian aid that contributes to the goals of the Tesoro Beach (Costa del Sol) Agreement of 14 February 1989."

[458] This commission started to function on Sept. 6, 1989. As a first step, the Secretaries General of the UN and the OAS sent a mission to Honduras and Nicaragua "in order to make contacts for the carrying out of its responsibilities in the execution of the Joint Plan." See Press Releases SG/SM/432, Sept. 5 1989; SG/1875/Rev.1, Aug. 25 1989 and A/44/451, S/20778, both of Aug. 9, 1989. As indicated earlier, CIAV verified compliance by monitoring the implementation of the Tela Joint Declarations. This

task included the "voluntary demobilization, repatriation or relocation in Nicaragua or third parties, of members of the Nicaraguan Resistance and their families, as well as assistance in the demobilization of all those involved in armed actions in the countries of the region when they voluntarily seek it."

459 *Id.*

460 U.N. S/20895 (Oct. 11, 1989).

461 In fulfillment of the two basic goals suggested by the Central American Governments, ONUCA sought the cessation of all forms of military assistance, such as the provision of weapons, ammunition and logistical support, to irregular forces and insurrectionist movements in the region. ONUCA's mandate included also the cessation of all other forms of assistance to such forces and movements, with the exception of humanitarian assistance, in accordance with Section 5 of the Guatemala Agreement and the Declaration of El Salvador. On the commitment by the Governments to prevent the use of the territory of one State for attacks on another State, the mission had to prevent any act of aggression against one State from or through the territory of another State, including all its land territory, territorial sea and airspace; to prevent the territory of any State...from being used by third parties... for the purpose of providing assistance to irregular forces; and to prevent the establishment or use of facilities for radio or television transmissions for the specific purpose of directing or assisting the military operation of irregular forces or insurrectionist movements in any of the five countries. ONUCA is envisaged to exert observation, monitoring and preventive functions--and, as appropriate, a deterrent function--with regard to the possible non-fulfillment of the commitments referred to above. See *Id.* at 3-5.

462 *Id.* at 4.

463 See P. Taylor, *Nonstate Actors in International Politics: From Transregional to Substate Organizations*, at 141-151 (1984); L. Scheman, *The Inter-American Dilemma: The Search for Inter-American Cooperation At the Centennial of the Inter-American System*, (1988); F. García Amador, *The Rio de Janeiro Treaty: Genesis, Development, and Decline of a Regional System of Collective Security*, 17 Inter-American Law Rev. 1 (1985).

[464] *US Supports UN Force for Latin America*, The Boston Globe, Nov. 8, 1989, 1, reproduced in 4 Central America NewsPak 1, (Nov. 6-19, 1989).

[465] For a detailed discussion of the "face-saving" role of peacekeeping operations, see A. James, *Unit Veto Dominance in United Nations Peace-Keeping*, in L. Finkelstein, *Politics in the United Nations System*, at 84-94 (1988).

[466] *Id.* at 85.

[467] *Nicaragua: U.S. Appoints Consultant to Government-Rebel Talks*, Inter Press Service, Nov. 14, 1989.

[468] *United Nations: Central American Observer Mission Approved,* Inter Press Service, Nov. 8, 1989; UN Chief Concerned Over Fighting In El Salvador, 1989 Reuters, Nov. 13, 1989, AM cycle.

[469] *Advance Party of UN Troops Headed For Central America,* 1989 Reuters, Nov. 30, 1989, BC cycle.

[470] T. Pickering, **Peace Seen as a Growth Industry**, interview, 1989 the Christian Science Monitor, Nov. 22, 1989, 12.

CHAPTER IX

AN OBSERVATIONAL STANDPOINT: THE FACTUAL VARIABLES APPLIED

[471] See *The Deepening Morass*, L.A. Times 4, Col. 1 (Dec. 17, 1986); *After Years of Isolation Cuba Makes Comeback in Latin America*, Reuters Ltd. BC Cycle (Jul. 14, 1986); *Realists v. Administration Ideologues On Nicaragua,* N.Y. Times 26 (Apr. 7, 1986); *Nicaragua Trick or Treaty?*, N.Y. Times 22 (Sept. 27, 1984); Cupas, T., *Cuba and Contadora*, U.P.I. PM cycle (Apr. 9, 1984); *U.N. Delegates: Hands off Central America*, Xinhua Gen. Overseas News Serv., item 1109331 (Nov. 8, 1983).

[472] See Ch. Dickey, *The Crisis Areas: Central America: From Crisis to Cauldron?*, 62 Foreign Affairs 659 (1983); *Central American Nations Condemn Nicaragua*, 1982 U.P.I. PM Cycle (Jul. 8, 1982); *A Diplomatic Dilemma: U.S. Has Pacts With Feuding Nations,* 1982 Wash. Post A1 (Apr. 4, 1982); *Where Are*

America's Allies?, 1982 U.S. News & World Report 22 (Jan. 18, 1982).

473 *Central American Nations Condemn Nicaragua*, 1982 U.P.I., PM Cycle (Jul. 8, 1982).

474 See Ch. Dickey, *supra* note 472, at 687.

475 A. Chayes, *The Cuban Missile Crisis,* in Falk, R., et al., **International Law: A Contemporary Perspective,** at 344 (1985).

476 W. Gould and M. Barkum, *International Law and the Social Sciences*, citing Aubert, at 226 (1970).

477 See *Non-Aligned Countries Call for Relaxation of World Tensions*, The Xinhua Overseas News Service, Oct. 12, 1983, Wednesday; see also *Four Latin American Presidents End Summit,* The Xinhua General Overseas News Service, Jul. 18, 1983, Monday. The latter report indicates that "since the beginning of this year (1983), the four countries have held several meetings and adopted nonintervention and self determination as the basic principles for solving conflicts in Central America.

478 A. Chayes, *The Cuban Missile Crisis, supra* note 480, 343.

479 Though the CDC proposal adopted the collective means of forcible intervention under the Rio Pact, the actual behavior of the United States and the reported tolerance of some Central American countries to U.S. unilateral military action against Nicaragua suggested that the U.S. bloc found permissible all forms of intervention in Nicaragua.

480 See our discussion in Chapter IV(B) on the procedural uncertainty within the Contadora process.

481 In this regard one should mention the Inter-American Conference for the Consolidation of Peace, held at Buenos Aires on 1936, see *Conferencias Internacionales Americanas: 1889-1936,* Carnegie Endowment for Peace, 1938, 605. Also, Articles 18 through 22 of the OAS Charter were intended to eliminate much of the confusion as to the principle of nonintervention and its interplay with collective security. This and other instances for clearly defining permissible and non-permissible intervention in the Western Hemisphere may be found in Subsecretaría de Asuntos Jurídicos, OAS, *Sistema Interamericano*, 93-106.

482 The actors' diverging perceptions about facts are also important. However, that the parties share similar normative expectations facilitates their implementation of increasingly impartial and objective fact-finding means. The element of "good faith" is also important, but the way we understand normative restraint--as constraints deriving from the fact that most participants and target audiences share similar normative expectations--implies that actors' manipulative arguments tend to decrease along with their disposition to learn or adapt.

483 Ernst B. Haas warns us, however, that: "because the relationship between relatively specific-static goals and increasingly consensual knowledge is by its very nature volatile, we can expect hanging calculations of joint gains within and among coalitions....This changeability suggests the possibility of occasional elaborate agreements covering a variety of issues, but not a pattern of such agreements," E. B. Haas, *When Knowledge Is Power*, at 78 (1989).

484 *Id.* at 71-85.

485 Miguel D'Escoto, Nicaragua's Foreign Minister "rejected...that the political turmoil in Central America should be resolved through the Contadora countries of Mexico, Panama, Colombia and Venezuela." See Proprietary to the U.P.I., April 9, 1984. The Nicaraguan application to the Court in fact served D'Escoto's perception. Nicaragua only submitted its application to the Court when the possibility of a Contadora stalemate was imminent. "Contadora is not precisely a court of law," D'Escoto used to say. As a direct response to Nicaragua's diplomatic move before the Court, the U.S. Secretary of State George Shultz pushed for bilateral negotiations with the Sandinistas on May 1984. The move was significant because it was the first attempt of its kind since December 1981 when Secretary of State Alexander Haig met with D'Escoto at an Organization of American States meeting. See **Proprietary to the U.P.I.,** June 1, 1984, Friday AM cycle.

486 There is some truth to this statement. The mining of Nicaraguan ports by the United States was perhaps the most immediate cause of the Sandinista's hiring of two American lawyers to explore the possibilities of filing their suit at the World Court. See D. Lauter, *Playing Hardball for Nicaragua*, The National L. J. 1

(May 7, 1984); Two *U.S. Lawyers Battle Over Nicaragua at the World Court,* 1984 Time 57 (Apr. 30, 1984).

487 While Nicaragua's Ministry of Foreign Affairs D'Escoto insisted that going to the Court responded to the need to separate Nicaragua-U.S. bilateral issues from the Contadora negotiations, Nicaragua later submitted applications against Costa Rica and Honduras on similar facts and almost identical grounds.

488 92 Notably, the commentaries by various international legal experts in 81 AJIL 9 (1987). As pointed out before, the Nicaragua Case refers to the case **Military and Paramilitary Activities in and against Nicaragua (Nicar. v. U.S)**, Merits, 1986 ICJ Reports 14 (Judgment of June 27, 1986).

489 *Id.* at para. 205.

490 *Id.* at para. 207.

491 *Id.* at para. 266.

492 E. Haas, *supra* note 483, at 74.

493 *Id.* 41.

494 *Id.* at 41.

495 Schachter, *The Invisible College of International Lawyers*, 72 Northwestern Law Review 217 (No.2, 1977). See also, Hambro, *The Centenary of the Institut de Droit International*, 43 Nordisk Tidasskrift for International Ret 9 (1973), and De Visscher, *La Contribution de L' Institut de Droit International au Developpement du Droit International*, Livre du Centenaire 1873-1973: Evolution et Perspective Du Droit International 128 (1973). To say that international lawyers share a common intellectual enterprise and common methods to solve technical problems should not be affected by the fact that theories about international law remain significantly divided. The standpoint of the theorist, who tries to explain the role of law in decision making, is different from that of the lawyer who applies the law to specific problems and tries to translate the resulting *truth* of his/her technical operation into public policy. The techniques which are used by the latter type of professionals are those that are shared within the epistemic community of international lawyers to which we here refer.

496 For a larger demonstration of this assertion, see E. Brown Weiss, *Judicial Independence and Impartiality*, in Damrosch, L.,

The International court of Justice at a Crossroads, at 123 (1987).

497 E. B. Haas, *supra* note 483, at 42-46.

498 *Id.* at 45.

499 Our distinction here between *prevailing and surviving normative expectations from consensual knowledge* means to suggest that the former actually translate into the latter after having seeped into the public policy of most actors and target audiences.

500 *Id.* at 75.

501 See E. Effron, *Nicaragua Likely to Press on Ruling*, The National Law Journal 3 (Jul. 14, 1986). Mr. Effron interviewed several international legal scholars just a few days before the ruling of the court on the Nicaragua case. Most of the scholars he interviewed anticipated a favorable decision for Nicaragua.

502 Even on the jurisdictional issue, most international lawyers criticized President's Reagan's decision to refuse jurisdiction. See *U.S. Rejection of World Court's Role Has Deep Roots*, 1985 Reuters, Jan. 31, 1985, Thursday, AM Cycle.

503 J.N. Moore, *Debate: The ICJ case on the Merits-Legal and Moral Implications of U.S. Aid to the Contras*, 6 Saint Louis University Public Law Review 85-130 (Spr. 1987); Moore, *The Secret War in Central America: A response to James P. Rowles*, 27 Virginia Journal of International Law 77-183 (Jan. 1987); Moore, *The Secret War in Central America and the Future of World Order*, 80 A.J.I.L. 43 (Jan. 1986).

504 See Briggs, Boyle, Christenson, et al., *Appraisals of the ICJ's Decision: Nicaragua v. United States (merits)*, 81 A.J.I.L. 77 (Jan. 1987); Bialos, Robinson, D'Amato, et al., *Should the United States Reconsider its Acceptance of World Court Jurisdiction?*, 79 Proc, Ann. Meet. A.S.I.L. 95 (Apr. 1985).

505 See R.F. Turner, Force, U.S. *Diplomacy, and International Law*, 11 The Washington Quarterly 119 (Autumn 1988). See also *Sandinista makes his Case on a Brooklin Church Visit*, N.Y. Times, July 28, 1986; *Rambo Plays the Capitol*, The Nation, Nov. 2, 1985.

506 *U.S. Refusal to Accept a Ruling of the World Court on the (Mining of Nicaraguan Harbors) Turned Congress More Strongly*

Against the Once-Covert Aid Program, See U.P.I., August 27, 1984, Monday, BC cycle.

507 See *U.S. v. Oliver North: Deregulating Political Murder*, The Nation, June 26, 1989

508 The author witnessed a substantial part of the deliberation process in the Costa Rican Ministry of Foreign Affairs, where he worked as a member of the Costa Rican team of legal advisors during 1986 and 1987.

509 E.B. Haas, *supra* note 483, at 46-49.

510 *Id.* at 46.

511 *Id.* at 75.

512 When adapting, actors change not because they accept the prevailing expectations but because they are constrained to do so under the circumstances.

513 4 Latin America Weekly Report 9, WR-88-04, January 28, 1988.

514 According to Reuters, the five Presidents believed that "progress in implementing the Esquipulas Accords is scarce, and it is necessary to speed negotiations on questions of security, national reconciliation and establishing calendars for verifying compliance." 1988 Reuters; June 25, 1988.

515 *Border and Transborder Actions* (Nic. v. Hon.) 1988 ICJ reports, 106 (Judgment on Jurisdiction and Admissibility).

516 See Proprietary to the U.P.I., Feb. 12, 1989, Sunday BC cycle. "Agreement on a monitoring commission was considered central to the summit, and it was not clear whether the stalemate would affect another aspect of the meeting, a decision to invite an international team to monitor cross-border security. *Central Americans Quarrel as Summit Appears Deadlocked*, 1989 Reuters, Feb. 13, 1989, Monday, PM cycle.

517 Honduran Ambassador to the Hague Mario Carias told journalists that the case was resumed when Nicaragua requested the Court's help in March after 3,200 U.S. troops landed in Honduras to help the Contras and Honduran bombing raids on Nicaragua." 1988 Reuters, June 6, 1988, Monday, AM cycle.

518 "But Honduras made clear it had signed the [Costa del Sol Declaration] on the condition that Nicaragua drops its case against

Honduras before the World Court." UN Chronicle, September 1989.

519 O. Schachter, *The Nature and Process of Legal Development in International Society*, in Macdonald and Johnston, ed., **The Structure And Process of International Law**, at 747 (1983).

CHAPTER X

APPRAISING INDICATORS: ITS SEQUENTIAL APPLICATION TO PEACE NEGOTIATIONS IN CENTRAL AMERIA DURING THE 1980'S

520 25 See A. Lowenthal, *Partners In Conflict: The United States and Latin America*, at 25-47 (1987). Though Lowenthal does not make any specific reference to international law, he persuasively demonstrates how U.S. dominance in Latin America has declined because of underlying, economic, social, technological, and military trends in the hemisphere since 1960. All these trends, he argues, "reflect and reinforce the growing tendency of Latin American and Caribbean nations to pursue their own interests, even in opposition to Washington's preferences" (p. 36). Under these circumstances, "the Reagan administration's attempt to reimpose U.S. dominance in the Hemisphere has begun to backfire..." (p. 47). I argue that international law and institutions are the major instruments the Latin American countries have used to pursue their own interests.

521 See for example L. Moreno, *Historia de las Relaciones Interestatales de Centro America*, (1928); E. Van der Haag and T. Farer *U.S. Ends and Means in Central America*, (1988); Ch. Chukwma, *International Law Perspectives of the Developing Countries*, (1980); M. Flory, *Adapting International Law to the Development of the Third World*, 26 Journal of African Law 12 (Spring 1982); J. Quigley, *The Reagan Administration and Third World Self-determination*, 45 Nat. Lawyers Guild Pract. 54, 1988.

522 Tomas Franck's concept of "symbolic validation" is intended here to encompass the ideas of "ritual" and "pedigree" that Professor Franck distinguished in his original discussion of the term. Franck defines "symbolic validation" of a "rule" or a "rule-making process or institution...a signal [that] is used as a cue to

elicit compliance with a command." He cites as an example of symbolic validation "the singing of a national anthem, as a vocal and [on public occasions] a visual signal symbolically reinforcing the citizen's relationship to the state, a relationship of rights and duties." See T. Franck, *Legitimacy in the International System*, 82 A.J.I.L. 725 (1988).

523 I extensively illustrated indeterminacy on nonintervention and its interplay with other fundamental principles of the Inter-American system in Part II when discussing uncertainty within Contadora. Further authority in this regard may be found in A. Thomas and Thomas, *Non-intervention: The Law and its Import in the Americas,* (1956). See also F.G. Dawson, *The Influence of Andres Bello on Latin American Perceptions of Nonintervention and State Responsibility*, 57 British Yearbook of International Law 283-284 (1986).

524 See our discussion supra pages 112-113. Among other studies offering a more or less complete picture of the matter, see C. Joyner and M.A. Grimaldi, *The United States and Nicaragua: Reflections on the Lawfulness of Contemporary Intervention*, 25 Virginia Journal of International Law 621-689 (1985); K. Quigley, *Framework for Evaluating the Legality of the United States Intervention in Nicaragua*, 17 N.Y.U. Journal of Int'l Law and Politics 155-185 (1984); and B. Dean, *Self-Determination and U.S. Support of Insurgents: A Policy-Analysis Model*, 122 Military Law Review 149-220 (1988).

525 For a complete description of the principle of nonintervention in the Inter-American System and concrete examples of its validation in Latin America, see Garcia-Amador, F., *Sistema Interamericano a traves de tratados, convenciones y otros documentos*, Vol. I, 1981, 47-49, 93-96. See also A. Cassese, *International Law in a Divided World*, at 143-148 (1986).

526 The Calvo doctrine has two main elements: a) a sovereign independent state is entitled, by reason of the principle of equality, to complete freedom from interference in any form, whether by diplomacy or diplomatic force, from other states; b) aliens are entitled to no greater rights and privileges than those available to nationals. Therefore, national courts of the host state have exclusive jurisdiction over disputes involving aliens, and aliens can seek redress only in such national courts. See Henkin, L. et al.,

International Law: Cases and Materials, at 1040 (1987). The Drago doctrine, elaborated by Luis Drago in 1902, stipulates that "the public debt can not occasion armed intervention nor even the actual occupation of the territory of American nations by a European power." See 1903 Foreign Relations of the United States 4; see also L. Drago, *State Loans in ther Relation to International Policy*, 1 A.J.I.L. 695 (1907).

527 The Estrada doctrine, first adopted by Mexico in 1930, has become very popular in Latin America. Most recently, it has been applied by most Latin American countries for the tacit recognition of Manuel Endara's government in Panama, right after the overthrown of Manuel Noriega by U.S. military forces on December 1989. For the complete text of the Declaration that originated the doctrine, see G. Estrada, *Declaración del 27 de septiembre de 1930*, in Casanovas y La Rosa, **Casos y Textos de Derecho Internacional Publico,** 165 (1984).

528 See M. Sorensen, ed., *Manual de Derecho Internacional Publico*, at 276-296 (1973).

529 In spite of the interests and purposes of an international actor, the utilization of a legal framework will also require that he or she elaborates some kind of legal rationale. When claims are persistently based on legal grounds, the persuasiveness of a legal argument rests mainly on the actor's more or less sophisticated correlations of customary and/or conventional legal sources with actual behavior. In this connection, the causal relationship between the framing of arguments in legal terms and the operation of the law is what has been called by some commentators as the *communications function* of international law. Defenders of this concept propose that international law not only aims at governing and proscribing desirable modes of conduct, but also supplies a means of argumentation based upon those modes. "Through this function, policy is legitimated, claims are made, situations are defined, and components of the actor's models as well as other models are discussed and interpreted....This function describes the operative dimension," see A. Nilsson, *Political Uses of International Law*, 1987, 52.

530 With regard to practice of the International Court of Justice, and in particular with the Nicaragua case, see K. Highet, *Evidence, The Court, and the Nicaragua Case*, 81 A.J.I.L 1-56 (1987).

531 Not only was the Court itself united on the technical issues, but little opposition has since been raised against the judgment in the international legal community. See 1986 Reuters Ltd., July 3, 1986. See also Highet, K., *Litigation Implications of the U.S. Withdrawal from the Nicaragua Case*, 79 A.J.I.L. 992-1005 (1985).

532 Article 53 of the Statute of the International Court of Justice provides that "Whenever one of the parties does not appear before the Court, or fails to defend its case, the other party may call upon the Court to decide in favour of its claim."

533 According to Oscar Schachter those elements are: "the selection of relevant facts, the need to give specific meaning to broad, undefined concepts, the subtle process of generalizing from past cases, the uses of analogy and metaphor, the inevitable choices between competing rules and principles." O. Schachter, *supra* note 524, at 66.

534 This is not to say that the factual and evidenciary material supporting the Court's decision represents the true facts. I do not mean to imply that the evidence submitted by Nicaragua--in all the phases of the case--and the United States--during the jurisdiction phase--was complete, accurate, and valid. That the United States did not participate in the merits phase of the litigation clearly suggests the contrary. In his dissenting opinion Judge Schwebel, the American member of the Court, criticizes some of the holdings because they do not rely on exhaustive evidence. See *Military and Paramilitary Activities in and against Nicaragua*, (Nicar. v. U.S.) Judgment (Merits), 1986 ICJ Reports 14, paras. 17-41.

535 For definition of "epistemic community", see *supra* note 189.

536 See F. Ikle, *How Nations Negotiate*, at 214 (1964); A. Lall, *Modern International Negotiation*, at 348-349 (1966), citing C. Wilfred Jenks.

537 We are not concerned either with the effectiveness or the success or failure of the negotiation process. Our interest is exclusively to appraise the impact of international law in a negotiating context.

538 I have suggested above that when a negotiation is not conducted in legal terms, it directly indicates the ineffectiveness of the myth system in attracting the actors' attention. A negotiation where the major issues are posed in legal terms is one in which the

most important questions are first evaluated by the parties according to some kind of normative principle. The Contadora Group's requirement that border tensions in Central America be resolved in strict observance of the prohibition against the threat or use of force in international relations and with absolute fondness to the definition of aggression by the United Nations is one such example.

539 The search for some form of consensus is accepted here as common to all diplomatic negotiations. See J. Kaufmann, *Effective Negotiation: Case Studies in Conference Diplomacy*, at 299 (1989).

540 See *Negotiations Still Ahead On Peace Plan*, 1987 Wash. Post, Aug. 9, 1987, Sunday, Final Edition, A1.

541 *Central American Peace; Arias: Whom Can We Trust?*, 1988 N.Y. Times, A32, Column 1, Jan. 10, 1988, Sunday, Late City Final Edition.

542 *Id.* at A32.

543 See E.B. Haas, *supra* note 488, at 79. Haas's typology of decision-making styles and issue linkage is summarized in Figure 4 in his book.

544 Haas, *supra* note 483, at 92.

545 See *Role for Contras in U.S. Central American Policy To End*, 1988 Reuters, Oct. 29, 1988, Saturday, BC cycle; *Latin Leaders Watching for Hints of Bush Policy: Attitude About Contras Among Key Concerns*, 1988 Wash. Post, Nov. 13, 1988, Sunday, Final Edition, A35; *US Seeking Way to Keep Contras Viable*, 1988 Wash. Post, Jul. 3, 1988, Sunday, Final Edition, A31.

546 *The Postinvasion Blues*, 1990 Time Inc. 28 (Jan. 29, 1990); *Panama Action a "Catch-22" for Latin Relations*, 1990 The L.A. Times 1, Col. 6, (Jan. 6, 1990); *OAS Votes To Censure U.S. for Intervention; Peru Suspends Cooperation in Drug Fight*, 1989 Wash. Post A7, (Dec. 23, 1989).

CONCLUDING REMARKS

547 I must acknowledge that this position has been opposed by some commentators. See for example, G. Schwarzenberger, *The Province of the Doctrine of International Law*, cited by M. Lachs, **The Teacher in International Law,** at 211 (1987). But see J. Brierly's

statement that "the codifier, if he is competent for his work, will make suggestions of his own...he will be suggesting legislation...he will be working on *lex ferenda* not the *lex lata*...he will be extending the law and not merely stating the law that exists," also cited by M. Lachs, *Id.* 210.

548 The work of Sixth Committee of the U.N. General Assembly, for example, may lead to important progress in this connection. See *Peaceful Settlement of Disputes Between State*, Report of the Sixth Committee, U.N. Doc. A/44/764 (1989).

549 For example, the proposal submitted to a Special Committee of the United Nations by Romania on a commission of good offices, mediation or conciliation within the United Nations. See, *Report of the Special Committee on the Charter of the United Nations and on the Strengthening of the Role of the Organization,* U.N. Doc. GAOR 44th Session, Supplement 33 (A/44/33), paras. 119-123.

INDEX